Futures of the Contemporary

Contemporaneity, Untimeliness, and Artistic Research

FUTURES OF THE CONTEMPORARY

CONTEMPORANEITY, UNTIMELINESS, AND ARTISTIC RESEARCH

Edited by Paulo de Assis and Michael Schwab

Leuven University Press

Table of Contents

Introduction

Paulo de Assis

Orpheus Institute, Ghent

Michael Schwab

Journal for Artistic Research (JAR)

The *contemporary* points towards incommensurable definitions. Largely debated in the fields of visual arts, art theory, and philosophy, the concept of the contemporary describes different practices, addressing diverse realities, and relating to disparate conceptual horizons. However, if distinguished from the *contemporaneous* of a given historical time, the *contemporary* becomes a selective concept that promotes or excludes things and practices according to their ability to respond to ahistorical or transhistorical aspects of the present. In this sense, the contemporary gains a critical function, involving particular modes of relating to history and to one's own time.

Since the contemporary is itself a historical concept that inscribes into its very diagnosis an image of the (global) present, problematisations are required that further complicate our relationship to history. Taking Roland Barthes's famous claim that "the contemporary is the untimely" as a seminal idea (quoted and expanded on by Agamben 2009), this book uses the link proposed between the notions of "the contemporary" and "the untimely" to engage anew with the temporality of artistic practices, in particular those that run against their own time and epoch, thus challenging history by engaging with its productive ground rather than by fleeing from it. The reader will see this link return again and again throughout the different chapters (starting with a discussion of these concepts in Chapter 1 by Paulo de Assis). By emphasising the notion of the untimely (Nietzsche's *Unzeitgemäss*), a relationship to contemporaneity's historical blind spot is developed, offering more diverse entry points to pasts, presents, and futures. More than futures of the present, what is at stake are futures of the contemporary, implying a move beyond historicising frameworks, and asking which futures are possible for an untimely contemporariness.

With contributions from scholars and artists who have been highly engaged with the topic for several years—coming from fields as diverse as music performance, composition, art theory, visual arts, art history, critical studies, and philosophy—*Futures of the Contemporary* offers different perspectives on contemporary art practices, the temporality of artistic works and phenomena, and new modes of problematising the production of art and its public apprehension. The variety of the chapters offers not only different views on "the contemporary" but also different critical attitudes and creative gestures towards it, including different literary styles and formats that range from more speculative and abstract essays to concrete discussion of artworks done today. Bringing together artists, musicians, and philosophers, the book moves the field of discussion from where it has been for the last decades, namely the fields of philosophy and art theory, to the emerging area of artistic research, thus pointing towards future work that might have the power to critically disentangle our global present and our presence within it (a topic that is discussed in the final chapter by Michael Schwab).

Diverse threads run throughout the essays, including ontological queries (What is the contemporary? What is the untimely?), epistemological discussions (Which forms of knowledge does the contemporary entail and how are they affected by the untimely?), methodological frameworks (Which artistic practices might be labelled *contemporary*?), ethical debates (How can the contemporary positively disturb and offset dominant structures?), and a transdisciplinary opening of horizons (What is the relationship between the contemporary and artistic research?).

Without proposing clear definitions of what "artistic research" might be—an almost futile endeavour given the institutional investments in the term—we use it to signal the possibility for new departures bewildered as we are by philosophy's distance from the motivations of artists as well as a certain outdatedness if not superficiality of artistic discourse. "Artistic research," if deployed as a speculative concept, may signal the arrival of a new paradigm for sense-making; it aims to work through—in all possible ways—a phenomenon's implications, accepting the disturbance of long-held beliefs, disciplinary striation, and taste to the point at which artistic labour becomes unrecognisable to those bound up by whatever presupposition they bring to the table. It is in this sense that we see artistic research implied in the *futures* of the contemporary.

The origins of this book go back to the Fourteenth International Orpheus Academy for Music and Theory, held on 8–10 May 2017 in Ghent, where some of the authors gave lectures, namely Babette Babich, Zsuzsa Baross, Heiner Goebbels, and Peter Osborne, as well as both editors (Paulo de Assis and Michael Schwab). During these lectures, but also in the preparatory work leading to the Academy, a tension between two different understandings of the word *contemporary* became relevant. On the one hand, the word has been used in recent decades to refer to a specific concept that critically scrutinises any historical time and period, thus being "ahistorical" (the *contemporary* as an untimely category); on the other hand, it has also been used as a word describing current (global) artistic practices, thus being highly situated in time (*contemporaneity* as the radical now of the global present). This tension between "untimely" and "timely" modes of expression—which is implied in the Barthes–Agamben statement "the contemporary is the untimely"—lends itself to becoming a cultural and philosophical *aporia*, risking repeating the old song of the end of history, not positively contributing to renewed artistic practices, and actually excluding art and music practitioners from the debate. However, for the practitioner, ideas of the end of history or of a perpetual state of ending can have a positive effect, allowing for the recalibration and reinvention of concrete practices and phenomena. While a philosophical or art-theoretical notion of a "concluding history" is certainly possible, it comes at a price, namely the curtailing of the practitioner's agency. And this is why the voice of artistic research matters today. It is not a question of how we can solve or contain the *aporia* of the contemporary, but of whether questioning the contemporary in this way actually does justice to what is happening on the ground. For maybe, contemporaneity is not a description of something but a mode in which certain temporal phenomena are proposed to be conceptualised. Are we getting these phenomena right when we speak of "the contemporary"? To be sure, we have no answer to this question; all we can do is try again in confronting practice with the notion of the contemporary—this time within the horizon of artistic research—observing the effects this has not only on possible understandings of "contemporaneity" but also on practice itself.

The book is organised in three parts: Part 1 (The Contemporary and the Untimely; Assis, Babich, Baross) considers the contemporary in relation to Nietzsche's "untimely" (*Unzeitgemäss*), including elaborations on texts and concepts not only by Giorgio Agamben, Alain Badiou, and Jean-Luc Nancy, but also by Michel Foucault, Gilles Deleuze, Charles Péguy, Paul Virilio, and Arthur C. Danto; Part 2 (Contemporary Practices; Goebbels, Cox, Prior, and Nolan, and Capdevila) presents and discusses recent artworks and practices by composers and visual artists such as Heiner Goebbels himself, Martin Howse, Shintaro Miyazaki, Christina Kubisch, Joyce Hinterding, Antonio Vega Macotela, and the Forensic Architecture studio; Part 3 (Problematising the Contemporary; Osborne, Lund, Schwab) returns to philosophical questions, but from a perspective that situates "the contemporary" as having been "worked" by history itself into a global form.

Starting from Nietzsche's notion of the untimely, Paulo de Assis's "The Contemporary: In the Midst of Multiple Hurricanes of Time" develops reflections on time, temporality, and the contemporary, extending Nietzsche's remarks on history to other concepts, such as Barthes's *contemporary*, Foucault's *actual*, Péguy's *aternal*, and Deleuze's *haecceity*. All these notions help define a new regime of temporality, a proto-theory of time in which art-makers (not only visual artists and others, but also composers and performers) can effectively operate and generate new problematisations of (and at) any given historical time. To live in a given time is to be contemporaneous with it, which is a piece of factual evidence and does not carry any critical stance over one's own presence in that particular time. This chapter claims that the most important role of "the contemporary" is to establish a critique of one's own time, otherwise the artist's surrounding contemporaneousness will condemn him or her to historicism. Critically, if distinguished from the contemporaneous of a given historically situated present, the contemporary becomes an ahistorical mode of relating to any given presence. It gains a critical function (on the identity of the present), enabling a clinical glance (symptomatology) at our own time. The present, and our presence within that present, is surrounded and over-layered by a multiplicity of temporalities, which are at work in every single thinkable and experienceable here and now, and which are perceptible as otherness or uncanniness. The present is not One, and it is not a stable entity. Like the inner eye of a hurricane, it is a complex arrangement of different temporalities moving at different paces (fast and slow), with different accelerations (strata and becomings), and different temperatures (hot and cold). Problematising the archive, Michel Foucault ([1972] 2002, 147) identified a "border of time that surrounds our presence," a particular zone in which human beings problematise what they are, what they do, and the world in which they live. But this differential critical temporality can also be explored and creatively expanded in relation to the future. The fundamental step is to grasp the extent to which these borders of time are out of phase with the zeitgeist of their present, which they surround and latently threaten. To be at the border of time is to resist the centre, to resist servitude, habits, clichés, intolerance, common sense, and consensuality that is, the present. Looking toward the future (and not to the archive) with the aim of constructing futures (and not at idealising them) is simply the desire to actualise different configurations of materials, connectors, and affects in a new present, which exists in the present but remains concealed to itself Questioning our own presence and our responsibility within any given temporality, this chapter aims at opening discourses and practices to the simultaneous co-presence of different times and temporalities in the historical, social, political, and artistic worlds.

Babette Babich questions the notion of the contemporary in and through the works of Giorgio Agamben, Paul Virilio, and Arthur C. Danto, which are brought into dialogue with Nietzsche's artist's and spectator's aesthetic, as well as with the art historians Terry Smith and Michael Fried. For Babich, beyond the currently contemporary, the notion of "contemporary art" cannot but be problematic in the one-upmanship of art history and art theory where failure to use categories properly not only risks the categoriser's reputation as a historian and a theorist but leaves the categoriser embroiled in what Jean-Luc Nancy (2010, 93) identifies as a "great dispute about art." In this sense, the contemporaneity of contemporaries reflects the fact that "contemporary art" takes "the form of a question." According to Babich, Giorgio Agamben's essay *What Is the Contemporary?* points to an ecstatic "irrelevance" [*inattuale*] characteristic of those contemporary to, in, and with their own time. The reference, via Roland Barthes, as Agamben emphasises, cites Nietzsche's reflections on history and life. If Nietzsche uttered his reservations contra theatricality in art, as Fried would come to do, Nietzsche specifically indicted what he named a "spectator's art" in his effort to write on behalf of an "artist's art," contra the dominant cult of the spectator that however and forever sets the spectator out of bounds, as a non-performer, non-congregant, non-participant, lacking a literal presence; as Fried ([1967] 1998, 168) concludes with a quasi-mystical recollection of the literal: "Presentness is grace." Reflecting on Pater's ([1893] 1998, 86) maxim "All art constantly aspires towards the condition of music," Babich's conclusion seeks to raise the question of the "artist's art" of contemporary music to ask whether, in music, we are left yet more exposed to what Nancy, after Heidegger, calls "the question."

Scrutinising the question of the contemporary today, Zsuzsa Baross, explores three artworks—a poem by Paul Celan, a song by a throat singer, a composition by György Kurtág—from the perspective of "the instant," which is understood as an instance of contemporaneity actualised. Instead of entering a debate with three of the most influential voices speaking on the subject currently (Nancy, Agamben, and Badiou), Baross works toward opening a space for posing a series of questions regarding contemporaneity today, not as an aesthetic category, genre, or period in art history, but as a historical and historically determined "sensibility," an endeavour that she considers difficult yet imperative today. Qualifying our current present as "dark times," Baross argues that it is art that will guide the passage toward a formulation, or indeed, provide a concrete demonstration of contemporaneity as a relation to be imposed, accomplished, or actualised.

Heiner Goebbels's essay "On Aesthetic Experience as Anachronic Experience" discusses the singular character of aesthetic experience in works of the performing arts. To get around the trap of familiarity and recognition, Goebbels seeks to avoid the vicinity of common text structures, linearity of narration, stereotypic images, and representation. He considers the work as an anachronic reality in itself; interpretations and the "contemporary" are not intentional and can only occur as a discovery by the listener or spectator—as a result of perception.

With "The Crackle of Contemporaneity" Geoff Cox, Andrew Prior, and Ryan Nolan move away from questions like "What is the contemporary?" or "What constitutes contemporary (visual) art?," engaging instead in a discussion about how artists are embracing and interrogating contemporaneity as opposed to breaking from it—either through nostalgic art-making, or through the so-called modernising avant-gardes. Through a reading of Martin Howse and Shintaro Miyazaki's project *Detektors* (2011), they look at artistic interrogations of the contemporary that place emphasis on reflective practices. *Detektors* represents research into the profusion of electromagnetic signals that populate our environment, explored particularly through the demodulation of these signals into the audible frequency spectrum. In part it sits within a sonic art tradition, close to the work of Christina Kubisch and Joyce Hinterding—both of whom are interested in sonifying the hidden electromagnetic soundscape—but it is framed specifically by Miyazaki and Howse in archaeological terms as a means to interrogate the material and processual conditions of contemporary information technology. This chapter's focus on *Detekors* provides a means to think through the slowing down and deep (forensic) consideration of an extended present. *Detektors* operates onto-epistemologically in approaching contemporaneity by simultaneously representing both what is in the world (via demodulated signals), and what we know about what is in the world. And, at the same time, it is illustrative of a "hacker" ethos that combines applied technological research, aesthetics, and planetary connectivity (through the sharing of circuit diagrams and instruction manuals, along with a project website where users can upload their own "detektions"). In this sense the project highlights an important feature of the contemporary as the ongoing temporalisation of history, which is to say that it cannot be fully grasped through symbolic transcription (as written history is, for example). It presents a new way of understanding contemporary (signal) conditions through the combination of human (aesthetic, affective) and non-human (the *Detektor* as techno-archaeologist) means.

In "Aporetic Temporalisations and Postconceptual Realism," Pol Capdevila works from the hypothesis that contemporary art, as such, is not to be defined as an art of our time but as an art that questions dominant historical narratives and, through its critical potential, the very structures of those narratives. Art produces temporal experiences that, from the narrativity standpoint, are aporetic. However, by virtue of contemporary art's performativity, these experiences motivate a reactivation of the historical sense. Capdevila argues that contemporary art, by generating aporetic temporalisations of aspects of our reality, seeks an immediate effect on the present: not only as a semantic rearticulation of the horizon of meaning but above all through an active participation, on however small a scale, in the production of the material conditions of our lives. First, this chapter contextualises artistic practices as a critical reaction to the dominant cultural tendency to impose closed narratives. Narrations are temporally articulated visions about the world and the subjects that inhabit it. Regarding narratives, Capdevila follows Agamben's critical insight that being contemporary consists of looking at the darkness of one's own time. That which is contemporary is anachronistic and introduces anachronism in the predetermined historical evolution in order to reactivate the historical course (Rancière). Next, the chapter addresses the question of the "resumption of history" by contemporary art (Osborne), understood here as a self-conscious reaction to the postmodern narrative model, which explains the historical social and artistic evolution as a process that has come to an end, either as a happy end of time (Danto) or as an attitude of resistance (Foster). After briefly explaining three main artistic strategies used by contemporary art—the appropriation of different pasts, the performative articulation of their elements, and, finally, the willingness to involve the public in an active reception—this essay presents two artistic projects that were shown at documenta 14: Antonio Vega Macotela's *The Mill of Blood*, and Forensic Architecture's *The Society of Friends of Halit*.

Peter Osborne's "Working the Contemporary: History as a Project of Crisis, Today" considers what it might mean to "work" the concept of the contemporary, under current conditions, in the sense of Georges Canguilhem's famous account of "working a concept." The contemporary, it is argued, has been "worked" by history itself into a global form. Two aspects are especially stressed: its immanent relationship to the temporality of crisis, and a renewed sense of history itself as a "project of crisis" (Tafuri), a putting into crisis, or a production of the present as crisis. This essay suggests that history as a project is the negativity of the unity of global crisis.

In "Untimeliness in Contemporary Times" Jacob Lund claims that we live in a crisis of time, marked by the uncritical radicalisation of the present, the sense that only the present exists, generating an overwhelming "presentism." At the same time, Lund identifies that we have lost the future as a political object, and his essay discusses the temporal complexity of our current situation, to which extent it even makes sense to speak of *our* situation. Agamben's influential text "What Is the Contemporary?" (2008) includes notions such as "of their time," "their own time," and "the epoch," but Lund asks, "What is *our* own time and *our* epoch? Who in the post- or decolonial situation actually takes part in the possessive determiner *our*?" This chapter argues that it has becoming increasingly difficult to identify a hegemonic time in relation to which one can be untimely; that the current contemporaneity—understood with Peter Osborne as a technical term designating the coming together of different times in the same historical present—makes it practically impossible today to be untimely and thus avant-garde in the traditional sense. Thus, for Lund it is no longer useful to employ Agamben's notion of *untimeliness* when trying to engage with the present in order to reinstall a futural moment, nor other temporal horizons than the one in which we live. The artistic practice of Kader Attia is discussed as a possible example of how a contemporary kind of untimeliness—characterised by operating in relation to several times at once and thus differentiating the presentist present—may find ways of expression.

Appropriating Hans-Jörg Rheinberger's work on *experimental systems*, Michael Schwab's essay establishes links to theories of contemporary art, suggesting a possible departure of artistic research from contemporary art by deploying Nietzsche's notion of the *untimely* against Barthes's claim that "the contemporary is the untimely." More specifically, this chapter traces the temporality of epistemic things as they emerge from an experimental system and how Rheinberger can—through Derrida's notion of historiality—claim that experimental systems are designed to make history. Aligning this discourse to theories of contemporary art (Peter Osborne, Boris Groys) this chapter highlights differences and overlaps in an attempt to situate both approaches within Nietzsche's problematisation of "history," suggesting that artistic research, rather than a philosophy of contemporary art, is able to deliver a Nietzschean solution to the problem of art in contemporary—that is, globalised—conditions. This entails both a criticism towards "contemporary art" and an opening towards "untimely" research practices.

References

Agamben, Giorgio. 2008. *Che cos'è il contemporaneo?* Rome: Nottetempo. Translated by David Kishik and Stefan Pedatella as Agamben 2009.

———. 2009. "What Is the Contemporary?" In *What Is an Apparatus? and Other Essays*, translated by David Kishik and Stefan Pedatella, 39–54. Stanford, CA: Stanford University Press. Essay first published as Agamben 2008.

Foucault, Michel. (1972) 2002. *The Archaeology of Knowledge*. Translated by A. M. Sheridan Smith. Abingdon, UK: Routledge. First published 1969 as *L'archéologie du savoir* (Paris: Gallimard). This translation first published 1972 (London: Tavistock).

Fried, Michael. (1967) 1998. "Art and Objecthood." In *Art and Objecthood: Essays and Reviews*, 148–72. Chicago: University of Chicago Press. Essay first published 1967 (*Artforum* 5 [June]: 12–23).

Nancy, Jean-Luc. 2010. "Art Today." Translated by Charlotte Mandell. *Journal of Visual Culture* 9 (1): 91–99. First delivered as a lecture, Milan, 2006.

Pater, Walter. (1893) 1998. *The Renaissance: Studies in Art and Poetry*. Edited by Adam Phillips. Oxford: Oxford University Press. Contains the text of the 4th ed. first published 1893 (London: Macmillan).

Part 1

The Contemporary and the Untimely

The Contemporary

In the Midst of
Multiple Hurricanes of Time[*]

Paulo de Assis

Orpheus Institute

CONTEMPORARY MUSIC

The expression *contemporary music*, especially for all those who studied music in the last quarter of the twentieth century, refers in the first place to a specific mode of conceiving and making music that is associated with a particular set of works and composers active in the post-World War II period. In general, these have been composers who strongly challenged common views on music perception, who devised new modes of composition and performance, and who thoroughly reflected their specific art forms and media. Their works seem to resist quick judgements and understandings, requiring attention, dedication, and discussion. In music, *the contemporary* has a fundamental quality of *resistance*, of overcoming habits and clichés, relating to a critical attitude towards conventional or commonsense understandings of art, thus arguing for a world and to a people still to come. To talk about *contemporary music* is very different from talking about *contemporary art* or *contemporary philosophy*. The qualifier "contemporary" has different meanings and different affordances according to the specific discursive practice to which it refers. In the sciences, to give a counter example, it would be redundant (if not absurd) to talk about *contemporary science*.

In music, the term *contemporary music* gained wider use in the second half (maybe, even more precisely, in the last quarter) of the twentieth century. Music composed in the first half of the century was not labelled "contemporary" but "new" (in German "Neue Musik") or "modern." So-called modernity in music usually refers to diverse new orientations in music composition observable in the first quarter of the twentieth century[1] (though the crucial events hap-

---

[*] This text is a revised and extended version of a lecture given at the Fourteenth International Orpheus Academy for Music and Theory 2017, first published as chapter 8 (". . . at the borders of time that surround our presence . . .") of my book *Logic of Experimentation: Rethinking Music Performance through Artistic Research* (Assis 2018a, 201–13).

1 As the music philosopher Gunnar Hindrichs (2004, 133) observed: "Generally, for music there are two options of interpretation [for the term "modern"]: used as an overall term, the 'modern' age is taken as the period beginning around the end of the 18th century, while in more specific usage it refers to the time since the start of the 20th century."

pened in a shorter period, probably between 1908 and 1913), including impressionism (Debussy, Ravel, Dukas), expressionism (Schoenberg, Berg, Webern, Scriabin, certain works by Stravinsky), atonality (Schoenberg, Scriabin), and dodecaphony (Schoenberg, Webern, Berg). Each of these different perspectives, with their different techniques and aesthetic approaches to composition, shared a common trait: the manifestation of the limits (actually, "the end") of "tonality," of music understood in terms of functional harmony. They each critically reflected upon the exhaustion of the Classical-Romantic set of forms, harmonic material, and instrumental choices, and they each proposed alternative paths. These composers operated what Jean-François Lyotard (1984)—in relation to knowledge in general—described as processes of "deligitimation" of previous modes of knowledge production and consumption. In the case of music, these included the dominant structures of functional tonality, standard forms, instrumental set-ups, concert rules, and so on.

A "second modernity" in music is usually associated with post-1950 developments, particularly related to the Darmstadt Summer Courses and their consequences. Especially between 1946 and 1961, under the direction of Wolfgang Steinecke, the Darmstadt Summer Courses for New Music (Internationale Ferienkurse für Neue Musik) became the main point of reference for theorising, discussing, and presenting what was then called the avant-garde. It included lectures by music philosophers (Theodor W. Adorno, Heinz-Klaus Metzger), musicologists (Carl Dahlhaus, Rudolf Stephan), older-generation composers (Edgard Varèse, Olivier Messiaen, Ernst Krenek), and young composers (Karlheinz Stockhausen, Pierre Boulez, and Luigi Nono, and later also John Cage, Helmut Lachenmann, and Brian Ferneyhough). The courses functioned as the international forum for new music, the place where compositional strategies and concrete modes of doing were openly presented and analysed in detail.

In Paris, the Domaine Musical (1954–73), founded by Pierre Boulez, had a different scope, mainly that of producing performances, but shared the idea of presenting avant-garde, cutting-edge musical works in dialogue with and alongside older pieces. Works by Stockhausen, Boulez, Pousseur, Berio, Kagel, or Boucourechliev were performed, but so too were pieces by Guillaume de Machaut, Dufay, Bach, Debussy, Schoenberg, Stravinsky, and Messiaen. According to Boulez's foundational statement, the Domaine Musical was meant to "produce concerts that would enable the re-establishment of communication between *composers of our time* and an *audience interested in the promotion of its own epoch*" (quoted in Steinegger 2012, 107, my translation, my emphasis).[2] This statement seems to indicate that contemporary music requires not only a special kind of composition but also a special kind of audience, one that is "interested" in "promoting" its own time. It seems to indicate that, in the period in which Boulez made the statement (the 1950s), people were more inclined to appreciate older epochs of music history than they were the contemporary.

---

2 "créer des concerts pour qu'une communication se rétablisse entre les compositeurs de notre temps et le public intéressé à la promotion de son époque."

Therefore, an effort was deemed necessary to "promote" the present, to support a completely new mode of making, thinking, and apprehending music. The composers named above, as well as the concert series discussed, include the composers and festivals that from the late 1960s on widely became labelled "contemporary." These composers lived in periods, in historical epochs, where in general there was little interest in their work—they thus needed a special kind of audience. From then on, music festivals featuring this type of music were known as festivals of contemporary music, and they attracted a specific kind of public.

It is important to draw a distinction here between *the coeval—the contemporaneous* of a given historically situated time—and *the contemporary*, which has a fundamental critical function (on the identity of the present) and which enables a clinical glance (symptomatology) at one's own time. The notion of *contemporary music* does not apply to all music that is composed "today," which in fact in the vast majority of cases is not *contemporary* at all. Music of today is certainly *contemporaneous*, it is coeval to us, but nobody would say that, for example, a composer today composing a Classical symphony in the style of Haydn is making "contemporary music." As Jean-Luc Nancy writes, "it can be said that some works of art produced today somewhere in the world do not belong to contemporary art. If today a painter makes a figurative painting with classical techniques, it will not be contemporary art; it will lack the cachet, the distinctive criterion of what we call 'contemporary'" (Nancy 2010, 91). Thus, contemporary music, like contemporary art, implies a critical dimension, a distance from the everyday world, a detachment from habitus, conventions, and stratifications of forms and media. But what, then, is the contemporary?

A first, very simple definition is the one offered by Alain Badiou in 2014—actually not one, but two definitions of contemporary art: (1) contemporary art is a *critical* art that is critical of Classical, Romantic, or even modern forms of artistic creation; and (2) contemporary art is an art that is *separated from the real*, and which aims at creating a new real by the mediation of new forms (Badiou 2014, 6'12"–6'53"). These apparently simple definitions require the acknowledgement of two distances: distance from art itself, and distance from the world. Both distances imply the presence, and importantly the *simultaneous* presence, of diverse planes of "reality," that is, of diverse times and spaces in spatio-temporal overlaying. This multiple temporality, the gap between the present and the present, between different planes of the present, is the main topic of this chapter, and in what follows I will address it from a variety of perspectives: first through Giorgio Agamben's attempt to define the contemporary, which is indebted to Roland Barthes's theories of writing and to Friedrich Nietzsche's central notion of *Unzeitgemäss* (and its problematic translations into other languages); then through Foucault's distinction between the *present* and the *actual*, Charles Péguy's *fringes of time* and his notion of the *aternal*, Deleuze and Guattari's central concept of *haecceity*, and my own *micro-haecceity*. All these notions and concepts share, in my view, a similar constitutive principle, namely the gap between the present and our presence within it, and they define different temporalities,[3] as well as different zones of indeterminacy situated at the borders of time; finally, I will conclude with a plea for artistic research as the contemporaneous carrier of the spirit of the contemporary.

Giorgio Agamben's *contemporary*, or: Roland Barthes reading Nietzsche

In October 2005, Giorgio Agamben opened his seminar at the faculty of architecture in Venice with a presentation entitled "What Is the Contemporary?" Agamben's "problem" in "What Is the Contemporary?" (2009), or, better, the question he poses, is, "Of whom and of what are we contemporaries?" This question could also be given as: How can past artists, philosophers, and artworks be considered as being contemporary to us? In this sense, Agamben's major concern is the relation of the present to the *past*, how this present is defined by its own past, and how some moments of the past remain *active* in the present. Agamben's questioning remains implicitly hermeneutic and interpretative, not addressing the experimental production of newness outside the actuality of our present. According to Agamben, the contemporary relates to the present through mechanisms of recognition of the present ("actuality") as something fundamentally archaic. Only those able to perceive and identify "the clues and signals of the archaic in the most modern and recent" things and events (Agamben 2009, 50) can really be considered one's *contemporaries*.

Beginning with a discussion of Friedrich Nietzsche's notion of the *untimely*, read through the eyes of Roland Barthes, Agamben's essay explores the concept of the contemporary in relation to a poem by Osip Mandelstam, to the interactions of light and darkness in astrophysics, to fashion, to the notion of *arkhē*, and to the fundamental heterogeneity of different (Pauline) times. Strongly inspired by Barthes's Nietzschean statement that "the contemporary is the untimely,"[4] Agamben defines the contemporary as "that relationship with time that adheres to it through a disjunction and an anachronism" (Agamben 2009, 41, emphasis removed). For Agamben, contemporariness is a paradoxical structure: those who are contemporary see and grasp their own time more clearly than others, by virtue of their very disjunction with it. This idea derives from Nietzsche's introduction to his second *Untimely Meditation*, where he posits that the untimely is that which "act[s] counter to our time and thereby act[s] on our time and, let us hope, for the benefit of a time to come" (Nietzsche 1997, 60). *On our time, counter to our time, for a time to come*. But how is it possible to be in our time and to act against it? Only through a disconnection and a positive anachronism. As Agamben (2009, 40) puts it: "precisely because of this condition, precisely through this disconnection and this anachronism, they [the untimely] are more capable than others of perceiving and grasping their own

---

3 On the simultaneous co-presence of different times and temporalities in the historical, social, and political worlds, see Koselleck (2000).

4 Agamben doesn't provide a specific reference for this quotation, which seems to have been pronounced by Barthes during his seminars at the Collège de France in 1978–80, in which he communicated this idea several times. However, and despite my efforts, I couldn't find this precise quotation in the published volume *La préparation du roman I et II: Cours au collège de France, 1978–1980* (Barthes 2003).

20

time." "Contemporariness," Agamben (ibid., 41) continues, "is, then, a singular relationship with one's own time, which adheres to it and, at the same time, keeps a distance from it." Through Nietzsche and Barthes, Agamben stresses the fundamental, both existential and experienceable, gap between the present and the present: between the present as "what arrives to us," our presence in it, and our potential departure from it. It is this gap that makes possible criticality, problematisation, and the invention of a new world. This gap is the untimely. To explore this gap creatively is to become-contemporary. That's how, for Barthes (as quoted by Agamben 2009, 40), "the contemporary is the untimely."

Roland Barthes's *inactuel*

Barthes introduced the idea that the contemporary is the untimely in the last series of his seminars at the Collège de France, in 1979–80, under the general title of "The Preparation of the Novel." He presented a conception of the act of writing as an act of resistance against the writer's own time. In this frame, Barthes referred to the untimely character (what he called *l'inactualité*) of the writer as a form of marginalisation, a discrepancy between his interior time and the time of the world around him. In the seminar of 16 February 1980, he specified this relationship in detail and observed that "actuality constantly blackmails whoever intends to forget it" (Barthes 2003, 352, my translation). The writer's responsibility is to counter this blackmail, to offer it a resistance, enabling the affirmation of alternative, infinite possible worlds. As Jean-Luc Nancy (2010) writes, criticising forms of art with explicit political or timely content: "Yes, there is form in these works, but a message precedes it and dominates it" (95). Art that directly responds to the actuality of its day is "not at all art, precisely because [it is] pure signification" (96). Actuality must be challenged, and that is one of the powers of art. The untimely then would be the result of such resistance against actuality. To make contemporary art would be to generate art objects that operate in an untimely manner, that create or enhance the gap between the world and the world, between the present and the present.

Barthes's choice of words (*inactuel*), leaves no doubt that he is referring to Nietzsche's second *Untimely Meditation*, "On the Uses and Disadvantages of History for Life," dated February 1874. As is well known, Nietzsche expresses in this text his annoyance at many of the most prominent features of the political, philosophical, and intellectual landscape of the European culture of his time. Central to his critique is the "cultivation of history," which makes people live in a state of suffering, consumed by the "fever of history" (Nietzsche 1997, 60). Nietzsche translator and commentator Daniel Breazeale (1997) notes:

> It was in the *Untimely Meditations* that Nietzsche first found the courage to "say No" to his age and to his fellow scholars, and, hence, to significant parts of his own self. (xxv–xxvi)

> A perhaps more important feature of the second *Meditation* is precisely the way in which [Nietzsche] seeks simultaneously to concede the inescapable historicity of human existence and to affirm the creative capacity of human beings to overcome

themselves and their past. . . . [Nietzsche's] project is to show how human life requires us to adopt *both* a "historical" and an "ahistorical" perspective upon ourselves. (xv)

The specific use of the term "untimely" (*Unzeitgemäss*)—with which Nietzsche even signed his postcards in that period—deserves a brief commentary. He used it for the first time in a letter to Erwin Rhode dated 17 August 1869. In that letter, the subject of which is Wagner's music, which at that time Nietzsche still admired unconditionally, Nietzsche looks for an explanation for Wagner's inability to gain public acknowledgement. Contrary to those artists that obtain immediate praise from the public, Wagner is described by Nietzsche as someone clinging firmly to his own power, with his glance strongly fixed beyond the transient and ephemeral—"'untimely' in the best sense of the word" (Nietzsche quoted in Breazeale 1997, xlv). According to Breazeale (1997, xlv–xlvi): "Any doubt about how Nietzsche understood the term 'untimely' is removed by a careful reading of *Strauss* [the First Meditation], which is very largely an attack upon the sovereignty of 'public opinion' as an arbiter of taste, values and truth itself. ('Ours,' he reminds us in section 2 of *Schopenhauer as Educator* [the Third Meditation], 'is "the age of public opinion."') Whereas the slave of public opinion strives always to be 'timely,' a declared critic of the same will instead flaunt his deliberate 'untimeliness.'"

The untimely in Nietzsche is opposed to the actual, to everything that in a given time contributes to strengthen the archaic structures of timeliness itself. It is a way to escape the enormous burden of inherited or dictated values, of habits and of all sorts of gregarious practices. What Nietzsche had in mind and what he was most powerfully attacking was his time, which was "consumed by the fever of history." Of course, today things have changed significantly, and I think our age is even more problematically consumed by the fever not of the past but of the present, by the overwhelming dictatorship of the quotidian, what some call "presentism." But, whether we are consumed by history or the present, Nietzsche's core message is how to escape this consumption, how to create a line of escape, how to act in our time, counter to our time.

NIETZSCHE'S *UNTIMELY* (LOST IN TRANSLATION)

The translation of Nietzsche's word *untimely* has been problematic in many ways, and one of these problems affects the translation of Agamben's essay "What Is the Contemporary?," making obscure for English-speaking readers a very important point of his argumentation. In an early discussion of Agamben's essay with my colleague Michael Schwab, I referred to the *untimely* as the "inactual," as something distinct from the *actual*, from dominant, prevailing, and commonsense modes of thought. Michael listened to me, and called me back later that day to tell me that what I was saying, specifically the word *inactual*, was not to be found in Agamben's essay. Fearing I had misunderstood Agamben, I read the essay once more, and there it was, at the beginning of its second paragraph: "Le contemporain est l'*inactuel* [intempestivo]" (Agamben

2008b, 8); and, further down, "le vrai contemporain . . . se définit comme *inactuel* [inattuale]" (ibid., 10). I suddenly realised that I was reading it in French and that Michael was reading it in English. Thus, I checked the English translation, where to my puzzlement I discovered the following: "the contemporary is the *untimely* [intempestivo]" (Agamben 2009, 40), and "those who are truly contemporary . . . are *irrelevant* [inattuale]" (ibid.). I went then to the Italian version, where it reads: "il contemporaneo è l'*intempestivo*," and "è veramente contemporaneo colui che non coincide perfettamente con (il suo tempo) né si adegua alle sue pretese ed è perciò, in questo senso, *inattuale*" (Agamben 2008a). The English translator seems to be unaware of the origin of the word, not to know that Agamben is referring back to Nietzsche's *Unzeitgemäss*, thus eliminating from the whole text the dual dimension of *actual* versus *inactual* that is so crucial to the argument. Instead of a gap between the present and our presence in it, one is misled by the assumption that the untimely is something simply of the order of the irrelevant.[5]

Deleuze and Guattari's *haecceity*

Before being discussed by Giorgio Agamben, Nietzsche's *untimely* (*Unzeitgemäss*) had been the object of important reflections by Gilles Deleuze and Félix Guattari, who developed it from Nietzsche, Foucault, and the French poet and essayist Charles Péguy. In 1980, in the section "Memories and Becomings, Points and Blocks" of *A Thousand Plateaus* (Deleuze and Guattari 1987, 291–98), just after describing how every musician, painter, writer, or philosopher fabricates a punctual system "in order to oppose it, like a springboard to jump from," Deleuze and Guattari make the Nietzschean claim that "history is made only by those who oppose history (not by those who insert themselves into it, or even reshape it)" (ibid., 295). They continue: "This is not done for provocation but happens because the punctual system they found ready-made, or themselves invented, must have allowed this operation: free the line and the diagonal, draw the line instead of plotting a point, produce an imperceptible diagonal. . . . When this is done it always goes down in History but never comes from it" (ibid., 295–96). Insisting on the centrality of drawing a cutting plane that cuts across chaos to produce a plane of composition, Deleuze and Guattari (1987, 296) stress the importance of "multilinear assemblages, which are in no way eternal: they have to do with becoming; they are a bit of becoming in the pure state; they are transhistorical." In this sense, they continue, "there is no act of creation that is not transhistorical and does not come up from behind or proceed by way of a liberated line. Nietzsche opposes history not to the eternal but to the subhistorical or superhistorical: the Untimely, which is another name for *haecceity*" (ibid., my emphasis).

---

5 Beyond the translation of Agamben's essay, the difficulty of translating Nietzsche's title *Unzeitgemässe Betrachtungen* into other languages is manifest in the various attempts officially made in English: *Thoughts Out of Season, Untimely Considerations, Unmodern Observations, Unfashionable Observations, Unconventional Observations*, and *Inopportune Speculations* (with the subtitle "Essays in Sham-Smashing"). In Neo-Latin languages, there is always the option of going for *intempestivo* (Italian, Portuguese, and Spanish), *inactual* or *inatuale* (Portuguese and Italian), or *extemporaneo* (sometimes in Brazilian Portuguese).

With the notion of haecceity, we find yet another way of conceiving the untimely. *Haecceity* is a concept developed by Deleuze and Guattari[6] that describes the emergence of a singularity at any given scale and field. Crucially, a haecceity does not refer to a fully qualified space–time, but to a spatio-temporal dynamism. A haecceity is a passage, a singular point in space–time that dramatises it, curving it, folding it, giving it transient form and temporal structure. In this sense, haecceities can be seen as the piercing points, the geometric place of a perforation in a given space–time surface (*chronos*) that opens a passage, a tunnel towards an empty form of time (*aîon*). If so, a haecceity would have strong links to the notion of *kairos*, the inescapable here-and-now of the event.

Deleuze and Guattari (1987, 260–65) appropriated and refabricated the medieval concept of *haecceitas* to suggest a mode of individuation that is not confused with that of a thing or a subject. In response to a clarification requested by the translators of the American edition of *Dialogues* (Deleuze and Parnet 1987), Deleuze stated that "Haecceitas is a term frequently used in the school of Duns Scotus, in order to designate the individuation of beings. [I use it] in a more special sense: in the sense of an individuation which is not that of an object, nor of a person, but rather of an event (wind, river, day or even hour of the day)" (Deleuze and Parnet 1987, 151n9). The difference from Duns Scotus's usage is crucial and can only be perfectly understood in light of Gilbert Simondon's misspelling of *hecceité* as *ecceité* (without the *h*), which gives the term a modal (rather than essential) quality. In a famous footnote to *A Thousand Plateaus*, Deleuze and Guattari (1987, 540–41n33) explained precisely this crucial difference: "[Haecceity] is sometimes written 'ecceity,' deriving the word from *ecce*, 'here is.' This is an error, since Duns Scotus created the word and the concept from *haec*, 'this thing.' But it is a fruitful error because it suggests a mode of individuation that is distinct from that of a thing or a subject" (my emphasis). And in the main text they explain further: "A season, a winter, a summer, an hour, a date have a perfect individuality lacking nothing, even though this individuality is different from that of a thing or a subject. They are haecceities in the sense that they consist entirely of relations of movement and rest between molecules or particles, capacities to affect and be affected" (ibid., 261).

MICRO-HAECCEITIES

I have appropriated this notion of *haecceity* for the performing arts, applying it to music, dance, theatre, and performance. Specifically focusing on intense and fast-moving haecceities, I introduced the notion of *micro-haecceity* (Assis 2018a, 149; 2018b, 257), a temporal radicalisation of the concept, collapsing it into an infinitesimal fraction of a second, into the radical here-and-now of the

---

6　For further details on the concept of haecceity see chapter 5 of my book *Logic of Experimentation*, especially section 7 (Assis 2018a, 148–52).

evolving performance. Such micro-haecceities are characterised by intensive negentropic properties, unfolding at very high speed. These special kinds of haecceities do not suggest (stable) contemplation, but rather rash (metastable) actions. The performers acting onstage navigate high-speed successions of *prolonged singularities*. There is no time for contemplation;[7] things must happen in the unavoidable urgency and imperative sequentially of the here-and-now. Micro-haecceities are high-energy-loaded and high-speed-moving singularities that carry a force of potential from one position to the next. They make up the visible or audible part of artistic transductive processes. In their functioning as radical becoming they never appear as stable *beings*, remaining an impulse of virtuality from one actualisation to the next. If one thinks, or does, or experiences artistic performances with these operations in mind, the Deleuzian notion of *capture of forces* becomes more graspable than ever: the virtual becomes actual in order to be instantly dissolved into the virtual again. A performer onstage exemplifies such a capture: he or she is not merely reproducing a stratified pre-existing entity, but operating a capture of forces (from the virtual) that produces a new individuation (actual) as a highly intensive becoming, which immediately—as soon as it is generated—points forward to other virtual pre- and after-individualities. Micro-haecceities reveal, therefore, the non-deterministic pasts of their individuated constitutive forces and energies, as much as their unpredictable futures. In doing so, micro-haecceities reveal that the making of art is a fundamentally problematic field—generating and enhancing heterogeneous tensions that produce the conditions of their own (transient) resolutions. If we understand the untimely also as the production of *micro-haecceities* we access the *now* of our becoming, a radical machine capable of piercing the surface of our epoch, the strata of our habits, the skin of our *self*.

Charles Péguy's *aternal*, Plato's *nun*, Foucault's *actual*, or: Gilles Deleuze reading Péguy

In 1991 Deleuze and Guattari once again returned to Nietzsche's notion of the untimely, in *What Is Philosophy?*, in the context of theorising the present as an assemblage (*agencement*), not as a stable entity but as an arrangement of complex relations, interactions, and psychological processes. For them, there is not *one* present but a simultaneous multiplicity of temporalities. In a dense page devoted to the French writer and novelist Charles Péguy and his definition of an event, Deleuze and Guattari (1994, 112) briefly introduce Péguy's concept of the *aternal*, Plato's *nun*, and Foucault's *actual*. Interestingly, these concepts are presented in relation to Nietzsche's *untimely*, on which they seem to be variations.

---

7   Here the contrast to Deleuze and Guattari's concept is clear. For their characteristic example of haecceity—Lorca's "at five in the afternoon" (see Lorca 1997, 263, 265)—has a scenic/contemplative quality, evoking a particular landscape, time of day, temperature, sunlight, inner memories, and so on. It requires a (rather long) duration and length.

Péguy's explanation of the event in his novel *Clio* led him to create a neologism, the *aternal* (in French *l'internel*), a term that describes something that "is no longer the historical, and . . . is not the eternal" (Deleuze and Guattari 1994, 111). Deleuze and Guattari write: "Péguy had to create this noun to designate a new concept. Is this not something similar to that which a thinker far from Péguy designated *Untimely* [*Intempestif*] or *Inactual* [*Inactuel*]—the unhistorical vapor that has nothing to do with the eternal, the becoming without which nothing would come about in history but that does not merge with history?" (ibid., 111–12). Quoting from Nietzsche's second *Untimely Meditation*, Deleuze and Guattari then discuss the temporal relations between past, present, and future, in a passage that recalls similar paragraphs from Deleuze's *Logic of Sense*, in which a stoic conception of time had been presented. What is new in the section on Péguy in *What Is Philosophy?* is the link to Foucault's notion of the *actual*, which Deleuze and Guattari derive from Plato's *nun*. Nietzsche's "acting counter to the past, and therefore on the present, for the benefit . . . of a future" points to a future that "is not a historical future, not even a utopian history, it is the *infinite Now*, the *Nun* that Plato already distinguished from every present: the Intensive or Untimely, not an instant but a becoming" (Deleuze and Guattari 1994, 112, my emphasis). To complicate things a bit more, Deleuze and Guattari ask whether Péguy's *aternal* [*internel*], Nieztsche's *untimely* [*inactuel*], and Foucault's *actual* are not the same thing:

> But how could the concept now be called the *actual* when Nietzsche called it the *inactual*? Because, for Foucault, what matters is the difference between the *present* and the *actual*. The actual is not what we are but, rather, what we become, what we are in the process of becoming. . . . The present, on the contrary, is what we are and, thereby, what already we are ceasing to be. We must distinguish not only the share that belongs to the past and the one that belongs to the present but, more profoundly, the share that belongs to the present and that belonging to the actual. It is not that the actual is the utopian prefiguration of a future that is still part of our history. Rather, it is the now of our becoming. (Deleuze and Guattari 1994, 112)

Deleuze and Guattari's very specific reference here is to chapter 5 of part 3 of Michel Foucault's *The Archaeology of Knowledge*, significantly entitled "The Historical *a priori* and the Archive" (see Foucault [1972] 2002, 142–48). Theorising the archive, Foucault claims that the "the proper task of a history of thought, as against a history of behaviors or representations . . . [is] to define the conditions in which human beings 'problematize' what they are, what they do, and the world in which they live" (Foucault [1985] 1992, 10). As part of this effort, Foucault identified a particular zone in which problematisation occurs, a zone where different temporalities come into contact, friction, and eventually destruction.

> The analysis of the archive, then, involves a privileged region: at once close to us, and different from our present existence, it is *the border of time that surrounds our presence*, which overhangs it, and which indicates it in its otherness; it is that which, outside ourselves, delimits us. The description of the archive deploys its possibilities . . . on the basis of the very discourses that have just ceased to be ours; its threshold

of existence is established by the discontinuity that separates us from what we can
no longer say, and from that which fails outside our discursive practice; it begins
with the outside of our own language . . . ; its locus is *the gap between our own discursive
practices.* (Foucault [1972] 2002, 147, my emphasis)

It is this gap—the gap between the present and the present, between the
present and our presence within it—that creates the conditions for a *diagnosis*.
Not a positivist diagnosis that would lead to a clear prescription and cure, but
a diagnosis that (paradoxically) creates its own problems, without which our
existence would be infinitely less interesting and less fruitful. It is a diagnosis that "deprives us of our continuities; it dissipates that temporal identity in
which we are pleased to look at ourselves when we wish to exorcise the discon-
tinuities of history. . . . In this sense, the diagnosis does not establish the fact of
our identity by the play of distinctions. It establishes that *we are difference*, that
our reason is the difference of discourses, our history *the difference of times*, our
selves the difference of masks. That difference, far from being the forgotten
and recovered origin, is this dispersion that we are and make" (Foucault [1972]
2002, 147–48, my emphasis).

This dispersion occurs in our lives, our activities, and our artistic practices.
It happens as a complex arrangement of different temporalities, discourses,
and masks—all moving at different paces (fast and slow), with different accelerations (stratifications and ruptures), and with different temperatures (hot
and cold). This means that no present is ever One, no present can ever be a
stable entity, no simultaneity can be fully grasped. As in the inner eye of a hurricane, we find ourselves in a dispersive and explosive column of air rotating
at high speed, a violent storm that doesn't blow forward towards the future
(Benjamin's progress) but that revolves around itself, throwing objects, things,
ideas, and feelings towards innumerable other compossible futures, which
exist *now*. If there is progress (in Benjamin's terms), it is convoluted rather than
linear progress, incoherent, not unifiable, not deductible in its succession, and
in centripetal rotation around an empty centre.

Multiple temporalities, or: artistic research as the carrier of the contemporary

Barthes, Agamben, and even Foucault relate to the *past*. Agamben's strongest
examples in *What Is the Contemporary?* are the notion of *arkhē* and Saint Paul.
In relation to *arkhē*, Agamben (2009) writes, "only he who perceives the indices and signatures of the archaic in the most modern and recent can be contemporary" (50). And he adds, "the key to the modern [in art and literature]
is hidden in the immemorial and the prehistoric" (51). He concludes, "to be
contemporary means in this sense to return to a present where we have never
been" (51–52). In this respect, my perspective is totally different: it is not about
a return, but about the *invention* of a present to which we have never been—
an invention that can only be accomplished by what Paul Klee referred to as

a people to come[8]—not a people from *the future* but people from today looking at our own time in a completely renewed way. However, Agamben does not refer to Paul Klee, nor to any kind of futurity, but to Saint Paul and his "being-contemporary with the Messiah, which he calls . . . the 'time of the now'" (52). For Agamben, the new present is to be built after insightful understanding of subtle signs from the remote past, a perspective that implies some sort of primordial lost paradise and some kind of lost sense that ought to be recuperated.

Foucault doesn't believe that history is a product of (modern) sense. But his continued obsession was the archive, and its many different modes of formation, stratification, and modulation. Foucault's archive is highly heterogeneous, articulating a multiplicity of historical dimensions without any clear-cut dialectics that would define its limits and borders. Foucault's historical methodology looks at the past not for the past's sake, but to understand how we became what we are today. Even if not historiographical in conventional terms, his approach remains that of a historian, of someone investigating past facts, documents, and events. This explains his numerous histories: of madness, of the hospital, of the prison, of knowledge, of infamous people, of sexuality. Self-ironically, Foucault said about himself, "I am a historian of ideas after all. But an ashamed, or, if you prefer, a presumptuous historian of ideas. . . . I cannot be satisfied until I have cut myself off from 'the history of ideas,' until I have shown in what way archaeological analysis differs from the descriptions of 'the history of ideas'" (Foucault [1972] 2002, 152).

Thus, moving beyond Agamben's, Barthes's, and Foucault's relation to history and historicity, my view and my proposal are different as I decidedly point towards *futures of the contemporary*, and those futures' manifold possibilities of constitution, formation, and reinvention. More so than other modes of research, artistic research has the power to reverse the arrow of research: where interpreters investigate the archive, looking into the past, into the *arkhē*, or into the *global present*, artistic researchers can look into the abysses of the present in order to grasp its futures, exploring the diagnostic function of art, contributing to a symptomatology of one's own epoch.

Artistic research can also be conceived as performing historical or historiographical research as a means to reactualise older forms, technical objects, or modes of expression. But artistic research's most interesting perspectives are those that more explicitly relate to the future. Such quests do not try to find out *how things really were in the past*, nor are they aiming at understanding *how we became what we are today* (this was Foucault's goal). Rather, the really challenging discoveries today are to find out *how we can become* today *what today we aim to be*.

---

8   Paul Klee's famous claim that modern art hadn't yet found its "people" can be found at the end of his short treatise *On Modern Art*, which he prepared as the basis for a lecture that he delivered in Jena in 1924 (see Read 1948, 7). More than "a people to come," he insists on the notion of a still "missing people." The passage is as follows: "Sometimes I dream of a work of really great breadth, ranging through the whole region of element, object, meaning and style. This, I fear, will remain a dream, but it is a good thing even now to bear the possibility occasionally in mind. Nothing can be rushed. It must grow, it should grow of itself, and if the time ever comes for that work—then so much the better! We must go on seeking it! We have found parts, but not the whole! *We still lack the ultimate power, for: the people are not with us.* But we seek a people" (Klee 1948, 54–55, my emphasis).

Or, *how we can depart from today, even without a clear destination in mind or safe ports to reach.* The future is contained in the present but remains concealed to itself. To be contemporary doesn't mean *to return* (Agamben) but *to invent* a present—a present where we have never been. At the borders of time and space defined by the violent hurricane of the present, we need to build the future rather than rescue the past. This future will not solve the storm, but it will generate new tensions and new inconsistencies, as well as new points of reference, new singularities in the ever-expanding manifold of art, life, and society. In this sense, I believe that artistic research has a very important role in the art world of today, especially in its capacity to generate new forms and modes of expression that are rigorous rather than accidental and at the same time indeterminate. Artistic research asks how we can create in the midst of complex arrangements of different temporalities, how we can artistically and creatively operate inside the furious inner eye of the multiple hurricanes we are living in—how we can live at the border of time that surrounds our presence and find the courage to jump into the core of the hurricane, from where we return *breathless and with bloodshot eyes.*

References

Agamben, Giorgio. 2008a. *Che cos'è il contemporaneo?* Rome: Nottetempo. Kindle. Translated by David Kishik and Stefan Pedatella as Agamben 2009.

———. 2008b. *Qu'est que le contemporain?* Translated by Maxime Rovere. Paris: Payot & Rivages. First published as Agamben 2008a.

———. 2009. "What Is the Contemporary?" In *What Is an Apparatus? And Other Essays*, translated by David Kishik and Stefan Pedatella, 39–54. Stanford, CA: Stanford University Press. Essay first published as Agamben 2008a.

Assis, Paulo de. 2018a. *Logic of Experimentation: Rethinking Performance through Artistic Research*. Orpheus Institute Series. Leuven: Leuven University Press.

———. 2018b. "Transduction and Ensembles of Transducers: Relaying Flows of Intensities." In *Transpositions: Aestherico-Epistemic Operators in Artistic Research*, edited by Michael Schwab, 245–65. Orpheus Institute Series. Leuven: Leuven University Press.

Badiou, Alain. 2014. "Alain Badiou and Judith Balso: Contemporary Art: Considered Philosophically and Poetologically." YouTube video, 38:06, posted by "European Graduate School Video Lectures," 30 September. Accessed 24 January 2018. https://www.youtube.com/watch?v=g83Qni9alYM.

Barthes, Roland. 2003. *La préparation du roman I et II: Cours au collège de France, 1978–1980*. Edited by Nathalie Léger. Paris: Seuil. Translated by Kate Briggs as *The Preparation of the Novel: Lecture Courses and Seminars at the Collège de France (1978–1979 and 1979–1980)* (New York: Columbia University Press, 2011).

Breazeale, Daniel. 1997. Introduction to Friedrich Nietzsche, *Untimely Meditations*, edited by Daniel Breazeale, translated by R. J. Hollingdale, vii–xxxiii. Cambridge: Cambridge University Press.

Deleuze, Gilles, and Félix Guattari. 1987. *A Thousand Plateaus: Capitalism and Schizophrenia*. Translated by Brian Massumi. Minneapolis: University of Minnesota Press. First published 1980 as *Mille plateaux* (Paris: Minuit).

———. 1994. *What Is Philosophy?* Translated by Hugh Tomlinson and Graham Burchell. New York: Columbia University Press. First published 1991 as *Qu'est-ce que la philosophie?* (Paris: Minuit).

Deleuze, Gilles, and Claire Parnet. 1987. *Dialogues*. Translated by Hugh Tomlinson and Barbara Habberjam. New York: Columbia University Press. First published 1977 as *Dialogues* (Paris:

Flammarion).

Foucault, Michel. (1972) 2002. *The Archaeology of Knowledge*. Translated by A. M. Sheridan Smith. Abingdon, UK: Routledge. First published 1969 as *L'archéologie du savoir* (Paris: Gallimard). This translation first published 1972 (London: Tavistock).

———. (1985) 1992. *The Use of Pleasure: The History of Sexuality: Volume Two*. Translated by Robert Hurley. London: Penguin. First published 1984 as *Histoire de la sexualité: 2. L'usage des plaisirs* (Paris: Gallimard). This translation first published 1985 (New York: Pantheon).

Hindrichs, Gunnar. 2004. "Musical Modernity: What Does It Mean Today?" In *The Foundations of Contemporary Composition*, edited by Claus-Steffen Mahnkopf, 133–51. Hofheim: Wolke.

Klee, Paul. 1948. *On Modern Art*. Translated by Paul Findlay. London: Faber and Faber. First published 1945 as *Über die moderne Kunst* (Bern: Bentelli), including an English translation by Douglas Cooper.

Koselleck, Reinhart. 2000. *Zeitschichten: Studien zur Historik*. Frankfurt am Main: Suhrkamp.

Lorca, Federico García. 1997. *Lament for Ignacio Sánchez Mejías*. Translated by Alan S. Trueblood. In *Federico García Lorca: Selected Poems*, edited by Christopher Maurer, 260–73. London: Penguin.

Lyotard, Jean-François. 1984. *The Postmodern Condition: A Report on Knowledge*. Translated by Geoff Bennington and Brian Massumi. Manchester: Manchester University Press. First published 1979 as *La condition postmoderne: Rapport sur le savoir* (Paris: Minuit).

Nancy, Jean-Luc. 2010. "Art Today." Translated by Charlotte Mandell. *Journal of Visual Culture* 9 (1): 91–99. First delivered as a lecture, Milan, 2006.

Nietzsche, Friedrich. 1997. "On the Uses and Disadvantages of History for Life." In *Untimely Meditations*, edited by Daniel Breazeale, translated by R. J. Hollingdale, 60–123. Cambridge: Cambridge University Press. Essay first published 1874 as "Vom Nutzen und Nachteil der Historie für das Leben," 2nd part of *Unzeitgemässe Betrachtungen* (Leipzig: Fritzsch, 1873–76).

Read, Herbert. 1948. Introduction to Klee 1948, [7]–[8].

Steinegger, Catherine. 2012. *Pierre Boulez et le théâtre: De la Compagnie Renaud-Barrault à Patrice Chéreau*. Wavre: Mardaga.

On the Question of Contemporaneity Today

Zsuzsa Baross

Trent University

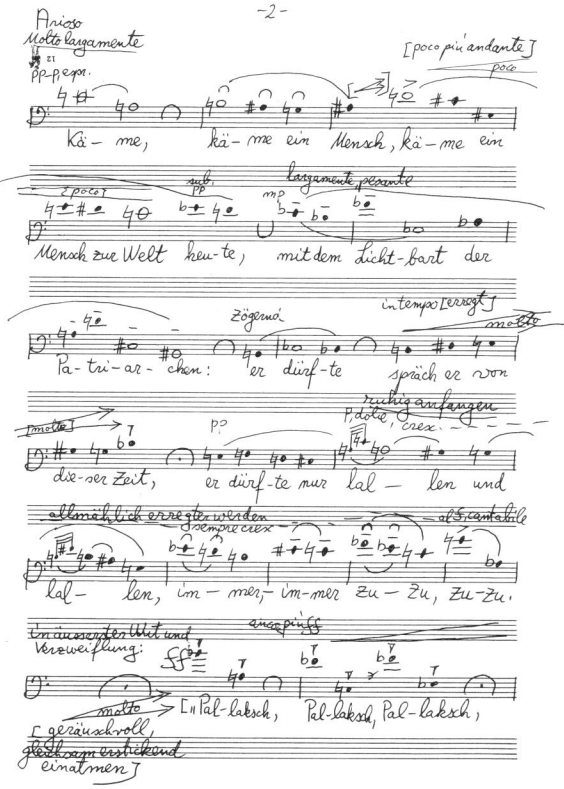

(In the place convention reserves for a motto or epigram at the head of the text, I am placing the image of a text or, as Derrida might have said, a medallion, which, in a just as condensed and enigmatic fashion—to be fully deciphered only at the end—intimates what the text is yet to come to say about its subject matter: contemporaneity in and of our present.[1])

---

1   The image is of the second page of the partition of György Kurtág's "Tübingen, Jänner"; both notes and text are in Kurtág's handwriting. Composed for a solo baritone, it is the last in Kurtág's *Hölderlin Gesänge* cycle (1990–95), but the words are Paul Celan's, from a poem whose eponymous title and text incorporate several of Hölderlin's singular markers, including the non-word "Pallaksch" that Hölderlin is said to have repeated, cried out, at times shouting, at times beating on his piano in the confinement of his tower in Tübingen, in the year before his death in 1843.

The writing here, which preserves the discursive style of the oral presentation on which it is based, is structured in the movement of three encounters, or rather, a collision and two encounters.[2] Steps taken a while ago in a longer journey that has anticipated the question of this Academy, they solicit the latter not with regard to the future but to the present—impasse? crisis?—of thinking the contemporary today.

Each of the steps comes in response to an invitation, irritation, or intervention arriving from the outside. The first, the collision (with a text by Éric Alliez), is the briefest contact. Instantaneous, it does not survive its own effects and the new direction in which it deflects the writing will not be traced back to it as source. Yet, it is not a negative, unproductive, or reactive event, a confrontation or an occasion for criticism. The collision matters. In the collision, the collision itself matters, even if it is not responsible and a fortiori does not oversee the future of its aftermath. Still, it is not an encounter, unlike the two other movements, which are set in motion by encounters—with Blanchot, or rather, by encountering Blanchot's encountering Bataille, and with Deleuze, who in turn encounters the song of a Tuvan throat singer from Siberia. . . . In an encounter, the contact endures, takes place in the writing that gives it a place, gives it the place of its taking place, whence it continues to guide, or as it were, watch over the patient working through the demands of the question, or dilemma, or contradiction it itself implants.

1. Éric Alliez: a collision

The contemporary as a question to reconstruct and a problem to reconstitute today first came to me at the first DARE conference here in Ghent at the Orpheus Institute, while listening to Éric Alliez's "On Contemporary Philosophy and Art" (see Alliez 2017). The ambitious presentation promised, "in the name of the *contemporary*," to introduce "an oscillation, a supplementary pulsation, between a philosophy that is *contemporary* with *contemporary* art and art that is *contemporary* with *contemporary* philosophy" (ibid., 293, emphasis added).

These prefatory statements gave only the vaguest indication or the symptom of the difficulty at the heart of Alliez's project, namely, that the threefold repetition will not properly fold (complicate) received concepts of the contemporary. But even if they did not yet point me—this will happen midway into the presentation—in the direction of the *differend* that will come to separate my work, not just from Alliez's, regarding precisely the contemporaneity of certain current notions of the contemporary, the images projected onto the screen—a cut-out by Matisse (*Swimming Pool*), two Duchamps, and a Warhol— did, immediately. It is they, and not the discourse or the theoretical apparatus assembled, that provoked the collision.

At the time, I was writing on/working with three singularly difficult if not painfully tormented works: Jean-Luc Godard's *Adieu au langage* (2014), a film

---

2   Unless otherwise noted, all translations are mine.

that does violence to the apparatus of the cinema and assaults the senses, in every sense of this word;[3] a single line from a poem by Paul Celan: "Die Welt is Fort," "The word is gone" (1967)[4]; and *La Rabbia*, Pier Paolo Pasolini's false documentary of the history of the present in 1964, whose title *Rage* is self-referential, directed at images of the very history it documents.[5] Received in the context of these concerns, Alliez's material evidence provoked the silent protest in me: "these are not my contemporaries." My contemporaries violently dismantle the apparatus of the cinema, break the word, make language stutter, write word holes into which other words disappear, rage against their present....

It may have been an impatient and, if only for this reason alone, an unjust reaction.[6] Yet it confirmed with the self-evidence of an intuition, immediately, instantaneously, something that I knew without knowing that I know it: that Godard, Celan, and Pasolini are contemporaries and, which is not the same thing, *my* contemporaries—not despite but because of the different distance that separates each from the other and from "my" present in historical time. To rephrase this intuition in a more theoretical language, the contemporary is simultaneously determined by a double negative condition: it cannot be universalised or generalised, that is, emptied of its content, which is its time; at the same time, it cannot be reduced to being of the same (chronological historical period or epoch of) time either. (The first of these propositions may appear self-evident; yet, one of the most influential texts on the subject in our time, Agamben's *What Is the Contemporary?*,[7] makes no reference to our present, asks not what characterises our time, what it is to be contemporary in this time. I will return to this lapsus.)

---

3 Baross (2015a).

4 Baross (2014).

5 Baross (2015b).

6 This is not the place for the justified and rigorous critique that Alliez's text deserves (Alliez 2017). I can only pose a few telegraphic questions regarding the concept or rather the different usages of the word *contemporary*, deployed, utilised, mobilised in several senses throughout the text. Even before attending to the sense of the ambition of speaking "in the name of the contemporary" (293) (will the text have to be or become a pragmatic/performative affirmation of the concept of its own construction?), or to the timeliness of affirming a "certain absolute of thought . . . in the figure of the 'untimely'" (294), one would need to ask about the meaning of being "contemporary with" in the double formulation and the *contemporaneity* it assumes and assures to link "art that is contemporary with contemporary philosophy" and "a philosophy that is contemporary with contemporary art" (293). Does the repetition differentiate the concept, introduce a productive difference in being, or becoming contemporary? In which case the sense of the first term in "contemporary with contemporary" must surpass the temporal horizon of the common usage of simply being of the same time. If not, if the relation remains confined to an epochal commonality (be it modernity or the urgent but epochal task of its transformation), inquiry will not pass beyond discovering analogies, resemblances, or even interactions or "reciprocal pulsations" (as in an early example of Matisse's *Swimming Pool*: the vitalism of Bergson, the flow of Nietzsche, a pragmatic constructivism [294])—neither of which folds the concept of the contemporary itself.

This difficulty is not uncommon to inquiries directed at "contemporary art." Alain Badiou diagnoses it as the difficulty inherent in the notion of "contemporary art" itself: "The expression itself is complicated because after all one could say of all art that it is contemporary and necessarily of its own time. It is rather strange to retain the adjective *contemporary* in a singular and particular fashion to define a particular sequence of art or the attribute of contemporaneity in a manner absolutely general" (Badiou 2012). Jean-Luc Nancy (2010) simply avoids the problem and exits from the difficulty by replacing the term "contemporary" with "art today."

7 The short Italian text *Che cos'e il contemporaneo* (Agamben 2008) appeared in several collections of Agamben's essays both in English and French translations. I will be citing here from the English text that appeared in *Nudities* (2011), while occasionally also referring to the Italian original as well as to the often more precise French translation (2009).

The radically different formulation that emerged from this collision and confrontation inscribes the question in the present as addressed to the present. It asks, what does it mean to be contemporary *today?* Or to dispense with the need for a subject, whose place falls away once we consider the contemporary as an event, how is writing (or dancing, or thinking, or filming, or composing, etc.) to *become* contemporary *today?* The double emphasis here is at once on time, on the timing of the question today, and on becoming, on contemporaneity as a becoming rather than being of an epoch or a period of time.

A few rapidly stated theoretical propositions:

To pose the question this way, to append the temporal adverb to Agamben's formulation "what does it mean to contemporary?" (2011, 10), "che cosa significa essere contemporanei?," is to start from the paradox: the "contemporary" is historical, historically overdetermined.

The concept, like any archaeological find, bears as symptoms the marks of the time of its provenance; but more importantly, its content, the conditions contemporaneity demands to be met by thought, action, writing, or figure, against which the latter will be measured, are themselves conditioned by time, by an each time singular and singularising today.

First, the concept itself has a history. By necessity: it inaugurates a new relation to time and to one's own time. Aristotle as we know defined the task of historical narrative as *immortalising*. When Agamben (2011, 10) cites Barthes (although this attribution is problematised by Paulo de Assis [see this volume, 20n4) "the contemporary is the untimely," the reference is to Nietzsche's *invention* of the contemporary—the invention of contemporaneity as itself an invention. But whether we trace its origin to Nietzsche or to Hegel's critique of a philosophy, which, for the purpose of teaching the world of what it ought to be, always comes too late, or in the domain of arts, where it appears with a certain *décalage*, to the *modernité* of a Mallarmé ("un present fait defaut"), Baudelaire or Rimbaud ("nous ne sommes pas au monde"[8])—or again, to all the "manifestos" that in the past century claim the future by reclaiming the present—the indices of this turn profoundly mark occidental modernity, are perhaps even synonymous with it.

Second, the content of the notion, the sense of the multiple sensibilities and their mutations it has come to gather to itself in its relatively short history, and which would not have made sense to the Greeks, is itself indexed for time. The "untimely" (of Nietzsche) is not timeless. The time of the contemporary, the "tempus" sheltered inside the word, itself has its time.

The question therefore is always of and for a today, never an abstraction or a transhistorical idea or ideal.

This determination, however, is not unidirectional, moving from time to action, to figure, or to writing. If the concept is to make sense, if there is to be a question, a problem, if the contemporary is to be a task or imperative, if there is

---

8   Quoted by Badiou (2014, 15).

to be the risk of failure, failing to be become contemporary, missing one's rendezvous with history—the contemporary must be a reciprocal co-relation, at once constitutive and constituted. We need to hear the prefix *con* of the vocable as referring to a figure or action, a work or *geste*, a writing or its "style" that composes with, is cut to the measure of its time, which in turn measures it—yields to its force, or not (neutralises it); composes with it, or not (remains indifferent to, unaffected by it, renders it impotent, ineffective, powerless).

Two consequences follow from this:

(a) First, the contemporary—*geste* and concept—constitutes an event, it arrives in *and* to a particular time; however minor, however imperceptible this event may be, it is an intervention *in* time. There is of course Nietzsche's monumental example of effective (*wirkliche*) history that simultaneously invents a past and opens the path to another future or rather gives itself another past so as to invent a wholly other future; or the exemplary of the figure of Paul in Agamben's texts who reorders relations of/in time itself,[9] or again, the writings of Heidegger that, precisely in times of crisis, intervene to convert the "contemporary" situation (in the 1929–30 lecture course, from boredom to the temporality of being [Heidegger 1995]; at the end of the war in 1945, from the poverty of things to spiritual riches [Heidegger 2004], again in 1945, from devastation to waiting, *attente* [Heidegger 2006]). And to look already ahead and cite an example from the domain of the arts, the painting of Bacon, of Deleuze's Bacon, for the writing of the philosopher is always a creative intervention, resumes the history of painting—otherwise (Deleuze 2003).

(b) The second consequence is yet another paradox: the contemporary is not contemporaneous (in the common usage of this term) either with itself (as the song says, "I'm not the same as I used to be") or with its time. It is situated on the other side of the interval that the constitutive gesture itself cuts into time.

But there is yet a third dimension, a more profound and critical complication, a fold on the interior of the historicity of the contemporary. If the first two aspects envelop the concept on the outside, this third dimension opens to a wholly other register of time on the interior. I owe its discovery to a silent distinction that Agamben makes in his seminar, which as we know develops a series of "indications" or definitions to answer the question of its title, "what is the contemporary?" or "who are our contemporaries?," by engaging a small number of texts of more or less distant origin—several centuries distant, more recent and very recent—*as contemporaries*: "it is important that we make ourselves contemporaries, in a certain manner, of these texts" (Agamben 2011, 10, translation modified).

The distinction (which permits this extraordinary folding of the question upon itself[10]) comes at the threshold of the seminar, before any of the texts would be encountered *as contemporaries*: "The 'time' of our seminar is contem-

---

9 See especially *The Time That Remains* (Agamben 2005).

10 Something that neither the redoubling/division of the contemporary, which remains mechanical, nor the genealogy/archaeology applied in Alliez's text succeeds in performing.

poraneity" (ibid., translation modified[11]), "Il 'tempo' del nostro seminario è la contemporaneità" (Agamben 2008a, 11).

It is a silent intervention (Agamben does not call our attention to it) but not any less crucial. It makes a *conceptual* distinction, is a decoupage that cuts things differently, draws a line between the *contemporary* as figure, task, act, or performative *geste*, which is yet to be defined and will be the work of the seminar, on the one hand, and on the other, *contemporaneity* as an order of time, a "chronologically indeterminate" temporal register (ibid., 18), in which the question, what is the contemporary? who are our contemporaries? will be asked and answered. For it is in this milieu that unfold the anachronic histories of contemporaries—of Kurtág whose music (*sprechgesang*) sings with Celan's poem; of Celan whose language stutters with Hölderlin's, of all three, Kurtág–Celan–Hölderlin, speaking together; or Paul, the Apostle, and Walter Benjamin, the philosopher; or again, of Pasolini and Godard. It is here, in this domain, that voices, works, music and texts, and *gestes* of more or less distant origin in chronological time, come to contact and contract, come to resonate, to resound in/with one another as contemporaries.

Now this conceptual contemporaneity designates not a relation, but a register of time, a register of temporal relations, of secret communications passing between images and texts, music and music, which, at a certain time in history, come to mutually resonate from their distant location in historical, chronological time. Such are the histories that take place in Agamben's seminar, the success of which depends on its discourse becoming contemporary of/with Mandelstam, Benjamin, Paul, and thereby, the recipient and the receptor of obscure missives/sendings from distant pasts.

So yes, contemporary *is always a question for a today, but its time, its temporal location, where it is actualised is contemporaneity: anachronic, discontinuous, heterogeneous with, yet inscribed in, chronological history and its calendar time.*

Contemporary versus contemporaneity: an absolutely critical distinction. It liberates the contemporary from its confinement to an epoch or period. In other words, it is the condition of possibility of both the concept and of making ourselves contemporaries, for example, of Racine,[12] or Benjamin and Paul, simultaneously; of forcing (for interpretation constitutes a forcing) an other to become our contemporary. Contemporaneity as a relation is therefore a creative act, perhaps even an act of resistance: creative, for the spatio-temporal zone of this relation does not precede the act; resistance, because it changes the world. It itself is an event.

---

11 Unnecessarily, the English translation substitutes the awkward "contemporariness" for "contemporaneity." For the difficulties in translating to English and several other languages Agamben's translations of Nietzsche's adjective in *Unzeitgemässe Betrachtungen* to Italian as "intempestiva" and "inattuale," see Paulo de Assis's essay in this volume.

12 On the day after the night of Trump's election victory, but referring to the planetary situation of the present, Alain Badiou (2016) opens his lecture at UCLA with a citation from Racine's *Athalie*: "C'était pendant l'horreur d'une profonde nuit" (It was during the horror of a profound night)—and in an instant actualises an instance of contemporaneity.

2. Blanchot/Batille: my contemporaries

In the massive corpus of Maurice Blanchot, I chance upon this critical passage:

> One can say that the political exigency was never absent from [Bataille's] thought, although it took on different shapes depending on the interior or exterior urgency. The opening lines of *Le Coupable* speak to this clearly. *To write under the pressure of war is not to write about the war* but to write inside its horizon and as if it were the companion with whom one shares one's bed (assuming that it leaves us room, a margin of freedom). (Blanchot 1988, 4, emphasis added)

I find it without looking for it, but once I find it, it immediately imposes itself as a contemporary, as the contemporary of my question. For Blanchot's reference may be to Bataille writing during the war but, as is often the case with Blanchot's writing, the passage carries what Benjamin calls (and which Agamben also cites as) a "historical index": a missive from the past to a particular future that is our present. Across the distance of time, of half a century, or rather, from inside another epoch—for the time when Blanchot (and Nancy and Derrida) was writing about "community," when writing could still gather us together around the question of community, even if it was its impossibility, is already another epoch—three critical indices in particular find us/target us today; they point in the direction of where our thinking should start, where it should install its worksite: in the middle of things, inside the horizon of the present, and under the pressures of the time, which are massive and multiple, incessantly multiplying.

Three key elements deserve closer attention:
• The first concerns the interdiction to write "about." To interrogate one's present, to ask "what characterises life in our time?" as does Bataille (2005, 92) or Badiou (2014, 17), whose question is already closer to ours, "of what present are we the *living* contemporaries *in* philosophy?"—but shall we not extend the domain to music, painting, or literature—is not to write "about" the present, but to write (or compose, or film, or dance, or think) inside its horizon, as if it were our companion sharing the same bed. (In another uncanny resonance of contemporaneity—in truth, a *web* of chronologically undetermined virtual relations, in the process of being continually actualised—Heidegger [1995, 75] writes around the same epochal time as Bataille of the "diagnoses and prognoses" of the present that do "not grasp us in our contemporary situation," and whose "contemporaneity . . . is entirely without us.")
• The second, concerns the condition of being "inside the horizon": that is, in a world closed upon itself, without an Outside; in other words, a world without a proper future, without the incalculable and the unforeseeable shimmering on the horizon, arriving unforeseen from the other side of a limit, open to the Outside. (In the same wartime text, *Le Coupable*, Bataille himself writes: "*When* this book is read, the outcome of this war taking place *now* will be known to the smallest schoolchild" [1988, 26, emphasis added]. It would be a mistake to think that Bataille here speaks of the future in the proper sense, that this

"when" refers to the future of his "now." The time of the "now" inside the horizon and of the "when" on the other side, which every schoolchild will know as past, as having passed, are not of the same order or genus of time. They may be contiguous but are radically discontinuous, at an infinite distance, just as the instant of my death is with the living duration of my life. The "when" [when the end of the war will be known] is, in fact, not a future at all but what Deleuze calls an "inclusive disjunction," the either/or [win or lose the war] which closes off *possible* futures, the possibility of futurity itself inside the horizon.)

· The third, to the condition of writing inside the horizon "under pressure," that is, *against* the pressure of the times. For pressure is tactile, *is* (in) contact. It is everywhere; like gases it occupies every space, fills up every place inside the horizon. In other words, it leaves "no margin of freedom." But writing against it is not in opposition to it, to negate its force. Opposition requires an interval, the gap of a distance whence to find one's footing, that is, the liberty for launching an opposing force—a force uncontaminated by it. Without such liberty, writing (dancing, thinking or filming) "against" will have to be a "composition" in the musical sense of this term, it will have to be composing with what weighs against it—lean into, strain against it, as one leans into the wind, strains against the force of the tide, of the current. For pressure is also weight, it weighs on or down; as such it leaves no room in between, permits no relation, if relation is contingent on an *écart*: the distance of a gap, of an interval of *differentiation*.

Closing here this detour explicating Blanchot's key terms, I return to the significance (both in the sense of meaning or *signifiance* and importance) of Badiou's exceptional formulation of the question: "of what present are we the *living* contemporaries *in* philosophy?" Or the *living* contemporaries *in* music? or *in* the theatre, or *in* literature? (We recall here that Artaud, mad, writing precisely against the pressure of diabolic forces that scatter his thoughts the instant they appear, claims existence *in* literature.[13]) For need we not ask the same *of* the arts as we ask of philosophy? Ask of their practices, works, compositions, that is, creations, not to describe or represent or narrate or lament or diagnose or save us from a world that is without a proper future, not to shelter us from or be a refuge in "an epoch without an epoch" (Stiegler 2016), in a world that is "a world without being a world." ("Il n'y a pas de monde," ours is a "situation de non-monde," as writes Badiou [2014, 93]), but they empower us to become the living contemporaries, in their domain, in and of precisely such a world. And art will meet this demand only if and when it composes with the formidable forces pressing against it; if and when it succeeds to exhibit as one exhibits paintings in a gallery, to render visible/sensible—on its skin—that immaterial field against which and with which it takes shape, at the same time as it lends it its own visibility/sensibility, the materiality of its corpus.

---

13 In one of his desperate letters to Jacques Rivière, the editor of La Nouvelle Revue Française, Artaud pleads, claims the right of an existence *in* literature: "Il m'importe beaucoup que les quelques manifestations d'existence *spirituelle* [original emphasis] que j'ai pu me donner à moi-même [my emphasis] ne soit pas considérées comme inexistantes" (Artaud 1927, 14, as translated in Artaud 1965, 8; It is very important to me that the few manifestations of *spiritual* [original emphasis] existence that I have been able to give *myself* [my emphasis] not be regarded as inexistent).

There are two ways to proceed from this radical point: inside the horizon, under pressure, without an outside or future:

(a) Ask "what is to be done?," as does Nancy (2016), who repeats Lenin's old question, which today translates as: what is left for art, what can it still be at the time of devastation, of planetary catastrophe? When time itself has mutated ("nous sommes dans une période intervallaire" [Badiou 2014, 72]), in "the epoch of the absence of epoch" (Stiegler 2016, 31), "without a predicate" (Badiou 2014, 35), in a mutation of which we cannot even say what mutation it is (Nancy 2016, 16); or perhaps even more radically, at a time when time itself has begun to end, is the time that remains, *le temps qui rest*?[14]

(b) Or, as philosophy has always done, turn to art, not for the salvation of the world but of the question, in the hope that in its intervention, intersession, and invention art may permit us, in its exceptional instances, to become the living contemporaries of *a* present.

Not the present, not the whole of the present but a present.

There are two ways of envisaging such a possibility, of art—in its creative invention/intervention—performing/effectuating/constituting an interruption of the homogeneity of our time, whether it is of a world that uncannily conjugates totality and infinity (infinitely totalising, as says Badiou),[15] or, it is a world where, as writes Nancy, capitalism is the only attempt to create another world: a second world, exactly like this world, but which now contains in itself its own proper end.[16] In either case, it is a world without an outside, whether its horizon reflects back to us images of images of reflections of the present. ("Ce sont des images d'images d'images" [Badiou 2014, 21]), or a world that takes the place of all possible worlds (Nancy 2016, 18).

(a) The one path is to follow the schema of Jean-Luc Nancy, which turns the *geste* of the painter—"la touche, la patte et la palette" (2016, 76)[17]—into a meta-phor or allegory for the act of creation, a "faire"—a making/a doing whose possibility, Nancy says, always remains; to entrust ourselves to art as a *geste* that concerns not the world, "il ne s'applique pas au monde, il fait plutôt monde qui

---

14 This path is pursued at length in my forthcoming *Contemporaneity, after Agamben: The Concept and Its Times* (2019).

15 "C'est un miroir fermé. Un miroir dans lequel on vient regarder le simulacre qu'on propose. Cette combinaison d l'illimitation des images d'un côté, de leur clôture de l'autre, est une allégorie possible de certains aspects de notre monde. C'est que cette combinaison touche à un problème capital. . . . à savoir: comment notre monde combine-t-il l'infinité et la clôture?" (Badiou 2014, 21; It is a closed mir-ror. A mirror in which one comes to look at the simulacrum one proposes. This combination of images without limit, on the one hand, and their closure, on the other, is a possible allegory of certain aspects of our world. It is that this combination touches upon a fundamental problem . . . namely: how does our world combine infinity and closure?).

16 "Le capitalisme représente la seule tentative effective de produire un second monde qui serait 'tout pa-reil au premier' comme disait Descartes et pourtant foncièrement distinct: un monde du remplacement du monde, c'est-à-dire de tous les monde possibles par un monde second comportant en lui-même sa propre fin" (Nancy 2016, 18; Capitalism represents the only effective attempt to produce a second world that would be "totally the same as the first," as Descartes said, and therefore fundamentally different: a world of the replacement of the world, that is to say of all possible worlds for a second world that entails its own end in itself.).

17 "the touch, the hand, and the palette" (Nancy 2014, 106).

est le sien" (ibid.),[18] it makes world, as one makes love or makes sense. It opens up a micro-world in the world, a world where sense circulates.

(In between parentheses: is this, has this not been the ambition of every avant-garde? Of "contemporary art"? The subversion of genre, the displacement of the centre, a rupture with the past, an interruption of local history, which makes world, a world of its own, "qui est le sien"? Is this not also a genre of discourse on art? Nostalgic for the time when placing a urinal in a museum sufficed to shock the (art) world? Does it still, even for a moment, disturb, make tremble a global and globalising determination that uncannily articulates closure and finitude with infinity?)

(b) The other path is opened in my third encounter. It is a cut; it cuts into the homogeneity of expanding time–space inside the horizon, in truth, a confinement without walls. It leaves nothing behind and leads to nowhere. And yet, it supports "existence"—the being there of a *da-sein*.

3. Deleuze and the Siberian throat singer

This third step and second encounter is with a fragment of a passage in a letter by Deleuze who, unlike Badiou, or Nancy, or Agamben, or Derrida, refrained from commenting in his philosophy and by way of philosophy on the immediate present, the times of the day. It is in the few interviews and the posthumous testament that he speaks directly of a "desert time," "the assassination of literature," of us passing through a desert time, in a period of re-action/re-activity. As he says, and this is confirmed in the letter I cite below, "philosophy does not separate itself from the anger against its epoch, but nor from the serenity of which it assures us" (Deleuze 1990, 7).

Written a year before his suicide, the letter is addressed to a friend, André Bernold, also in a state of "chronic crisis" at the time:

> C'est curieux comme nos existences (je parle de nos deux existences) protègent leur état de crise chronique en trouvant un abri dans ce qu'il y a de plus violent en art, de plus terrible. C'est que cette terreur-là met en déroute l'abjection de ce monde (pas de jour qui ne nous apporte son lot de comique abject, et qui ne nous fasse haire notre époque), non pas au nom d'un passé regretté, mais au nom du plus profond présent. (Deleuze 2015, 98)[19]

"Curious," as he says. That it is not in the most savagely sublime beauty of art or in the timely or untimely wisdom of the poets, who address us, anticipate us across the distance of time, precisely as "contemporaries," that existence (and who could ask for less?) should find shelter in an abject world. (I am thinking of Hannah Arendt who "in dark times" turns to Schiller's or Goethe's verse,

---

18 "It does not apply itself to the world; rather, it creates a world in the way that a painter's gesture . . . makes a world that is its own" (ibid.).

19 "It is curious how our existences (I am speaking of our two existences) protect their own state of chronic crisis by finding shelter in what is most violent in art, the most terrible. It is that this terror deroutes the abjection of this world (no day passes that does not bring us its share of comic abjection, and make us hate our own time), not in the name of a regretted past, but in the name of the most profound present."

finding there consolation that language itself could not go mad; or of Marguerite Duras who, listening to Bach's *Art of the Fugue*, no. xviii, cries out, in pleasure, "quelle douleur!" (what pain!); or of Heidegger, whose *philosophy* finds more than once the signs pointing in the direction of a path toward an exit—from "boredom," from "poverty," and from "devastation"—in Hölderlin's verse.)

But then how could this not be the case, that instead of the "fine" arts, it is the most terrible, the most violent in art that would be the measure, measure up to and be cut to the measure of an abject time? That would have the force to "deroute" it, to expose its comically abject underside—its abjection as comic and its comedy as abject? (Would such *exposé* measure up to Badiou's notion that in our contemporary situation comedy *is* the "thought of the present"?) An abject time or world: without pathos or depth, at once ridiculously pathetic and lethal; lacking precisely the profundity of both tragedy and the properly abject, whose everyday examples psychoanalysis furnishes as excrement, the corpse, vomit, or sex, without the potency of the properly abject that is the reflection of the force of its constitution, namely, its exclusion and repression by the properly "proper."

The example Deleuze gives is neither sublime—sublime violence or horror, beyond the power of apprehension by concept, and beyond the limit of representation—nor is it the simply cruel, as in the cruelty of torment, torture, or even suspense.

It is at once curious, most extraordinary, and most unexpected that the example given be a song or rather the voice of a Mongolian throat singer.

I will attend to the question of violence momentarily, but first I need to pay closer attention as before to two key terms in these extraordinary and extraordinarily precise formulations:

· To shelter (existence): we need to ask what shelter (by art) could mean here, if it evidently does not mean either to transport (as in a fiction, as in a certain kind of cinema) to another space, to a wholly Other space: utopia (no space), or a regretted past, or another future (promised, yet to come); nor does it mean to shelter *from*, to give refuge, be a sanctuary from the present in the present. On the contrary, as it says, it shelters in the name of the most profound present, without blunting, weakening, or sublimating one's hatred for the epoch.

· Deroute: to deroute does not mean to oppose, to confront, to defeat in combat, or even to resist. The word means, among other things, to "throw off the tracks," to redirect force, away from its target. As in slapstick comedy, where the punch lands elsewhere, on the puncher himself, it is a *geste* of lightness, grace, eloquence, and irony (hence its difference from the *comic* of the abject); the gesture is characterised by a certain economy, it economises on expenditures: captures or hijacks (as one hijacks—deroutes—an aeroplane) the other's force. Like a martial artist of Silat, who does not exert him- or herself, but uses the opponent's force, turning it against him or her, derouting the abject, it turns it against itself, returns it to itself as comic and its comedy as abject. This is exactly what happens in Badiou's reading of Jean Genet's play *Balcony*, where, as we recall, the police chief decides to appear at the ball wearing the costume of a phallus. Outside, the revolution; inside, a masked ball, where power appears to show itself in its abject nudity. In Badiou's reading of the play, it is a demonstration that comedy, precisely in its power to deroute (although Badiou does not use this term), is "the thought of the present" today (2014, 19).[20]

But this is not what is happening in either of the two examples Deleuze gives in the letter: the voice of the throat singer and the inhuman beauty of a child (whose cruelty I cannot enter into here). He could have given yet other examples, of course. Elsewhere, he cites the terrible cry of Lulu, and Berg's other opera, *Wozzeck* (where in one short instant, Marie's voice approaches the inhuman, the sound of death comes out of her throat). If these are possible examples, it is because each has something in common with the voice of the throat singer: in each case, the most terrible, the most violent is not of representation, it is not the violence of/in the spectacle, it is not represented nor is it of representation. It is not even an absent violence reflected—as by the terrible cry of an open mouth, of *Pope Innocent X*, in Bacon's paintings. It is present and its presence falls outside representation.

"Terrible are the songs of the Mongolians that you sent me" writes Deleuze (2015, 98) in the letter. "A voice so hollow, terribly hollowed out that others would fill it in."[21] The violence is not of the song or even of the voice; it is what has arrived to the voice ("ils ont touché au vers," "they have done violence to verse" as Shoshana Felman [1992, 18] quotes Mallarmé), or rather, what is arriving to the voice in the present tense, as long as the song lasts, in the course of it being sung. It is being hollowed out, voided of its propensity of being, of becoming song. Such is its song. If the example given could have also been writing by Beckett or Duras, or the cinema of Godard, or a poem by Celan, it is because in these works the writing exhausts language itself, empties it of its words, writes word holes into which other words disappear; and in the theatre of the cinema, Godard's cinema turns against its own apparatus. It does not withhold the film image, as does the avant-garde. In his last (and not his latest) film, Godard destroys the apparatus "cinema," so that the last film bearing his signature becomes the very last film in/of the cinema.

But the song is still a singular example, eloquent in its economy: without melody and without words, or a narrative or a story. Its violence is without significance (signifiance), falls outside the regime and register of signification. Its violence is pure violence, it says nothing. It is a pure cut in what Jean-Luc Nancy calls the "world" (a space where sense circulates, where art *makes* sense), just as the slash in a Luciano Fontana canvas is a pure cut. It cuts into, without showing, revealing, representing, referring, or deferring to anything, without being some thing.

So the question is: How could such art shelter, without either giving or being a refuge?

---

20 As if to offer an unwitting confirmation of this thesis, at a masked ball on Long Island, Donald Trump's sidekick or spokesperson Kellyanne Conway appears wearing the costume of Superwoman, while Trump himself shows up as himself.

21 "Terrible sont les chants mongols que tu m'as envoyés, une voix si creuses, terriblement creuses, que les autres voudraient remplir."

How can existence, itself in chronic crisis, find protection from the abject comedy of the day in what is most terrible, most violent in art? Is it the purity of its violence, of being pure violence, without aim, purpose, or end? As opposed to the always hybrid mixity of the obscene, whose violence wears the mask of many names: the "market," "terrorism," "democracy," "law and order," "ethical oil," "economic migrant," "illegal alien," "patriotism," "all lives matter" . . . ?

Once again it is Blanchot who comes to my aid, shelters me from thinking I have reached an impasse: a paralysing contra-diction, without mediation, between shelter and violence; an obstacle that makes it impossible to reconnect, in the place of *the* or *a* concept of the contemporary, the violence of art with the contemporaneity of an epoch that never stops hyperbolising its abject comedy. In the text in question (where Blanchot [1997, 188] also cites Turgenev's last letter to Tolstoy, "I am writing you to tell you how happy I was to be your contemporary"), Blanchot refers to the (recent) deaths that struck Camus, Elio Vittorini, and Georges Bataille: "it is as if the *power* of being contemporaneous *with ourselves* . . . found itself gravely altered" (ibid., emphasis added).[22]

An extraordinary notion: to be contemporaneous—not with the world or with our fellow humans, but with ourselves. Such then would be, at the limit, in our limit situation and condition *and* at the limit of art having reached its own limit, the power of art: to empower to be both *in* and *of* our time.

If the philosophy of culture, as Heidegger names the diagnoses and prognoses of crises, is a point of view *on* the contemporary but is a contemporaneity "entirely without us," and belongs "to the eternal yesterday" (Heidegger 1995, 75), art's contemporaneity runs through us. In its most violent and most terrible, it does not shelter, does not transport/carry us to an elsewhere, outside the horizon where obscene, abject violence reigns everywhere, occupies every place and space, appropriates every gesture to itself, leaving no outside. Its power is not to offer a refuge (existence) in a regretted past or in a promised future; it empowers, opens to the possible an existence in the most profound present: of being present to what is present, without being invaded by it, becoming complicit with it, of being symptomatic of it, and yet, without being outside it. In other words, art's violence makes contemporaneity possible, not *with* the abject comedy of the time, but at a time of abject comedy.

The violence of art today—the forces it liberates on the canvas, the violence of the painter's hand "touching" paint; of the notes touching the "musical" in music, or the force of Godard's découpage, or again, of the naked razor blades covering the skin of Adel Abdemessed's figures—this violence is absolutely heterogeneous with the violence in and of the epoch. It is irreducible/untranslatable to the multiform violence done to the flesh, to the earth and the sky, to the body, animal and human, to such notions as "liberty," "communism," "revolution," "justice," "democracy" . . . and to the sense of words, that they make sense, in every sense of this word. . . . The two orders do not communicate, the violence of art, while also of this world, in which it claims a place for itself, does

---

22 "Comme si le pouvoir d'être contemporains de nous-mêmes . . . se voyait soudain altéré gravement" (Blanchot 1971, 214).

not compose with the obscene abject violence of the epoch, of the world; it cuts into it, it cuts a virtual line on the inside, opens a however narrow interval of a hair line, which is not a space of opposition, resistance, or renewed combat. On this thin line—drawn by the crushed voice of the throat singer—existence, being in and of this world—*without refuge*—becomes possible.

Of course, it is not the song as such that is our contemporary. It is ancient, as opposed to being timely; it is traditional, that is to say, timeless. The co-relation arrives to the song, from the direction of writing, of Deleuze's writing that turns to the song, turns it into its contemporary, situates it, listens to it, in the shared anachronic time of a contemporaneity.

Postscript

Celan–Hölderlin–Kurtág—in that order—contemporaries and, which is not exactly the same thing, my contemporaries. Such is the "solution" to the enigma that rises from the image at the head of this text that pictures Celan's poem "Tübingen, Jänner" set in *Sprechgesang* (and whose one line in the first strophe, not included on this page, cites from Hölderlin's "The Rhine": "An enigma is the pure sprung forth," "Ein Rätsel ist Reinentsprungenes"[23]).

A single page of a text in the broadest sense, such is my starting point. Or rather an image filled with handmade graphic marks, a veritable manuscript, and yet not yet saying or singing, not yet signifying anything. "To paint with texts,"[24] writes Simon Hantaï (2001, 31) in a letter to Jean-Luc Nancy, reporting on the progress of his project of writing out on the same white sheet, of paper or chiffon, a few pages from texts by Derrida and Jean-Luc Nancy, superimposing one over the other, making them "touch" one another ("touch, contact, *and* distance in the contact,"[25] writes Nancy in response [Hantaï 2001, 25]). Here too the writing hand writes out and in doing so touches, caresses, the letters of Celan's poem; it draws each word on the page under the five lines that at the same time also order and align the notes, the symbols and the marks that set the words into a virtually spoken song. It gives them the potentiality of a body, the virtual body of sound, that of a song arising from an actual, real body.

Certainly, the words, the broken language—which itself stutters and can only stutter, "lallen und lallen," more visibly in German on the page than in trans-lation; it babbles "immer immer zuzu" (this last non-word is a quick, anachronic attribution to Hölderlin by Celan, who borrows it from Wozzeck[26]), as much as it does today (*heute*) when it speaks of this time (*dieser Zeit*) today. These

---

23   The translation is the strange offspring of a vexatious translation problem: how to render in the English translation of Lacoue-Labarthe's *La Poesie comme experience*, Lacoue-Labarthe's own French translation of Hölderlin-Celan's German original (Lacoue-Labarthe 1986, 28). As it happens, Andrea Tarnowski's rendering as "pure sprung forth" of Lacoue-Labarthe's rendering of "Rein-entsprungenes" as "pur jaillis," comes closest to the strangeness of the German idiom, even if it separates "pure" from the uncommon verbal noun it qualifies (Lacoue-Labarthe 1999, 16).

24   "Peindre avec des textes."

25   "toucher, contact *et* écart dans le contact."

26   I owe this observation to a conversation with Kurtág, who also suggested the homophonic association between Hölderlin's "Pallaksch" and the Russian (not Polish as he thought) *Pallaksh*—"hóhér" as he said it in Hungarian: executioner or *bourreaux*.

words are significant. As is the nonsense of the other nonword borrowed from Hölderlin, *Pallaksch*. But I do not have to read or translate or to make reference to the words yet to see a threefold contemporaneity being instantly actualised, traced on the page. Threefold, for there is first Celan, who makes Hölderlin his contemporary, inlays his poem with fragments, with the singular markers of the mad poet, his broken words, the name of his tower, his tormented language. And this incorporation to the poem's body of the other's signs is not to draw an analogy or to create the semblance of a resemblance between the torments of life or the tormented writing. He who writes elsewhere, "The world is gone, I must carry you" (Celan 2002, 251)[27] carries Hölderlin, in and by the stuttering words of his own poem to his today, to the present of his time. He opens a clearing, clears the space inside the text for the other poet's words to speak—in the present, as a contemporary. Then there is Kurtág who some fifty years later in calendar time writes out these words by hand, makes them sing/speak with the single voice of a baritone, which voice then carries, transports *not one or the other* but this pair, this instance of being and becoming contemporary, to the present—as his contemporaries, in their contemporaneity.

The latter is not a relation held up by the sense of the words, or by the quasi-question, "if there came a man today," suggesting that it could be just as well asked, would make sense if asked, today. It is rather carried by the joining together, without mixing, of three geological layers of historical time that are laid over one another, are made to touch one another, without forming an amalgam. "Toucher, contact et écart dans le contact," to again cite Nancy in his letter to Hantaï. Touch is possible only when there is a gap, the distance of an interval—creative, productive, precisely of a relation.

It is across this gap of heterogeneous, discontinuous registers of time that the words begin to resonate, speak to one another, ask of one another "if a man came today," how could he speak of this time; it is across this interval that they deliver their secret missive destined for this time; so that Hölderlin's non-word, curse, and cry "Pallaksch" resounds with, or indeed, begins to speak Russian, to say—"after Auschwitz," which is the proper name of the date of Celan's poem—the word *paklash*, executioner or *bourreaux*.

Across the distance of time, Hölderlin sends a missive from the past to the future, of which missive Celan is the recipient, only as long as he hears the other poet, who spoke of our language "lost in foreign places"—"Schmerzlos sind wir und haben fast / Die Sprache in der Fremde verloen"[28]—as his contemporary.

Kurtág's song gives a body to the silent cry of this word, repeats it not twice as does Celan, but three times, and in the recording five times, differently, angrily, cursingly, in extreme range and desperation, then, as if frightened by it, by its own sound, quietly . . .

---

27 "Die Welt its fort, Ich muß dich tragen" (Celan 2002, 250).
28 "Without pain we are and have nearly / Lost our language in foreign lands" (Hölderlin 1984, 116 [original], 117 [translation]).

Tübingen, Jänner

. . .

Käme,
Käme ein Mensch,
kame ein Mensch zur Welt, heute, mit
dem Lichtbart der
Patriarchen: er dürfte,
spräch er von dieser
Zeit, er
dürfte nur lallen und lallen,
immer-, immer-
zuzu.

("Pallaksch. Pallaksch.")[29]

REFERENCES

Agamben, Giorgio. 2005. *The Time That Remains: A Commentary on the Letter to the Romans*. Translated by Patricia Dailey. Stanford, CA: Stanford University Press. First published 2000 as *Il tempo che resta: Una commento alla Lettera di Romani* (Turin: Bollati Boringhieri).

———. 2008a. *Che cos'e il contemporaneo*. Rome: Nottetempo. Translated into French as Agamben 2008b. Translated into English as Agamben 2011b.

———. 2008b. *Qu'est-ce le contemporain?* Translated by Maxime Rovere. Paris: Payot & Rivages. First published as Agamben 2008a.

———. 2011. "What Is the Contemporary." In *Nudities*, translated by David Kishik and Stefan Pedatella, 10–19. Stanford, CA: Stanford University Press. Essay first published as Agamben 2008a.

Alliez, Éric. 2017. "On Contemporary Art and Philosophy: Towards a Diagrammatic Critique of Aesthetics." In *The Dark Precursor: Deleuze and Artistic Research*, edited by Paulo de Assis and Paolo Giudici, 2 vols, 2:293–308. Orpheus Institute Series. Leuven: Leuven University Press.

Artaud, Antonin. 1927. *Correspondance avec Jacques Rivière*. Paris: Éditions de la Nouvelle Revue Française. Translated by Bernard Frechtman as Artaud 1965.

———. 1965. "Artaud–Rivière Correspondence." Translated by Bernard Frechtman. In *Antonin Artaud: Anthology*, edited by Jack Hirschman, 7–25. San Francisco: City Lights Books. Chapter first published as Artaud 1927.

Badiou, Alain. 2012. Discussion with Elie During. BNF, 14 December 2012. Accessed 18 February 2019. https://gallica.bnf.fr/ark:/12148/bpt6k1321098g/f1.

———. 2014. *Images du temps présent: 2001–2004*. Paris: Fayard.

———. 2016. "Reflections on the Recent Election," public lecture, UCLA, 9 November 2016. YouTube video, 1:15:06, posted by "Kenneth Reinhard," 10 November 2016. Accessed 12 January

---

29 "Tübingen, January" . . . "Should, / should a man, / should a man come into the world, today, with / the shining beard of the / patriarchs: he could, / if he spoke of this / time, he / could / only babble and babble / over, over / again again. // ("Pallaksch. Pallaksch.") (Celan 2002, 154 [original], 155 [translation]).

2019. https://www.youtube.com/watch?v=gRnUpVLc31w.

Baross, Zsuzsa. 2014. "'Die Welt ist fort.'" Paper read at the international conference "In Memoriam Jacques Derrida," Institut Français, Budapest, 17 October 2014.

———. 2015a. "*Adieu au langage*: Fragments of a Response to the Last Film." Unpublished manuscript.

———. 2015b. "In Praise of (La) Rabbia." In "Pier Paolo Pasolini entre régression et échec," edited by Paolo Desogus, Manuele Gragnolati, Christoph F. E. Holzhey, and Davide Luglio, special issue, *LaRivista* 4: 82–92.

———. 2019. *Contemporaneity, after Agamben: The Concept and Its Times*. Brighton, UK: Sussex Academic Press.

Bataille, Georges. 1961. *Le Coupable*. Paris: Gallimard. Translated by Bruce Boone as Bataille 1988.

———. 1988. *Guilty*. Translated by Bruce Boone. Venice, CA: Lapis Press. First published 1944 as *Le Coupable* (Paris: Gallimard).

———. 2005. "Sur *Humanisme et terreur* de Maurice Merelau-Ponty." *Les temps modernes* 629: 29–34.

Blanchot, Maurice. 1971. "Le détour vers la simplicité." In *L'Amitié*, 158–67. Paris: Gallimard. Translated by Elizabeth Rotternberg as Blanchot 1997.

———. 1988. *The Unavowable Community*. Translated by Pierre Joris. Barrytown, NY: Station Hill Press.

———. 1997. "The Detour Toward Simplicity." In *Friendship*, translated by Elizabeth Rottenberg, 188–200. Stanford, CA: Stanford University Press. First published as Blanchot 1971.

Celan, Paul. 2002a. "From *Atemwende*." In *Poems* of Paul Celan, translated by Michael Hamburger, 206–55. Rev. ed. New York: Persea Books. *Atemwende* first published 1967 (Frankfurt am Main: Suhrkamp).

———. 2002b. "From *Die Niemandsrose* (1963)." In *Poems of Paul Celan*, translated by Michael Hamburger, 130–203. Rev. ed. New York: Persea Books. *Die Niemandsrose* first published 1963 (Frankfurt am Main: S. Fischer).

Deleuze, Gilles. 1990. *Pourparlers: 1972–1990*. Paris: Minuit.

———. 2003. *Francis Bacon: The Logic of Sensation*. Translated by Daniel W. Smith. London: Continuum. First published 1981 as *Francis Bacon: Logique de la sensation* (Paris: Éditions de la Différence).

———. 2015. "À André Bernold." In *Lettres et Autres Textes*, edited by David Lapoujade, 98–100. Paris: Minuit.

Felman, Shoshana. 1992. "Education and Crisis, or the Vicissitudes of Teaching." In *Testimony: Crises of Witnessing in Literature, Psychoanalysis, and History*, by Shoshana Felman and Dori Laub, 1–56. New York: Routledge.

Hantaï, Simon. 2001. *La connaissance des textes: Lecture d'un manuscit illisible; Correspondances*. Written with Jacques Derrida and Jean-Luc Nancy. Paris: Galilée.

Heidegger, Martin. 1995. *The Fundamental Concepts of Metaphysics: World, Finitude, Solitude*. Translated by William McNeill and Nicholas Walker. Bloomington: Indiana University Press. Delivered as lectures in 1929–30. First published 1983 as *Die Grundbegriffe der Metaphysik: Welt—Endlichkeit—Einsamkeit* (Frankfurt am Main: Klostermann).

———. 2004. *La pauvreté (Die Armut)*. Translated by Philippe Lacoue-Labarthe. Strasbourg: Presses universitaires de Strasbourg. Written 1945. First published 1994 as "*Die Armut*" (Heidegger Studies 10: 5–11).

———. 2006. *La dévastation et l'attente: Entretien sur le chemin de campagne*. Translated by Philippe Arjakovsky and Hadrien France-Lanord. Paris: Gallimard. Written 1944–45. First published 1995 as *Feldweg-Gespräche: Gesamtausgabe*. Bd. 77: 3. Abteilung: Unveröffentliche abhandlungen—vorträge—gedachtes (Frankfurt am Main: Klostermann). Translated by Bret W. Davis as *Country Path Conversations* (Bloomington: Indian University Press, 2010).

Hölderlin, Friedrich. 1984. *Hymns and Fragments*. Translated by Richard Sieburth. Princeton, NJ: Princeton University Press.

Lacoue-Labarthe, Philippe. 1986. *La Poésie comme expérience*. Paris: Christian Bourgeois. Translated by Andrea Tarnowski as Lacoue-Labarthe 1999.

———. 1999. *Poetry as Experience.* Translation by Andrea Tarnowski. Stanford: Stanford University Press. First published as Lacoue-Labarthe 1986.

Nancy, Jean-Luc. 2010. "Art Today." Translated by Charlotte Mandell. *Journal of Visual Culture* 9 (1): 91–99. First delivered as a lecture, Milan, 2006.

———. 2014. "What Is to Be Done?" Translated by Irving Goh. *Diacritics* 42 (2): 100–117. First published 2012 as "Que faire?" (*Bulletin de la Société française de philosophie* 106 [2]). Also published in French in Nancy 2016.

———. 2016. *Que faire?* Paris: Galilée.

Stiegler, Bernard. 2016. *Dans la disruption: Comment ne pas devenir fou?* Paris: LLL.

The Question of the Contemporary in Agamben, Nancy, Danto

Between Nietzsche's Artist and Nietzsche's Spectator

Babette Babich

Fordham University, New York; University of Winchester, UK

THE QUESTION OF THE CONTEMPORARY, TIMELINESS, AND THE "COVER" IN ART AND MUSIC

How can anyone talk about the contemporary?[1] The target, the reference, the focus, the ambit moves as one attempts to address it: one moves oneself and not necessarily in lockstep with the contemporary. Some are more contemporary than others; some, as Nietzsche argued, are born posthumously, contemporaries of an era yet to come; or, and this is indistinguishable, there are those whose time is past and those who belong to no time at all. It is in this sense that Giorgio Agamben (2009, 40) defines the contemporary as *inattuale*, referring to Nietzsche's "contemporariness," expressed as Nietzsche articulates his timely "relevance (*attualità*)" (ibid.), qua what Nietzsche with all due historical precision designates as the "untimely" (*unzeitgemäß*). The question of the currency, the relevance of the untimely, is tied to the question of the timely as such: when is it? how is it? and how can we say (for sure)? How are we to know? Undergirded by a tendency toward nonbeing, as Augustine mused of time as such, precisely in its present immediacy: "we cannot rightly say that time *is*, except by reason of its impending state of *not being*" (*Confessions*, bk 11, chap. 14, as translated in Augustine 1961, 264). Like a moving sidewalk, the contemporary carries you along with it and passes as you pass, cliché, amenable to categorisation as belonging to a bygone present, the latest thing in its eclipse, already foreclosed.

The question of "the contemporary" has a specific meaning with reference to art, such as *modern* and *postmodern* art but also *conceptual* art and, perhaps especially significantly, *pop* art. In philosophy of art, Giorgio Agamben and Jean-Luc Nancy, along with other philosophers hailing from the analytic tradition, especially Arthur Danto, have made the theme of the contemporary central to their

---

1 Unless otherwise stated, all translations are my own.

thought. Likewise, and more colloquially, the contemporary is tied to remix culture (quite along with issues of piracy and profit[2]), remakes, and revivals, but also readymade and found and pop art—and now we are back to Danto—and, in music, at least pop music, also including the musical cover.[3]

The art graphic language of the "cover" is terminologically key to music covers (literally referring to the imprint of a studio album) (Babich 2018b, 385); but this also corresponds to today's contemporary art, for example, the political contemporary pop artist Wang Guangyi (1957–) who in his own poster art "covers" Andy Warhol's "covers" of, especially, Coca-Cola, riffing on capitalist iconology beyond Warhol's own 1964 *Brillo Boxes* just as philosopher Arthur Danto, a contemporary of Warhol, journalistically "covered" and so was—according to Wang Guangyi and others—instrumental in assuring Warhol's success.[4]

Nietzsche claims in *Human, All too Human*, writing on the "Human Being in Communication," that "it is not seldom that one meets copies of famous people" (Nietzsche [1878] 1980, 239), adding that the copies tend to be ranked higher than the originals, and we can expand this to include cover versions, contemporary remakes, new translations, or "updates," especially true of paintings (one may vary this to include music, as Adorno does).[5] Thus, not infrequently, as exemplified by Leonard Cohen's "Hallelujah" in the case of pop music, the cover version can be the version—via the rendering in an album tribute, *I'm Your Fan*, by John Cale—that assures a song's status as a "hit."[6]

Increasingly, there are covers of covers of older versions, sometimes adapted for film, like Anna Kendrick's cover of Lulu and the Lampshades' own YouTube cover of the traditional gospel and pop country song "You're Going to Miss Me When I'm Gone" (see Kendrick 2012; Lulu and the Lampshades 2009). In Lulu and the Lampshades' version, the London-based singers, Heloise Tunstall-Behrens and Luisa Gerstein, use a cup (in some versions, a pint glass is used), for rhythmic accompaniment, hence the metonymy of the title by which the song is commonly known, "The Cup Song." Kendrick's version of the Lulu and the Lampshades cover made a "hit" out of ninety years of recordings of "You're Going to Miss Me When I'm Gone."[7]

---

2 In addition to several discussions by Lawrence Lessig over the years, see Gunkel (2016); Borschke (2017).

3 I discuss this in an essay (Babich 2018b) that grew out of a lecture on the concept of the "cover," given on 11 May 2017 at the Orpheus Institute, Ghent. I am grateful to Paulo de Assis and for the inspiring questions and discussion at that conference and also, regarding an earlier version, to John Faithful Hamer who invited discussion of the theme in Leonard Cohen's hometown on 26 June 2015 at Concordia University, Montreal. In a first monograph on this complicated question (Babich [2013] 2016), backtracking from pop music to the current of music (Adorno) to Beethoven and the Greeks (Nietzsche), I track the pop music of Leonard Cohen (1934–2016) articulated *through* various "covers" of "Hallelujah"—specifically attending to k. d. lang, as a female singer typically ignored, while also reviewing the more iconic renderings of Cohen's song (these are the more universally preferred male artists associated with "Hallelujah," especially Bob Dylan and the universal favourite, Jeff Buckley).

4 For a discussion, see the contributions to Andina and Onnis (2019), including Babich (2019c, 112–14).

5 The complete aphorism is as follows: "*Copies.* It is not seldom that one encounters copies of famous persons; and as in the case of paintings, most people like the copies better than the original" (*Human, All Too Human* §294, Nietzsche [1878] 1980, 239).

6 Cohen first released the song as the centre of his *Various Positions* album in 1984 (see Babich [2013] 2016, chap. 4). For a popular retrospective account, see Runtagh (2017).

7 The song was recorded by the Carter Family back in the 1930s, the Mountain Ramblers, circa 1969, covering the New Lost City Ramblers, etc.

Here it is important to preface a discussion of the contemporary with reference to remixes and to covers because in many ways covers and (re)appropriations go hand in glove with the contemporary, even foregrounding it to the extent of deliberate hokeyness, as in the cup used in the cup song, fetishising the accidental, the incidental as prop, and in this way echoing the irrelevance of Agamben's *inattuale*.

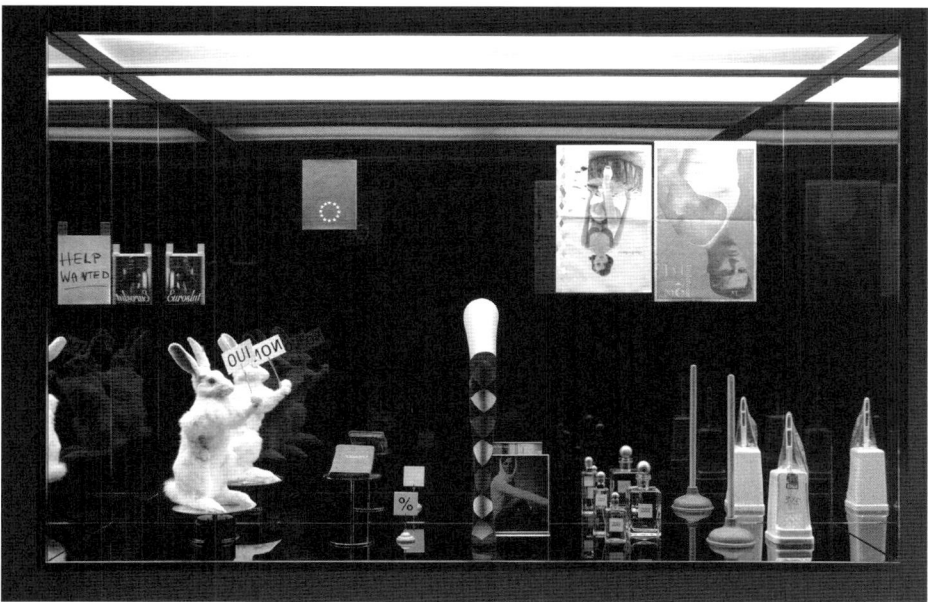

Figure 3.1.

CONTEMPORARY ART AS A CONCEPT: ARE WE THERE YET?

The Australian art historian Terry Smith relates the reception given to the then-new formation of the Society of Contemporary Art Historians in Los Angeles at the 2009 College Art Association Annual Conference. Struck by the "huge crowd" that turned out to hear the speakers speculating on the theme of contemporary art, Smith recounts the questions as they then haunted art history and which, as constitutive, continue to haunt the field:

> Can we do history of contemporary art? Should we do history that is like the art it studies? Are we really doing criticism, or perhaps theory (note to self: it may already be out of fashion)? Whatever happened to critical distance, scholarly objectivity, disinterested judgment? What counts as an archive? How do I claim a topic before all the others? What if "my artist" suddenly refuses to cooperate? How do I relate my topic to "the field" when no one seems to have any idea of its overall shape and direction? What do I do when my artist changes her work before I finish my dissertation? (Smith 2010, 366)

51

Figure 3.1. Josephine Meckseper (1964–), *The Complete History of Postcontemporary Art*, 2005. Credit: Photo: Josephine Meckseper. Courtesy: Galerie Reinhard Hauff.

To illustrate, Smith "reads" a particularly picturesque example of a "contemporary" concept: Josephine Meckseper's 2005 art window-display *The Complete History of Postcontemporary Art*.

Smith's example is relatively "safe," given the tensions involved in designating contemporary/postcontemporary art. Hence, and we will return to some of these questions via Paul Virilio's *Art and Fear*, below, it might have been interesting to see what Smith made of the masturbating "shock" performance artist, Vito Acconci (1940–2017) or, Marina Abramović (1946–).

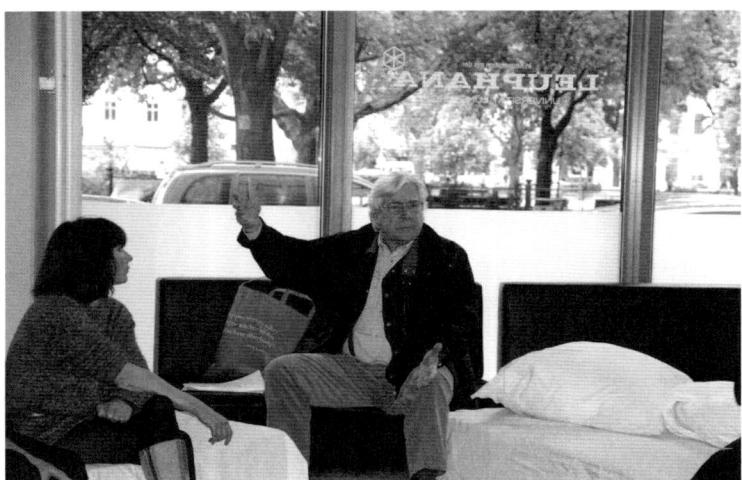

Figure 3.2.

On the continuum of art-window displays like Meckseper's 2005 *The Complete History of Postcontemporary Art*, one wonders what Smith, writing in 2009, would make of the Berlin *Denkerei* founded in 2011? A complete storefront animated by the action artist (part of the Fluxus group originally associated with Joseph Beuys) and—*nomen est omen*—longwinded contemporary conceptual artist/theorist Bazon Brock (1936–), Brock's *Denkerei* seems, to all appearances, an institution, down to inscriptions and official labels. As a concept, the *Denkerei* is an art installation: *Amt für Arbeit an unlösbaren Problemen und Maßnahmen der hohen Hand* (*Office for Work on Insoluble Problems and High Hand Measures*), featuring Brock himself: "thinker" at your service. What could be more contemporary/postcontemporary, inasmuch as the *Denkerei* has now closed its doors, following an eight-year run: 3 December 2011–9 April 2019?

Bracketing questions of artist choice (not that this is irrelevant: it animates Michael Fried, for example, as we briefly note below), by "reading" as Smith does Josephine Meckseper's "mixed media in a display window," as a rebus,[8] the

---

8   We are, to be sure, told to do this by many scholars—even bracketing the esotericism surrounding Poussin from Anthony Blunt and David Carrier onward—see, in addition to Bryson (1984), Mitchell (1994), Elkins (1999), and, not least, Berger ([1972] 2008), and even Gadamer (1986).

Figure 3.2. Bazon Brock (1936–), *Der neue Berliner Salon zu Gast in der Denkerei*, Denkerei, Berlin-Kreuzberg. 17 May 2012.

Credit: Photo: Babette Babich (1956–). With the permission of Bazon Brock.

art historian is enabled to count off its content, thus telling us, as art historians do, just what we are to look at in the pictures they discuss for us:

> the ironic title of her installation appears inside the display, inscribed in gold on the cover of a leather-bound volume: the book itself is clearly over a century old. It sits behind glass, in a shop that is closed, making it impossible to read. Nonetheless, the work's title taunts us with the thought that even postcontemporary art is, already, ancient history. Meckseper's larger argument is even stronger than what this array of failed allegories implies. She always shows her vitrines alongside sets of her photographs of antiglobalization demonstrations in Berlin, Washington, and elsewhere. (Smith 2010, 367)

The temporal placement of contemporary art is an issue for Jean-Luc Nancy, who reflects on a problem known to philosophers of science as the demarcation problem. Hence if the word "postmodern"[9] worked to upset academics and journalists, like "deconstruction," this was often in inverse proportion to their technical comprehension of the term (hence, in a post-truth era, we are still blaming postmodernism for ruining everything). In art, however, especially architecture, where the modern is stylistically well defined, things are more complicated. For Nancy, the modern is just where we find ourselves in time. Thus I began by noting that the contemporary *finds* us just as it carries us along with it—like moving walkways familiar in airline terminals, and if this seems sufficiently up to date, such moving walkways were featured at the 1883 World's Fair in Chicago and again in Paris in 1900.[10]

Designating the modern, the postmodern, the contemporary, the postcontemporary, can be *stylistically* confounding, co-incident in some cases, periodically overlapping, and constantly changing. For Nancy:

> contemporary art is a fixed phrase that belongs in its way to art history: there has been, as you well know, the era of impressionism, of fauvism, of cubism, of surrealism, of the avant-gardes, and then there were those movements that are beginning to form part (or not) of contemporary art, *l'arte povera* in Italy, hyperrealism. And contemporary art is also a strange historical category since it is a category whose borders are shifting, but which generally don't go back to much more than 20 or 30 years ago, and hence are continually moving. Concerning this category, it can be said that some works of art produced today somewhere in the world do not belong to contemporary art. If today a painter makes a figurative painting with classical techniques, it will not be contemporary art; it will lack the cachet, the distinctive criterion of what we call "contemporary." (Nancy 2010, 91)

Indeed, the focus of Nancy's title "Art Today" highlights what he names "a space of contradiction, quarrel, at times very violent, in the centre of which there is

---

9   For Lyotard who wrote on the postmodern condition in just such a circumstance, what was postmodern was not locatable as much as it was a condition of the future of knowledge and not less of aesthetics (see Babich 2010). Lyotard's distinctions are still too abstruse for most readers, including most philosophers of art who objected to his terminology rather for the same reasons that Danto challenges postmodern art, for being too inclusive and insufficiently specific about (Danto's thesis concerning) the end of art; thus, Danto recommends speaking of post-historical art.

10   I refer to such sidewalks among other contemporary tech signifiers in Babich ([2010] 2014, 264).

the question of art, because you are well aware that many people are ready to say, if you talk to them about contemporary art, that it's not art" (ibid., 93).

The contest between "it is art" and "it is not art" ought to be (though there is little space to consider this here) related to the enthusiasm for demarcation that characterises analytic philosophical reflections: what is art? This would include variants such as Danto's declarative 2013 retrospective, *What Art Is*:[11] when is art (where is art)—that is, it's philosophy/it's not philosophy or it's science/it's not science. The demarcation problem is the problem of what one decides, in line with the Trumpism of our era, to call art (or name as "news" as opposed to "fake news"), or designate as true (as opposed to alt or post-truth).[12] In the case of art, things are a little different: talking about what art is (or what is not art but only claimed as art) in the best or worst case can only be a matter of artistic deception—as Nietzsche describes art as "that in which exactly the *lie* sanctifies itself, in which the *will to deceive* has a good conscience" ([1887] 1980, 402). Beyond this there is the matter of certification, imprimatur, blessing as such. In this case, saying what art is or determining the scope of contemporary art also entails or permits inclusion and exclusion, in line with peer review and other gate-keeping standardisations. At issue is not only categorising art as art but also which artists should be known, which scholars are to be acknowledged and which can be left unread, and which exhibits must be seen and which may be safely forgotten.

Thus Danto offers his own explanation, without to be sure referring to Nancy or Agamben: "just as 'modern' has come to denote a style and even a period, and not just recent art, 'contemporary' has come to designate something more than simply the art of the present moment. In my view, however, it designates less a period than what happens after there are no more periods in some master narrative of art, and less a style of making art than a style of using styles" (Danto 1997, 10). Where Terry Smith writes about art historians among art historians, as theorists write about theorists and philosophers about philosophers, Danto himself was rather individual (not unique as there are others) in that he was originally a practitioner, an artist. Hence, Danto wrote not merely *about* the artists but regarded himself, in his origins, as one of those about whom he wrote.[13] One may argue that it is this performative or artist's perspective on cooperation

---

11 Danto's *What Art Is* (2013) borrows from (or "covers"), as he sometimes seems to do—his book *Nietzsche as Philosopher* silently echoes Hans Vaihinger's earlier book title—Oliver W. F. Lodge's *What Art Is* (1927). See too, albeit from very different frames or points of view, the contributions to Nina Felshin's *But Is It Art? The Spirit of Art as Activism* (1995) or Jane Kramer's *Whose Art Is It?* (1994) and Cynthia Freeland's monograph *But Is It Art? An Introduction to Art Theory* (2001) (which Arthur Danto endorsed and iconically seemed to model his own book on some dozen years later).

12 The disquiet matters as a dissonance inasmuch as the postmodern has a clear reference in architecture as in music. Nevertheless, until the end of his life, Danto remained uncomfortable with the rubric as such and in quite traditionally analytic or reactive ways. And today, Danto's discomfit seems, if anything, to be justified: one blames the "postmodern" for what is called "fake news" and "alt truths" can be blamed for Brexit and Trump.

13 It is not for nothing that Tiziana Andina (2010) names Danto a "pop philosopher of art," attuned as he is to popular tensions, including the natural habitat of art (in museums but also in galleries and studios, in public places) as Danto writes. Thus it has been argued that there was a certain synergy between Andy Warhol, the event, and Danto's art criticism, beginning with Danto's first gallery encounter with Warhol's *Brillo Boxes* in 1964, which for Danto encompassed an involvement with museum practice, including curators and artists.

and calculation (this is different from capital speculation) that drives Danto's book the *Transfiguration of the Commonplace* (1981).

NIETZSCHE'S ARTIST'S AESTHETICS CONTRA THE SPECTATOR'S AESTHETIC IN CONTEMPORARY ART

In his prolegomena to a "science of aesthetics," as one may also regard Nietzsche's first book, *The Birth of Tragedy out of the Spirit of Music*, Nietzsche distinguishes masculine and feminine forces of artistic creativity (see Nietzsche [1872] 1980, 25). He distinguishes the Apollonian and the Dionysian and further and more complicatedly distinguishes—a distinction he maintained throughout his life—between an artist's aesthetics and a spectator's aesthetics. Nietzsche takes the distinction from Empedocles's cosmology (B63) by way of Hölderlin's poetic expression of the "strife between lovers," where reconciliation and the tension of opposition abides, periodically—an exchange of desire and alienation, harmony and conflict.[14] Nietzsche distinguishes two kinds of creative artistic force, the active force of abundance and the reactive force that compensates for lack or deficiency (ibid., 30–34, 67–71).[15] In the course of his first book, Nietzsche argues for the contrast between the active spectator—part of and indistinguishable from the spectacle, as in ancient Greek ritual, such as the Dionysia where there is no contradiction between spectator and tragico-musical artwork—and the reactive spectator who keeps a proper distance as we do today, a spectator free to arrive late or leave early, for all the difference it makes.

Arguing in his preface to *Twilight of the Idols* that "only excess of force is the proof of force" (Nietzsche [1889] 1980b, 57), Nietzsche also argues that lack or deficit or need has traditionally been the most "interesting" source of human creativity, as he writes in *On the Genealogy of Morals* (Nietzsche [1887] 1980, 266), precisely by way of the same ascetic ideal that can characterise the artist. There is almost nothing discipline cannot remedy. The decadent, the moraline pathos of the slave, but also the depleted artist, can still be creative, sometimes triumphantly so, given ascetic rigour (or from a distance or with better lighting).

Recollecting the distinction Nietzsche makes between the aesthetics of the artist and the spectator, Agamben highlights receptive aesthetic judgement as the basis of all aesthetics. Regarding Kant's *Critique of Judgement*, he cites Nietzsche at length to argue:

---

14 In addition to Empedocles, Nietzsche draws on Heraclitus to echo the closing lines of Hölderlin's *Hyperion*, where Hölderlin in a beautifully musical metaphor, compares lovers, including those separated and lost, to "living tones" sounded together in nature's indestructible harmonies: "Wie der Zwist der Liebenden, sind die Dissonanzen der Welt. Versöhnung ist mitten im Streit und alles getrennte findet sich wieder" (Hölderlin [1799] 1920, 204; Like the quarrels of lovers, are the dissonances of the world. Reconciliation is amidst strife, and all things parted find one another again). Of course, the sentence, continues: ""Es scheiden und kehren im Herzen die Adern und einiges, ewiges, glühendes Leben ist Alles" (ibid.,The arteries separate and return in the heart and one, eternal, glowing life is all), and Hyperion concludes this last epistle: "So dacht' ich. Nächstens mehr" (So thought I. More soon.)

15 Thus in 1887, in the fifth book of *The Gay Science*, Nietzsche includes the key aphorism "What is Romanticism?" (§370) distinguishing between the creative inspiration of "hunger" by contrast with "abundance [*Überfluss*]" (Nietzsche [1882] 1980, 623).

> Kant, like all philosophers, instead of envisaging the aesthetic problem from the point of view of the artist (the creator), considered art and the beautiful purely from that of the "spectator," and unconsciously introduced the "spectator" into the concept "beautiful." It would not have been so bad if this "spectator" had at least been sufficiently familiar to the philosophers of beauty—namely, as a great *personal* fact and experience, as an abundance of vivid authentic experiences, desires, surprises, and delights in the realm of the beautiful! But I fear that the reverse has always been the case; and so they have offered us, from the beginning, definitions in which, as in Kant's famous definition of the beautiful, a lack of any refined first-hand experience reposes in the shape of a fat worm of error. "That is beautiful," said Kant, "which gives us pleasure *without interest*." Without interest! Compare with this definition one framed by a genuine "spectator" and artist—Stendhal, who once called the beautiful *une promesse de Bonheur*. At any rate he *rejected* and repudiated the one point about the aesthetic condition which Kant had stressed: *le désinteressement*. Who is right, Kant or Stendhal? (Nietzsche, *On the Genealogy of Morals*, as quoted in Agamben 1999, 1–2)

The passage Agamben cites both presupposes and implies a great deal (see Agamben 2009, 40). Nietzsche sought to comprehend the creative aesthetic of the artist contra Kant's claim of disinterested interest as this creative aesthetic exemplifies the Stendhalian promise of happiness, a promise that is at once forward-thinking optimism and the presentiment of misappointment. It is a promise as Stendhal observes—and as Alexander Nehamas (2007) argues—that speaks from a masculine view. The perspective informs Nehamas's reflections as reflected in his book *Only a Promise of Happiness: The Place of Beauty in a World of Art* (2007). In *The Hallelujah Effect* ([2013] 2016) I offer a counterpoise to Nehamas's account reading the theme of male and female desire in art by questioning, and contrasting, the aesthetic of the male spectator in a chapter entitled "On Male Desire and Music: Misogyny, Love, and the Beauty of Men" (Babich [2013] 2016, 48–78). At issue for Nietzsche is hardly the gendered aesthetics of contemporary feminist aesthetics. Hence to understand Nietzsche's project is to look at what makes the artist possible by raising what Nietzsche names the question of subject as such. In this respect, Nietzsche highlights the masculine referentiality of presumptively objective judgement: that is the neutral, disinterested power of judgement, just where the claim of objective, neutral, disinterest remains to this day. Intriguingly, we believe in this claim and in its neutrality never more than when a work of art has been singled out as best, an artist or a musician celebrated, or a philosopher or scientist or a novelist ranked with a prize or an award. In art, this is the *claim* of the beautiful.

Nietzsche's attention to the masculinist bias inspiring the "interest" haunting disinterested interest can also be used to read between today's reflections on male and female desire. It may thus be argued that male desire (largely heterosexual but also homosexual, the imperatives of which are interiorised by women as they are by men) dictates what we may see in museums, but above all in a digitally mediatised era, what we see onscreen, from Hollywood to YouTube music videos.[16] This dictates what we see in our fashion shows but also what appears in our magazines and online video advertisements, just as it is (male) desire that speaks in the pop music we hear, even when sung or composed by female artists, as well as what we see on display, what is chosen for the same, from traditional to modern to contemporary art in museums. This is in accord with, to use Nietzsche's distinction here, a masculine estimation or ranking. Nevertheless, only Simone de Beauvoir among all theorists has reflected on what she calls "complicity" by women with this arrangement in its totalisation in culture, be it as (the rare) object of that desire or as spectators of the same. Hence Adorno (1992, 49–50) will speak of the shop girl's fantasies[17]—as a side-lined non-choice, who forms herself, as Nietzsche will muse with no more sympathy than might otherwise be imagined, according to this male dictate.

Recall the articulation noted at the outset of Nietzsche's *The Birth of Tragedy*: "We shall have gained much for aesthetic science [*die aesthetische Wissenschaft*] when we have come to realise, not just via logical insight but also through the immediate certainty of intuition [*Anschauung*], that the ongoing evolution of art is bound up with the duality of the *Apollinian* and the *Dionysian*: in similar fashion, as reproduction depends on the duality of the sexes, through continuing battles and only periodic intervals of reconciliation" (Nietzsche [1872] 1980, 25).[18]

In his 1887 preface to the second edition of *The Gay Science*, a book that returns Nietzsche to many of the themes that inspired his first book, Nietzsche foregrounds "above all: an art for artists, only for artists!" (Nietzsche [1882] 1980, 351). As Agamben likewise does not fail to note, *both* hunger and abundance, the negative and the positive, are inspirations for the artist. For Agamben, distinguishing between artist and spectator, Nietzsche purifies the concept of "beauty" filtering out the αἴσθησις that corresponds to the sensory involvement of the spectator. Qua the martial art of conflict, aesthetics too is a spectator sport. But this also makes Nietzsche's project in *The Birth of Tragedy* nothing less than a phenomenology (Babich 2013): for Nietzsche, as for Heidegger, it is a Kantian affair dedicated to articulating—this is the *logos*—what comes to appearance in the phenomenon. For his part, Nietzsche highlights the non-metaphysical element of this phenomenology owing to the physical genius of the Greeks who had, as Nietzsche wrote, the unique gift of being able to remain at and to delight in the surface of things (Nietzsche [1882] 1980, 352).

Reflecting on spectatorship, Agamben reflects on taste, clarified as both high *and* low, as cultivated *and* vulgar.[19] Agamben thus covers Denis Diderot's point in *Rameau's Nephew*, updated, beyond Adorno, remixed beyond Lyotard,

---

16 Thus "male and female, we all listen with men's ears" (Babich [2013] 2016, 51, see for further discussion at the intersection between philosophy and pop music, 49–68).

17 The same complex reticulation of sexuality and difference may be found in Adorno's reflections on culture (and desire and music) in *Quasi una fantasia* (see Adorno 1992).

18 If Nietzsche coordinates the reference with the generative conflict between the sexes (this is Empedocles), he echoes this in his reflection on science as such—science as a question—viewed through what he calls the optic (*Optik*) of the artist, refracted on the ground of life in his 1886 preface to his re-issuing of *The Birth of Tragedy*.

19 See Agamben (1999).

beyond Pierre Bourdieu, post postmodern, and, in advance: post post-truth, meaning post-kitsch,[20] a point regarding vulgar taste precisely needed in an academic era long accustomed to contesting Adorno's views on jazz (levelling or ignoring their musicological specificity in the process) along with the contrast between culture, high and low.

Agamben quotes Paul Valéry in French, to be sure, but in translation it is immediately transposed into parenthetical English: "'le goût est fait de mille dégoûts' ('taste is made of a thousand distastes')" (Agamben 1999, 15). If you want, you may hear a thousand drops: gobs of disgust. Like negative theology, Agamben's negative aesthetics refigures kitsch in terms of "the transmissibility of culture" (ibid., 104). In other words, as Agamben reprises Valéry, "good taste is essentially made of bad taste" (ibid., 17).

Agamben transcends debates on Lyotard's aesthetic postmodern, beyond the notion of cultures high and low, thus: "we no longer even wonder (although it would be natural to do so) how it is possible that our taste is divided between objects as incompatible as the *Duino Elegies* and Ian Fleming's novels, Cézanne's canvases and knickknacks with floral patterns" (ibid., 19). Noting Rimbaud's confession of his debility in taste (i.e., outspokenly "bad"),[21] characteristic of the intellectual fond of Rilke and James Bond (or Karl May), Agamben quotes Schlegel's *Lucinde*—here, perhaps we begin to understand Roman Polanski, Woody Allen, and Louis C. K., just to name some predatory artists from way back, and we could, arguably, also include almost every film comedy ever made, the otherwise unimpeachable Chaplin and the Marx Brothers included—"So is not a certain *aesthetic cruelty [ästhetische Bösheit]* an essential part of harmonious education?" (Schlegel 1962, 28, as quoted in Agamben 1999, 22).

Clearly, Agamben is *not* addressing cinema's tacit sadism or its sexism, that is, its masculine delectation of virginal *opsis*, much less its fetishisation of youth or indeed the obliquity of the male subject as object (the male is not even in the optical frame for the most part). At issue is the compatibility of opposites in the case of Rameau's nephew: "a man of extraordinary good taste and at the same time a despicable rascal" (Agamben 1999, 22).[22]

---

20   For a discussion of kitsch and modernity, see Emmer (1998).

21   Agamben (1999, 21) quotes Rimbaud from *A Season in Hell*: "J'aimais les peintures idiotes, dessus de porte, décors, toiles de saitimbanques, enseignes, enluminures populaires; la littérature démodée, latin d'église, livres érotiques sans orthographe, romans de nos aïeules, contes de fées, petits livres de l'enfance, opéras vieux, refrains niais, rhythmes naïfs. (I loved stupid pictures, the panels over doors, stage sets, the backdrops of mountebanks, inn signs, popular prints; antiquated literature, church Latin, badly spelled erotic books, the novels of our grandmothers, fairy tales, children's books, old operas, inane refrains and artless rhythms.)" And Agamben goes on to say: "From the point of view of taste, what was eccentric in Rimbaud's time has become something like the *average taste* of the intellectual, and has penetrated so deeply into the heritage of *bon ton* that it now constitutes a real mark of that heritage" (ibid., 22).

22   Agamben (1999, 22) refers here to Diderot's "short satire that, having already been translated into German by Goethe at the manuscript stage, exerted a powerful influence on young Hegel. In the satire, Rameau's nephew is a man of extraordinary good taste and at the same time a despicable rascal. In him every difference between good and evil, nobility and commonness, virtue and vice, has disappeared: only taste, in the middle of the absolute perversion of everything into its opposite, has maintained its integrity and lucidity." Agamben here cites Diderot (1966, 107–8).

Agamben traces a genealogical reading of Nietzsche's less attributed sources, to the verge, if not quite, of including Nietzsche's reference to Memnon's column in *The Birth of Tragedy* via Diderot (and, we may add, Voltaire).[23] Agamben also summarises Kant's contribution to the science of aesthetics as distinguishing "four characteristics of beauty as the object of aesthetic judgment (namely, disinterested satisfaction, universality apart from concepts, purposiveness without purpose, and normality without a norm)" (ibid., 42). Accordingly, for Agamben, "it seems, that is, that every time aesthetic judgment attempts to determine what the beautiful is, it holds in its hands not the beautiful but its shadow, as though its true object were not so much what art is but what it is not: not art but non-art" (ibid.).[24]

The point to be made between Benjamin and Adorno and Heidegger is part of the point in Gadamer's *The Relevance of the Beautiful* for Agamben (1999, 49): "After aesthetic judgment taught us to distinguish art from its shadow and authenticity from inauthenticity, our experience, on the contrary, forces us to face the embarrassing truth that it is precisely to non-art that we owe, today, our most original aesthetic emotions." If Agamben follows Nietzsche through Heidegger he also echoes Hölderlin: "Everything is rhythm, the entire destiny of man is one heavenly rhythm, just as every work of art is one rhythm, and everything swings from the poetizing lips of the god" (ibid., 94). Although Agamben goes on to cite the archaic Greeks, he does not name the poet Archilochus, the poet who Nietzsche describes over the course of two full sections of his book on tragedy as the inventor of an astonishing array of musical modes (according to ancient authority) and whom he discusses at length in his lecture course on Greek lyric poetry, naming Archilochus the lyric poet of all lyric poets, to be ranked with or perhaps *above* Homer.[25]

---

23 When Diderot asks him why he has not been able to produce anything worthwhile despite his gift for hearing, remembering, and reproducing, Rameau's nephew justifies himself by invoking the fatality that has endowed him with the ability to judge but not the ability to create, and recalls the legend of the statue of Memnon: "Round the statue of Memnon there were a multitude of other statues on which the sun's rays shone just the same, but Memnon's was the only one that gave forth a sound . . . the others . . . are just so many pairs of ears stuck on the end of so many poles" (as translated in Agamben 1999, 23).

24 Here Agamben (1999, 47) invokes—as Nietzsche likewise invokes—Lessing's suggestion of the condition of a Raphael "without hands" (see Lessing 1772, 13); this last would, in a certain sense, correspond to the normal spiritual condition of any spectator who cares for the work of art, and the experience of art can only be the experience of an absolute split.

25 "Moreover, if we may believe Pindar, Terpander was the originator of drinking-songs. But it must be remembered that further innovations were made by Archilochus, the trimeter, the combination of unlike measures, the recitative or rhythmical recitation of poetry to music, and the style of music to which recitative was set. To him also are ascribed the epode, the tetrameter, the cretic, the prosodiac, and the lengthening of the 'heroic' or dactylic hexameter; and some authorities would add the elegiac, and not only that, but the combination of the epibatic paeon with the iambic, and that of the lengthened 'heroic' with the prosodiac and the cretic. He is also credited with the device of reciting some of a number of iambic lines to music and singing the others, a device afterwards employed by the tragic poets and introduced by Crexus into the dithyramb. He is also thought to have been the first to set the music of the accompanying instrument an octave higher than the voice, instead of in the same register with it as had been the custom before his day" (Plutarch, *De Musica* 28, as translated in Edmonds 1931, 87, 89). Or as Nietzsche explains in the second lecture of his Winter Semester 1878 to 1879 lecture course on Greek Lyric Poetry, which drew on his earlier research on rhythm and echo points made in *The Birth of Tragedy*, "Die Lyrik ist [die] älteste Form der Poesie: das Epos entwickelt sich aus einer gewissen Art des Liedes, der Götter- und Heroenhymne. Die Lyrik uberall verbunden mit dem religiösen Cult, wo Musik und Tanz mit ihr zusammenkommen der Rhythmus in das Wort hineinewählen, gruppirt die Atome des Satzes; der Rhythmus in Bez[iehung] auf den λόγος heißt μέτρον" (Nietzsche [1878–79] 1993, 372;

As Nietzsche's Zarathustra remonstrates with his heart, so Archilochus originally addressed himself: "Soul, soul! stricken with overwhelming troubles.... But in joys delight, and in evils grieve—not overmuch; so learn what rhythm holds men" (Archilochus, as translated in Taylor 1911, 240). Archilochus's rhythm, Nietzsche's rhythm, and also Aristotle on rhythm and structure yield the calculus Agamben invokes: "It is only because rhythm situates itself in a dimension in which the very essence of the work of art is at stake that the ambiguity is possible in which the work of art presents itself on the one hand as rational and necessary structure and on the other as pure, disinterested play, in a space in which calculation and play appear to blur into each other" (Agamben 1999, 99). Rhythm (and tone) are key to Nietzsche's musically phenomenological discussion of tragedy. Glossing the phenomenological *epoché* with Nietzsche's reflection on forgetting as this appears at the outset of Nietzsche's meditation on the relevance (and "irrelevance") of history for "life," as Nietzsche says, for Agamben, "rhythm—as we commonly understand it—appears to introduce into this eternal flow a split and a stop. Thus in a musical piece, although it is somehow in time, we perceive rhythm as something that escapes the incessant flight of instants and appears almost as the presence of an atemporal dimension in time" (ibid.).[26] Thus as Agamben goes on to say: "In this sense one can say that on the one hand, *kitsch*, which considers beauty as the immediate goal of the work of art, is the specific product of aesthetics, while on the other hand, the ghost of beauty that kitsch evokes in the work of art is nothing but the destruction of the transmissibility of culture, in which aesthetics is founded" (ibid., 111, my emphasis).

Through the skein of Agamben's references, his discussion of Diderot–Rousseau–Valéry constitutes a high cultural reflection on one of the lowest denominations in popular culture. If Agamben invokes Ian Fleming by name—James Bond novels and films—a low/high cultural reference has the Bond du jour, to date and still, Daniel Craig, and the Queen herself, still, jumping from planes (in effigy of course) to open the 2012 London Olympics. For similar reasons, a particular holiday season sets digital culture in search of the right film, from *Miracle on 34th Street* (1947), named for its location in a department store, the better to dislodge the suspiciously Marxist-minded *It's a Wonderful Life* (1946), to something more "relevant" or contemporary—like *Love, Actually* (2003), a mixed bag of love stories in search of a movie, featuring Alan Rickman (cheating on Emma Thompson), as well as Hugh Grant and Colin Firth and Liam Neeson for good masculine measure, or else perhaps, and more datedly

---

The lyric is [the] oldest form of poesie: the epic is developed out of a certain kind of song, the hymns of the gods and the heroes. The lyric is everywhere connected with the religious cult, wherein music and dance come together selecting the rhythm into the word, grouping the atoms of the sentence; the rhythm in re[lation] to the λόγος is called μέτρον). See further, Babich (2017a).

26 "In the same way, when we are before a work of art or a landscape bathed in the light of its own presence, we perceive a stop in time, as though we were suddenly thrown into a more original time. There is a stop, an interruption in the incessant flow of instants that, coming from the future, sinks into the past, and this interruption, this stop, is precisely what gives and reveals the particular status, the mode of presence proper to the work of art or the landscape we have before our eyes. We are as though held, arrested before something, but this being arrested is also a being-outside, an *ek-stasis* in a more original dimension" (Agamben 1999, 99).

still, *Die Hard* (1988), with a youthful but untidy Bruce Willis besting a younger, better dressed Alan Rickman at a Christmas party besieged by faux-terrorists. As I write, the culture industry is working on the latest candidate, complete with a screenplay co-written by Emma Thompson with "unreleased" music by the late pop singer George Michael, underscoring a clear bid for novelty, and titled with reference to Wham!'s 1986 classic *Last Christmas* (2019). What else is, better said, *could be* new?

THE RHYTHM OF INVENTION OR EDGAR ALLAN POE CALCULATING "NEVERMORE"

In *What Is the Contemporary?*, Agamben (2009, 40) highlights the irrelevance (*inattuale*) necessarily associated with those who are contemporary in and with their era. This also entails that contemporary figures tend to be unaware of one another, irrelevant to one another. Those on the cutting edge do not, perhaps because they cannot, catch sight of others on the edge. Roger Scruton, the contemporary philosopher of art, as he is, whatever his tastes, denounces Adorno, who, dead as he is, is presumably beyond minding. Scruton also omits the names of other current thinkers: thus he does not mention Agamben or Nancy any more than Danto did, just as he does not mention Virilio. Which is heretical to point out just because, so precise is Agamben's estimation of the *inattuale*, contemporary thinkers, if they are leading thinkers, are not meant to notice other thinkers. Sovereign, they are oblivious. In philosophy, whether one is Heidegger or Wittgenstein, Vattimo or Cavell, one mentions only sparely, naming only the rarest of canonic names. Even here, writing about authors like Nancy and Agamben, I couch what I write, as they do, by referring (mostly) to Nietzsche as Agamben himself glosses Diderot, Voltaire, and Valéry.

Nietzsche tells us that only the irrelevant can be untimely, as a temporal tactic, as he concludes his foreword to his second *Untimely Meditation*, "to work against our time and thereby on our time and hopefully to the benefit of a time to come" (Nietzsche [1874] 1980, 247). It is forgetting timeliness, one's time-bound condition, that "makes happiness happiness," that is to say, as Nietzsche explains: "to feel unhistorically through and through" (Nietzsche [1874] 1980, 250). In consequence all our joy is oblivion. It is the forgetting of the memory of past feeling that gives us, yet once more, pleasure. This corresponds to the delight of recognition that is for Adorno all we need to like anything, be it music, traditional or new, films, photographs, any work of art. As Nietzsche writes: "Whoever cannot settle down on the threshold of moment, forgetting all the past, who is incapable of standing on one point like a goddess of victory without dizziness and fear, such a one will never know what happiness is and worse yet: he will never do anything that makes others happy" (ibid.).

By contrast, memory is a sentence to unhappiness. Thus the satirically "mocking" Lucian, the provocative second-century Syrian author who was as influential for Nietzsche as he was for Erasmus and for Jonathan Swift and likewise David Hume, underlines the punishment reserved for those deemed exceptionally unjust in the afterlife, to wit, the case of the tyrant. Contra the underworld rule according to which "it is customary . . . for all the dead to drink the water of Lethe" (Lucian 1915, 55), the tyrant caught in the shadows of the underworld is condemned to "review . . . his life of luxury," doomed "to remember what he did in life" (ibid., 57). Repetition is the compulsion of memory.

In a digital era, we are surrounded by an enormous tide of priming prompts: via our phones, or where online ads interrupt our internet, like the commercial interruptions that we are programmed to expect on television and radio. Thus our social media pages ask us to help curate and design the kind of ads we would *like* to see—there is never an option of not seeing any ads at all: instead, if anything, these proliferate. If you want to avoid advertising, you need to avoid not only the internet but also any cultural event, including museum visits, opera, and theatre.

And almost all this has been true for centuries, and can be confirmed, had we need of this, in centuries past, if we care to consider Michelangelo's efforts to secure his fortune (Lenain 2011, but also Vasari 2008, 423, and see Babich 2017b, 116–119) or Schiller and his own efforts to attain market success (see Woodmansee 1994; Mortensen 1997), ditto Nietzsche and his dependence on sales ultimately not forthcoming, which is another way to read the subtitle of his *Thus Spoke Zarathustra: A Book for All and None* and perhaps his calculated decline.

Nietzsche argued—and this argument continues to be rejected by established Nietzsche scholars, even by those interested in Nietzsche and rhythm, just as it is excluded by contemporary scholars of ancient Greek music (in both cases for *normative* reasons, as Kuhn described this as key to "normal science")—that it is our modern rhythm that deafens us to the Greeks (Nietzsche 2016). The mainstream judgement seems justified: surely we have never had more rhythm—thus I began the current chapter with a riff on pop music covers, tricked out in a gesture towards the up-to-date with the rhythms of the "The Cup Song"—and I could go on to add a reflection on jazz and rock and roll, punk and rap, and so on. But it may help to add a poetic reflection on rhythm by the poetic master of the same, Edgar Allan Poe, as the poet details his formulaic and famously rhythmical poem *The Raven*.

Highlighting composition, emphasising the refrain qua deliberate keynote of melancholy, Poe (1846, 164) tells us that: "As commonly used, the *refrain*, or burden, not only is limited to lyric verse, but depends for its impression upon the force of monotone—both in sound and thought." As Plato reflects on the role of poetry and rhetoric in the *Republic* and the *Ion*, the artist, just in order to be an artist, calculates the reception of his work. In *The Raven*, Poe tells us that the poet compels the reader. Thus the line and its emphasis, the story of sorrow, bereaved love, and the almost mechanical ictus of the bird's utterance, was not a matter of typical poetic inspiration, the muse did not seize the author in this case but much rather the poet tells us that he sought to find a word from which the poem would follow, taking the reader along with him, in accord with a certain necessity, which search engendered, as refrain, *Nevermore*. Poe writes: "That such a close, to have force, must be sonorous and susceptible of protracted emphasis, admitted no doubt: and these considerations inevitably led me to the long *o* as the most sonorous vowel, in connection with *r* as the most producible consonant" (ibid., 165). This musical reflection on the assonance of poetic composition is significant: repetition and its calculated deployment[27] are more important to Poe, as he underscores for us, than the content of the poem as such, a fact Poe highlights with reference to two names, one now standardised sufficiently, that would be Dickens, the other now less well known.[28] Meaning is, to this extent subordinate: "the chief use of the 'meaning' of a poem ... may be to satisfy one habit of the reader, to keep his mind diverted and quiet, while the poem," so T. S. Eliot tells us, "does its work upon him" ([1933] 1964, 151).

Negating claims: not art—not music—not philosophy

I began with an unmarked phenomenology of the contemporary for and in art history and philosophy of art, focusing on contemporary art, including Agamben's deficits, that is, bad taste and rhythmology, and Poe's poetic calculations, along with passing allusions to fashion as well as the commonplace of desire, however gendered. Recall the earlier reflection on demarcation—what counts as art and what does not—to Nancy's bemusement: "a space of contradiction, quarrel, at times very violent, in the centre of which there is the question of art, because you are well aware that many people are ready to say, if you talk to them about contemporary art, that it's not art" (Nancy 2010, 93).

The demarcation problem remains: thus the battle of high and low culture and Agamben's reference to our easy ability to like *both* Rilke *and* Bond, especially when it comes to film versions of Bond, such as Daniel Craig's, rather as one might order a cocktail or vote for one's favourite filmic Bond—for nostalgia's sake, Roger Moore or Sean Connery, or else to hold out for another favourite who might be next. In philosophy, demarcation is the functional point of having the analytic–continental divide: one wants to say, in advance, this is about authorisation, what counts as philosophy.

---

27 "And here it was that I saw at once the opportunity afforded for the effect on which I had been depending—that is to say, the effect of the *variation of application*. I saw that I could make the first query propounded by the lover—the first query to which the Raven should reply 'Nevermore'—that I could make this first query a commonplace one—the second less so—the third still less, and so on—until at length the lover, startled from his original *nonchalance* by the melancholy character of the word itself—by its frequent repetition—and by a consideration of the ominous reputation of the fowl that uttered it—is at length excited to superstition, and wildly propounds queries of a far different character—queries whose solution he has passionately at heart—propounds them half in superstition and half in that species of despair which delights in self-torture—propounds them not altogether because he believes in the prophetic or demoniac character of the bird (which, reason assures him, is merely repeating a lesson learned by rote) but because he experiences a phrenzied pleasure in so modeling his questions as to receive from the *expected* 'Nevermore' the most delicious because the most intolerable of sorrow" (Poe 1846, 165).

28 The first name Poe refers to is that of Charles Dickens, the second that of William Godwin. Poe refers specifically to Godwin's *Things as They Are; or The Adventures of Caleb Williams*, which was published on 12 May 1794 to coincide with the suspension of habeas corpus and banned from booksellers and the stage almost immediately. One can rather see why it was banned, even if only for the title epigraph: "Amidst the woods the leopard knows his kind; / The tyger preys not on the tyger brood; / Man only is the common foe of man" (Godwin 1794, title page).

In consequence, we may draw an indexical phenomenology of sorts, modelled to be sure on Heidegger's question concerning translation: tell me whether you think there is a difference between "analytic" and "continental," and I will tell you who you are. If you think there is a divide, you may be on the continental side (or you are not, but chances are good). And if you *don't think there is a difference* between analytic and continental approaches to philosophy *or* else if you *think it unimportant/irrelevant*, you are more than likely to be on the analytic side. What is at stake concerns the style of philosophy tolerated and even more crucially, which thinkers are to be counted and which not.

Michael Fried raises the question of art theatre, and thus the parallel with kitsch, as Agamben specifically mentions Fleming's pulp fiction, which may be read in Fried's case as a negative shadow of Walter Pater's "*all art constantly aspires towards the condition of music*" ([1893] 1998, 86). As Fried argues,

> *Art degenerates as it approaches the condition of theater.* Theater is the common denominator that binds together a large and seemingly disparate variety of activities, and that distinguishes those activities from the radically different enterprises of the modernist arts. Here as elsewhere the question of value or level is central. For example, a failure to register the enormous difference in quality between, say, the music of Elliott Carter and that of John Cage or between the paintings of [Morris] Louis and those of Robert Rauschenberg means that the real distinctions—between music and theatre in the first instance and between painting and theatre in the second—are displaced by the illusion that the barriers between the arts are in the process of crumbling (Cage and Rauschenberg being seen, correctly, as similar) and that the arts themselves are at last sliding towards some kind of final, implosive, hugely desirable synthesis. (Fried [1967] 1998, 164)[29]

Fried opposes this synthesis but not by invoking Agamben much less Nietzsche, who declared as a kind of closing imperative in 1888 "*that the theatre not become the lord of the arts*" (*The Case of Wagner*, §12, Nietzsche [1889] 1980a, 39). Nor was this a new development for Nietzsche as he had uttered similar reservations on the matter in *The Birth of Tragedy*, writing contra Shakespeare (in passing) and contra Euripides–Socrates–Plato in 1872. Thus, as I emphasised above, Nietzsche initially wrote against the theatrical cult of the spectator and hence in opposition to a feminine aesthetics (which he often extended to a screed against feminine artists—who were, as the term *histrionic* also makes plain, sometimes male), criticising the traditional "I" conception of tragedy and lyric poetry (re poetic subjectivity), raising the question of the subject as a spectator set out of bounds, qua non-performer, non-congregant, onlooker.[30] In a contemporary

---

29 I am thankful to Tracy B. Strong's engagement with Fried. Strong's reading is enriched with references to Rousseau and to Stanley Cavell. Here Fried appropriates—I would argue that he does this innocently—the claim that animates Friedrich Nietzsche's preface to the original edition of *The Birth of Tragedy Out of the Spirit of Music* inviting Wagner to make common cause with the project of his new book for the sake of a genuine artwork of the future, just to speak of the futures of the contemporary. Strong has repeatedly (and rightly to my mind) emphasised the rhetorical force of the first preface addressed to Richard Wagner as *Vorkämpfer* both for its apotropaic directionality but also for, as I hear this, a possible project of waging a common battle for the soul of culture (see Strong 2017).

30 This is a very complex issue as Agamben makes plain in his own discussion, which I turn to below. See, too, reflections on Nietzsche's critique of the subject in Babich (2017a, esp. 421–27), as well as Rampley (2000, 50–77).

context, to return to the postcontemporary theme, note the quasi-mystical literality of the literal, as Fried ([1967] 1998, 168) writes, "Presentness is grace."

We could ask: whose grace? Still more importantly perhaps: whose presentness? One answer (noted above) invokes Stanley Cavell and a certain enthusiasm for "the ordinary" among the chosen ones of American academia and elsewhere. And there are other replies. But all the academic collateral in the world does not help us with this conundrum. Writing about "the subject," Nietzsche writes of what Fried calls "presentness," and also writes with every offensively misogynist vein in his body about what Nietzsche calls the "spectator's art," an art as he specifies, before witnesses, an art for appearance's sake, "theatre," quite as Fried details. And there is theatre in any museum installation but also and explicitly so in performance art: the artist as art, the spectacle/scandal of masturbating occlusion in the case of Vito Acconci, as mentioned above or else simply face to face, to refer to Marina Abramović's exhibition *The Artist Is Present*, exemplifying, the oblivion, as Nietzsche writes, of every "monologic art or art before witnesses " (Nietzsche [1882] 1980, 616).[31] This corresponds to Nietzsche's spectator's aesthetics, and a good deal of conceptual art, performance art, and protest art depends on this.

The next section turns to, and I must apologise because it is unpleasant— perhaps it will help if we pretend these are "pictures at an exhibition"—the pitilessness of art between artist and spectator.

Paul Virilio on "the pitilessness of art": from performance pain to Danto's fur

The introduction to the English translation of the late Paul Virilio's *Art and Fear* (2003) informs the reader that Virilio offers "an aide-memoire of a further precise obligation to poetry or as an awareness of the aesthetics of Auschwitz" (Armitage 2003, 12; see also Danto 1997).[32] Virilio undertakes to articulate the dispassion of our disinterested interest as what he calls the "pitiless[ness] of contemporary art" (Armitage 2003, 10). It is relevant to add that Virilio's reference to contemporary art is especially to shock art, or "gut art," here using biblical language as Ivan Illich does for his gut-wrenching invocation (to pity).[33] Other contemporary artists that could be discussed include Abramović: her self-cutting or self-burning, her covers of the work of other artists (including

---

31 The counterpoint for Fried's observation in Greenberg is useful for the next section, along with the turn to music as the focus on what Greenberg names the "condition of non-art" and Fried's objecthood, for Fried, quoting (and partly eliding) Greenberg: "No matter how simple the object may be, there remain the relations and interrelations of surface, contour, and spatial interval. Minimal works are readable as art, as almost anything is today—including a door, a table, or a blank sheet of paper. . . . Yet it would seem that a kind of art nearer the condition of non-art could not be envisaged or ideated at this moment" (Greenberg [1967] 1993, 253, as quoted in Fried [1967] 1998, 152).

32 For Armitage (2003, 12), what is at stake is politics and not less awareness (and this goes beyond context): "Contemporary art is then the expression of all those artists who take for granted that today's transformation of the field of aesthetics into a kind of terroristic performance also implies the elimination of silence. As a constant critic of the art of technology and the current attack on representation, Virilio is intensely uneasy about the development of pitiless art."

33 See further my discussion of compassion in the New Testament account of the Good Samaritan in Babich (2018d, 24), including reference to Ivan Illich (ibid., 26).

Joseph Beuys), or her self-stimulation, including a re-creation of Acconci's 1972 New York performance suggesting (it did not show) autoeroticism. If the shock of Acconci is one thing (hidden beneath a fake floor, Acconci was in no danger of exposure), shame and shaming highlights the stress that is caused simply being looked at, harder for a woman, even an artist, than we like to suppose—"installed" at MOMA in 2010, "The Artist is Present" day nine, let's take the other artists on display in this case, the actors James Franco or Alan Rickman. Thus, Abramović tells us, "The hardest thing is to do something that is close to nothing" (quoted in Jacques 2012).

For Virilio, pitilessness corresponds, on the side of the exhibiting artist, to Petr Andreevich Pavlensky, whom I note as a more recent example who was *not* Virilio's much more shocking reference but qua an instantiation of a certain, now already *passé*, contemporaneity. Virilio's book was first written in 2000, and on 10 November 2013 Pavlensky in an act of protest art (meaning and not only as an act of protest) nailed his scrotum to Red Square.

Phenomenologically, we approach contemporary and protest art by reflecting on what we have always already bracketed, just in order to see such art as and qua art. Thus Virilio (2003, 16) shatters our neatly enclosed perspective vantage point, asking: "Hasn't the universality of the extermination of bodies as well as of the environment, from AUSCHWITZ to CHERNOBYL, succeeded in *dehumanizing us from without* by shattering our ethic and aesthetic bearings, our very perception of our surroundings?"

Virilio is not alone in highlighting the irrelevance of (still) contemporary and (still) ongoing political shock or terror. Benjamin ([1968] 2007, 241) reminds us of "the violation of the masses, whom Fascism, with its *Führer* cult, forces to their knees," but the aesthetic reference is to Filippo Tommaso Marinetti, the Italian Futurist who writes: "War is beautiful because it establishes man's dominion over the subjugated machinery by means of gas masks" (quoted in ibid.). Thus Virilio (2003, 16) recalls "The slogan of the First Futurist Manifesto of 1909—'War is the world's only hygiene'—led directly, though thirty years later this time, to the shower block of Auschwitz-Birkenau." Peter Sloterdijk who writes on the terrors of atmospheric war technologies,[34] along with Walter Benjamin and Marinetti, reminds us that war remains the articulation of *techne* today, including as Agamben speaks of it, both *poiesis* and *praxis*—if we wished we could add other names, but Virilio's point is that there are relatively few such names when speaking of art.

As insistently as Benjamin's cousin, Günther Anders—a traditionally discounted theorist, even by those most expert in Benjamin's thought—insisted on emphasising the nuclear violence inherent in the peaceful uses of atomic power in his *Gewalt ja oder nein* (1987),[35] Virilio underlines the more ubiquitous and more calculated construction of "the *balance of terror* along with the opening of the laboratories of a science that was gearing up to programme the end of the world—notably with the invention, in 1951, of thermonuclear

---

34 See for discussion of Sloterdijk and atmosphere or weather, Babich (2019b).
35 See for the Heideggerian subtleties of Anders's discussion, Babich (2018c).

weapons" (Virilio 2003, 17).[36] Keeping to the self-mutilation of artists, Virilio invokes the art-science that is medical technology, biology, and embryology, which he gives the technical name *teratology*, the creation of monsters, research science dedicated to "the hybridization of man and animal" (ibid., 27). Art and science come together in the hacking of tissue, sliced and diced, fractionated for human-animal chimeras, embryological mosaics almost wholly human, 80 per cent or more, raised in, raised as animals, on factory farms,[37] for the sake of the medical industry.

Focusing on what pain reveals of the subject, Virilio invokes the spectator's sensibility. The performance art supposed by artists like Abramović and Pavlensky—or Beuys explaining his art to his dead hare or larding a chair with animal fats, even the insistent Bazon Brock, repeating word-shocks through academic fabulance (to vary Bracha Lichtenberg Ettinger's Lacanian *fascinance*)—all depend, qua performance, qua art, on shock per se. The bourgeoisie exists to be well and truly—and this is getting harder and harder—*epaté*.[38]

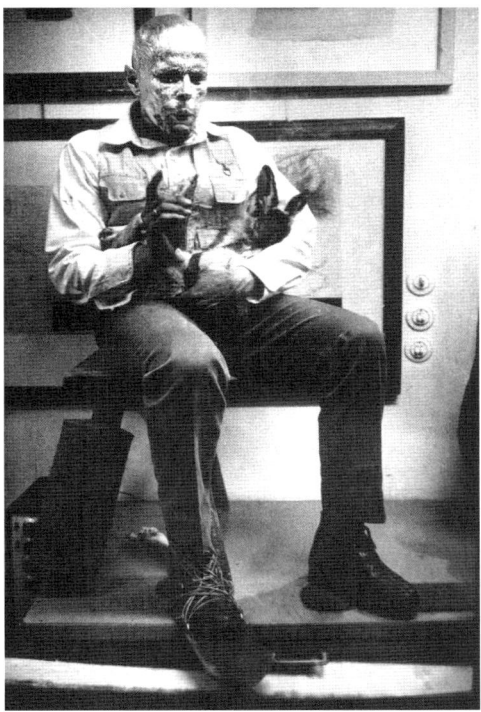

Figure 3.3

---

36 Here Virilio (2003, 18) seems to anticipate the age of Trump and "the desolation of modern times with their cardboard cut-out dictator that keeps popping up, whether it be Hitler or the 'Futurist' Mussolini, Stalin or Mao Zedong."

37 I discuss this in a contemporary context in Babich (2018a).

38 To this extent, Danto maintains, this is the expected disdain of the "art critic," that and if only to prove one's artworld cachet, one is expected to "dislike" contemporary art. See for one discussion, Sassower and Cicotello (2000).

Figure 3.3. *Joseph Beuys in the Action "Explaining Pictures to a Dead Hare"* 1965, printed 1997. Credit: Ute Klophaus (Germany, b. 1940, d. 2010), Joseph Beuys (Germany, b. 1921, d. 1986), gelatin silver photograph, 30.7 × 20.5 cm, Art Gallery of New South Wales, Mervyn Horton Bequest Fund 1997. © Ute Klophaus. Photo: Brenton McGeachie, AGNSW. 434.1997.9.

If Bazon Brock is seriously unserious, serially moving through tactics as he does, in search of whatever works, Virilio was unremittingly constant, emphasising that Auschwitz-Birkenau was a leading research laboratory for both pain *and* genetics.[39] Armitage (2003) ventures that such sensibilities are perhaps to be attributed to concerns deriving from Virilio's Catholicism. But Christianity, Catholic or otherwise, does not much mind what is done to animals, indeed, Judaism doesn't much mind, and nor does Islam. This seems to cross all faiths as, apart from Pythagoreanism or Jainism or some (not all) kinds of Buddhism, it's hard to find a religion that minds.

Virilio's talk of pain and pity raises the question of artist and spectator, dispassionate interest, as "art." By contrast, to move to the fetish of contemporary art, Danto (2013, 128) reflects on the use of materials usually inspiring disgust, from elephant dung to blood and fur, invoking Duchamp's urinal in terms of male "comfort," urine, and semen, and characterises Beuys's animal fat as a signature material, emblematising "nourishment and healing." Thus Danto treats the issue of pain and cruelty as a philosophical problem with an uncertain referentiality. In this respect, Danto notes Bentham's philosophic puzzle of animal pain (do they feel pain?) along with the then trend (exactly no longer contemporary) for animal rights activists to splash the fur coats of society matrons with dashes of paint, gestures that were never held to be the working dynamism of art, and which duly ruined private property as Danto notes (ibid., 141).[40]

Concerned with art and fear, for Virilio (2003), contemporary museum goers are conditioned, trained, neither to interfere nor indeed to respond to "art." We are thus unsurprised to learn that spectators would come and go, watching as a dog installed as an "installation" starved to death. To be sure, it wasn't only "art lovers," as the installation came with the blessing, that is the institutional complicity, of museum curators, museum staff, and the artist himself.

This impotent, passive, feminine aesthetic of the spectator, as Nietzsche speaks of it, characterises everyone from the artist seeking the effect to the curator to museum goers and critics, even those who wrote to deplore the event: this is also the perspective Kant dictates, and in Nietzsche's variation, the objective perspective of disinterested interest qua spectator. Note that this characterisation includes even art theorists who otherwise dispute the notion of "disinterested interest." Danto (2013, 131), who was worried about the victims of art animal activism, has no concern for the animals transformed into art by David Hammons's "fur coats on stands, slathered with paint." This is the point

---

39 Modern physiology, do not fail to note, has hardly abandoned pain experiments to this day, the legacy of a research science seemingly dedicated, as Simon Richter reminds us, "to determin[ing] how all the different body parts react to pain" (1992, 32).

40 These protests had no effect on the fur industry apart from inducing designers to, Hiawatha-like, make coats that put the furside inside, revealing only glimpses of the unthinking coldness of the wearer. At issue is not Danto's insensibility with respect to the question of animals, but his contention that "philosophy never presented itself as a candidate for deconstruction" (Danto 2013, 141). For Danto, the reason that this is the case is because mainstream analytic philosophy has already been there, done that: "most of the main movements in twentieth-century philosophy already consisted of programs for the reform of the discipline" (ibid.). And, oblivion clearly has its rewards: there is no need for continental philosophy or indeed feminist philosophy as Danto's female philosopher friends, so he tells us, "do not see a need for deeply altering the nature of the institution" (ibid., 142).

of Virilio's *Art and Fear* and it is also the literal aesthetics of Auschwitz, as artists continue to experiment with our own spectatorship as part of the spectacle of the exhibition as such. Thus, Hammons's paint-splattered display of fur coats could be characterised by Okwui Enwezor (2007) as mixing fashion and cruelty as a "Sadean coup de theatre."[41] But Danto focuses on object-ontology, asking what art is, and so varies analytic philosophy of art, here asking "how could a constellation of ruined ladies garments be a work of art?" (Danto 2013, 133). By this point in Danto's reflections, the theorist is so far from any reference to the issue of living, brutalised, and skinned animals that he has moved on to Andy Warhol's portrait of Liz Taylor by contrast with Warhol's 1962 *Campbell's Soup Cans*.

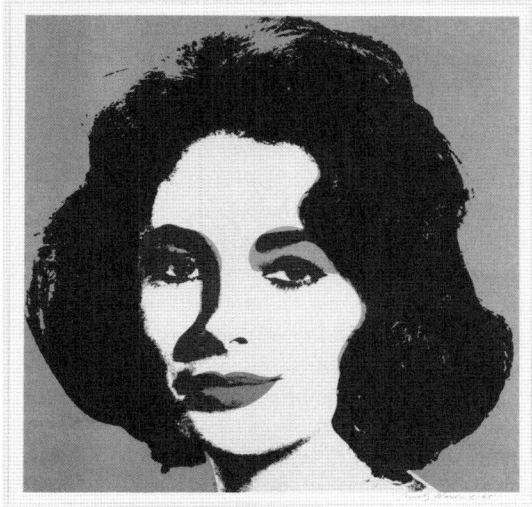

Figure 3.4.

What is at stake is one-upmanship: thereby Danto shifts—among artworld moves this is a power move—to the taste cognate issue of value. Speculation is the real meaning of futures in art (along with bitcoin and pork bellies). Hence, rather than discuss the issue of furs and such, Danto (2013, 133) goes on to mock "a certain Charles Lisanby" for his thickness in turning down Andy Warhol's offer of a portrait of Elizabeth Taylor, retailing then in 1962, as Danto, who was on the scene, tells us, for $200, but valued at auction today, to quote Danto at "$2–$4 million." Danto's valuation is on point but falls short: at the time of writing, Christie's has the painting on actual offer between 10 and 15 million.

---

41 This is not to say that Enwezor is attuned to animal rights or any such art-insensitive thing. At the end of his short paragraph, Enwezor (2007) writes that he was reminded of "Federico García Lorca's line in *Ode to Walt Whitman*: 'The rich give their mistresses small illuminated dying things. . . .'"; Enwezor's conclusion is that "No one is better than Hammons at wresting poetry from obsolescence."

The reference to value—lasting, appreciating cash value—is the point behind the judgement of taste for no one less than David Hume:[42] How can one evaluate a good wine? A good book? A good painting? A good philosopher? If art, to be art, must have enduring value, we need to know how to predict what things esteemed today will also be esteemed in future times.

THE FATE OF DUCHAMP'S *FOUNTAIN*

The relation between art and investment, which is often discussed by scholars as if this were some kind of new revelation, heretofore unexpected, constitutes one of the more patent meanings of "futures of the contemporary," which is thus not a Nietzschean gateway of the moment colliding with a series of moments yet to come. Hence, where Thierry de Duve (1993) invokes Duchamp via a return to Kant, Danto recalls the tale of Duchamp's *Fountain* retold in a Hegelian modality, emphasising that the story can never have an end: the object is no object: the fetish is missing: the original porcelain fixture long since vanished. If a certain habitus of bafflement or embarrassment—*ist das Kunst oder kann das weg?* (is this art or can it be chucked?)—is an earmark of contemporary art, then it is not merely the question of demarcation as noted above and as discussed by Danto when he points to the indistinguishability of a work of art no matter whether Warhol's *Campbell's Soup Cans* or his *Brillo Box*, by contrast with an ordinary work of commercial industrial production (as if the Warhol Foundation did not proceed accordingly, no less than Jeff Koons for his own part),[43] but, much more perniciously, as the indistinguishability of art from junk, detritus, or garbage. Patently—and to be sure, it is a frequent enough occurrence, arguably more frequent at the beginning and end of an installation—cleaning crews at museums can happen to "clean up," thus disposing of art installations in error. And in the case of Duchamp's *Fountain* at issue is also a question of media—all we have is a photograph of the "work," a photograph of a plumbing unit that appears to have been a one-off, and exactly not mass produced.

Thus, Danto (2013, 26) writes: "The most famous readymade is a urinal, lying on its back and crudely signed with the false signature 'R. Mutt 1917,' splashed onto the urinal's rim. That was the year when America entered the war and Alfred Stieglitz's 291 gallery (so-named because it was located at 291 Fifth Avenue in New York) closed shop." But Duchamp's famous ready-made was the kind of artwork almost picture-made for analytic philosophy. And Danto, as an analytic philosopher but also as a once-aspiring artist himself, knowing what he knows about reading rules, reminds us that the only criterion for exhibition, as Duchamp certainly realised, was a matter of paying the fee.[44] In other words: "anything would be shown if the artist paid the admission fee and

---

42 See, including Hume's original "Of the Standard of Taste," the various contributions to Babich (2019a).

43 See for a discussion, my contribution to the catalogue for the Jeff Koons sculpture exhibition in Frankfurt, 20 June–23 September 2012 (Babich 2012, 64–65).

44 Contemporary academics and certain contemporary artists will also recognise this as a matter of securing the fees needed for open access publication or the academic obligation of registering for a conference.

[adding an important further detail] there were to be no prizes" (ibid., 26–27). Thus it might reasonably be expected that *anything* ought to count as a submission precisely because the admitting society had not only said as much but also absolved itself of any need for discrimination or judgement—no prizes to distinguish entries also entails that no distinction be made between entries one way or the other.

Yet consistency has never been a problem for any institution, thus "the society managed to reject *Fountain*, as Duchamp ironically named it" (Danto 2013, 27). But after it was refused for exhibition at the Grand Central Palace, the fact was duly recorded in a photograph, and we all know the photograph.

The case may be made, as Danto contends, that Duchamp's *Fountain* is that photograph (ibid.). All extant physical exemplars on display, however legitimated and authorised by Duchamp himself, are to this extent three-dimensional *ekphrases* of this two-dimensional Stieglitz photograph. Nor is this irrelevant: the "original" Stieglitz gives the aura of the photographer, the tonalism Danto duly highlights.

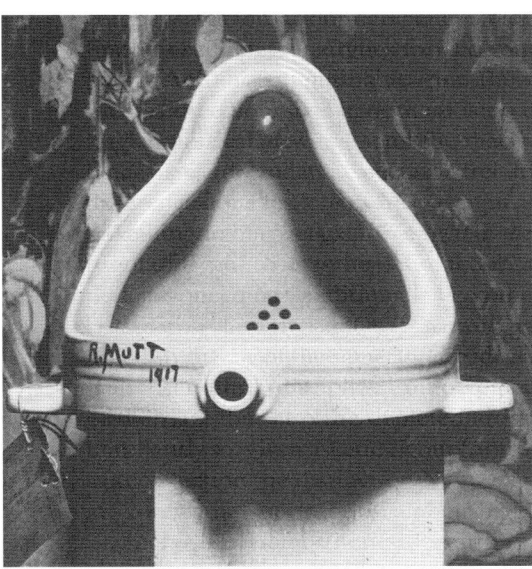

Figure 3.5.

Writing a "defence" of Duchamp's specifically ready-made urinal, qua urinal, Danto emphasised that part of the point of the ready-made was exactly its disposition as seeming disposable; in this way, it explicitly resisted the then (and still popular) convention of art appreciation.[45] Thus Danto, in the millennial

---

45 Hence, Danto (2000) writes: "We can see how little Duchamp's closest associates understood his agenda from the fact that Duchamp's patron, Walter Arensberg, imagined the artist's intent in submitting the urinal was to draw attention to 'a lovely form,' and to the formal parallels between this piece of industrial plumbing and the sculpture of Constantin Brancusi! It was no intention of Duchamp to have the

Figure 3.5. Alfred Stieglitz (1864–1946), *Fountain by R. Mutt. The Blind Man (No. 2), May 1917.* 291 Gallery. Credit: The Philadelphia Museum of Art / Art Resource, NY.

Published by Beatrice Wood (1893–1998), in collaboration with Marcel Duchamp (1887–1968), and Henri-Pierre Roch (1879–1959).

year of 2000, begins with a quotation that might remind us of Agamben's referencing of disgust—easy enough as Agamben borrows his reference from Valéry and Danto is citing Jean Clair, the then-director of the Musée Picasso in Paris, with his "new aesthetic category" as a terminus of evolution: "'From taste . . . we have passed on to disgust'" (Danto 2000). But for Danto the language of disgust entails,

> *Il catologo e questo*, as Leporello says. "If we cast about for predecessors for this abject or repulsive or excremental art, examples of which present themselves in ever growing numbers to our eyes, there is no shortage of examples to choose from." He [Clair] mentions various artists of varying degrees of stature, from Piero Manzoni, who presented *Merda d'artista* in cans, certainly as an avant-garde joke, and Joseph Beuys, who used animal fat as a symbolic material in his art. It would have to be a very squeamish individual, and perhaps a vegetarian as well, who finds lard—or felt, which was Beuys's other signature substance—disgusting. (Ibid.)

What matters for Danto is the Hegelian impetus of the thesis of the end of art, now instigated in 1907 by Duchamp: "After Duchamp, one could in principle make art out of anything. The era of turpentine and taste had come to an end. The era of finding a definition of art to replace the one based on aesthetic delectation had begun" (ibid.).

As Jean Clair (2000a) observed as the curator of the Pompidou celebration of Duchamp: "Every man is an artist. Every gesture is a work of art. Every work of art can be anything at all." Clair's book on Duchamp (Clair 2000b) perhaps unsurprisingly yields a Duchamp more complex than Danto's, including references to Joris-Karl Huysmans, to Edwin Abbott's *Flatland*, to Henri Poincaré, Heinrich Hertz, Ernst Haeckel and Sándor Ferenczi, Jacques Lacan and Thomas W. Laqueur, not to mention an ongoing discussion of Klein bottles, Leonardo and Paul Valéry and Novalis, in addition to Hannah Arendt (*The Origins of Totalitarianism*), and, very centrally, Hans Magnus Enzensberger, emphasising not the need to secure definition between designations in (Danto's word) "paroxysm" but much rather in terror.[46] Via Arendt, herself a reader of Nietzsche, if often unsung as such, Clair notes the working dynamic of failure, insignificance, Nietzschean *ressentiment*. Updating the reference for a then-contemporary reader, the allusion works even if it is no longer "contemporary." As Clair explains: "the idea of being a loser, a pariah, an outcast, a *Sonderling* or whatever leads a person to finding out at the age of fifteen or sixteen that they're not in the 'in' crowd."

---

urinal sublated under aesthetic perception, and appreciated as something after all beautiful—something to which we had heretofore been blind. 'I threw . . . the urinal in their faces as a challenge, and now they admire it for its aesthetic beauty.' Its beauty, if beauty there is, is neither here nor there. He was submitting it as a work of art. . . ." Cf., by contrast Kuspit (1995).

46 "Enzensberger recalled some facts that France, sole remaining nation managing the arts in Europe, continues to ignore. 'From Paris to Saint Petersburg, the fin de siècle intelligentsia flirted with terror. The premier expressionists called [it] the war of their wishes, just like the futurists. . . . In large countries, the cult of violence and the "nostalgia for mud" in favor of industrializing the culture of the masses, became an integral part of heritage. Because the notion of the avant-garde took an unfortunate turn, its first supporters would never have imagined'" (Clair 2000a, interpolating a quotation from Enzensberger 1995).

Including the early seventies, the generation of the sixties, that is, Clair's own generation, was the era of Leonard Cohen's *Beautiful Losers* (1966, published in French as *Les perdants magnifiques*, 1972). But the point to be made here relates more to Danto's point, because Clair's reading—no wonder Danto could not read this—set Danto's thesis back more than half a century, by fixing its original expression in Duchamp's own inspiring insight: "Duchamp was one of the rare [onlookers] to acutely grasp that which others were refusing to admit: art—art such as we knew it, the art of painting, with its rules, techniques, and enslavement to style and schools, art with its status, social recognition, academies, salons, glory—had no reason to exist any longer. Art, an invention of the XVth century, had had its day . . ." (Clair 2000a).[47]

Clair's allusions only intensify owing to his tendency to provocation, isolation; that is, he uses Stirner (not Nietzsche) to claim "The idea of the unique pupil in advance of the obsession. Nothing owed to anybody and nothing repeating itself" (ibid.). Thus, Clair reads the backstory of Duchamp's *Bride Stripped Bare by Her Bachelors, Even* (1915–23), setting Duchamp as a "bachelor," in advance of the mode that continues to be current today, as part of Duchamp's own transgender efforts (which perhaps can and should be read back to the *Fountain* but which Clair unpacks as part of the essential misogyny of masculinist "subjectivity," a point Luce Irigaray repeats in her own *This Sex Which Is Not One* [1985] in a very different direction).[48]

For Clair (2000a), precisely by contrast with our simple and straightforward vision of Duchamp as the "prophet" of the avant-garde,[49] we would rather follow our theoretical indolence and consider "Duchamp a Dadaist, a provocateur, an ancestor of New Realism, of kinetics, of the conceptual, of action, or more generally of the nihilism of art. That he managed, contrary to this caricature, a strong, thoughtful method, reasoned, and founded upon mathematical speculations . . ." Clair founds his point with reference to Linda Dalrymple Henderson's *The Fourth Dimension and Non-Euclidean Geometry in Modern Art* (1983) (but not less on an unacknowledged earlier philosophical—and mathematical—discussion of Van Gogh), points that Danto might have good familiar cause to engage with but which make no appearance in his own discussion.[50]

---

47 As Clair (2000a) goes on to observe, Duchamp "was the first to understand that he belonged to a world 'without art,' in the same way one speaks of a world 'without history.' When he began his work, the death of art had taken place. In this respect, Duchamp is a survivor, not a precursor." As a counterpoint—arch, to be sure—see, again, Kuspit (1995).

48 See in general, Irigaray (1985). If Brancusi must be read as a counterpart to points made here, if only on the other side of a more consistent point, one to be realised in film with Fritz Lang's 1927 *Metropolis*, the female machine, the machine to replace the female, then "The unsurpassable perfection of airplane propellers that Duchamp remarks upon during a visit to the aeronautical museum in the Grand Palais in 1912, crosses the mind of the hero of Huysmans. 'The beauty of woman is, in everyone's opinion, the most original and the most perfect.' In revenge man makes 'an animated and artificial being who is amply worthwhile from the point of view of fabricated beauty'" (Clair 2000a, interpolating a quotation from Huysmans, *À rebours*; see Huysmans 1998, 20).

49 See, more broadly, to be sure, Kuspit (1993).

50 Danto knew the philosopher of science Patrick A. Heelan and his interest in art, geometry, and visual perception and thus Danto might well have pointed to this dimension (Heelan 1972; see also 1983, 114–28) had he considered it, as he did not. Clair, who was interested specifically in the fourth dimension and was not familiar with New York City philosophers, would have had no reason to advertise this specific point; I note it here only to suggest the limits of Danto's response.

Art Futures

Overnight what counts as contemporary art changes, there is the "New Contemporary," and we have already invoked the postcontemporary. For the same reason, like the children's game musical chairs, gallery and museum curators can be anxious about missing out and so exchange now-outmoded "contemporary" pieces from time to time, as collectors do, as museums do, to make space—*Ist das Kunst oder kann das Weg?*—for up-and-coming contemporary art. This is perhaps the best meaning of "futures of the contemporary," which takes us back to Schiller's concern to cultivate a market, as we may also read in Horst Wagenführ's *Kunst als Kapitalanlage* (1965)[51] or Judith Benhamou-Huet's *Art Business: Le marché de l'art ou l'art du marché* (2001), or indeed, Marc Shell's *Art and Money* (1995). In Theodor Adorno's words, "The entire practice of the culture industry transfers the profit motive naked onto cultural forms" ([1975] 1991, 99).

As noted in the case of pop music covers, the work of art becomes a commodity form, and this commodification willy-nilly enters aesthetic criteriology: what is good versus what is bad. As Adorno argues, what counts as good is what sells and what sells is what is recognisable, what we know is what we like, which is also to say that what sells is what is marketed to us. In *Current of Music*, Adorno points out that radio programming, true to its name, "programs" its listeners: "the 'plugging' of songs," Adorno emphasises, "does not follow the response they elicit but the vested interests of song publishers. The identification of the successful with the most frequently played is thus an illusion, an illusion, to be sure, that may become an operating social force and in turn really make the much-played a success: because through such an identification the listeners follow what they believe to be the crowd and thus come to constitute one" (Adorno [2006] 2009, 140–41). This is not Adorno's curmudgeonly opinion—many are pleased to characterise him as being antagonistic to jazz, or opposed to kitsch, things that Teddie, one teases, ought to find redemptive, things which, as we have seen Agamben argues, even high-culture academics ultimately, that is, "really," like.

Adorno's "programming" is featured (albeit not by name) in Gadamer's "The Relevance of the Beautiful," in relation to the critical "relevance" of the beautiful. Speaking of new music, Gadamer introduces his point with the effective rhetorical expedient of saying that he is not going to talk about it (the jury may disregard the witness's remarks, to recall Perry Mason or other legal television dramas): "I should like to maintain a tactful silence about the extreme difficulty faced by performing artists when they bring modern music to the concert hall. It can usually only be performed as the middle item in a program—otherwise listeners will arrive later or leave early" (Gadamer 1986, 7). Thus Gadamer invokes "the conflict between art as a 'religion of culture' on the one hand and art as a provocation by the modern artist on the other" (ibid.), and in this way

---

51 More recently, see, with the same title, Carsten Kunze's *Kunst als Kapitalanlage* (2002), as well as—it seems that a variation of the main title is too much to ask—Eric Bernhard's *Kunst als Kapitalanlage* (2005).

he highlights this conflict as being at "the origin of kitsch and all bad art" (ibid., 52). The point is underscored for the "connoisseur" dedicated to the piety of the "religion of culture," which returns us here to the fetish notion of the cover: Who is it who is playing? Who is conducting? Who is singing? Thus Gadamer writes, "We go to the opera because Callas is singing, rather than because a particular opera is being performed" (ibid.).[52]

The liking that general audiences or non-connoisseurs get to indulge is the affective corollary of programmed recognition as such. This programming is the motor of what I name the "Hallelujah Effect," whereby, as Adorno and Eisler write in their *Composing for the Films* ([1947] 1994, 15), music can be "unveiled as the drug that it is in reality." The recognition effect also permits one ethnographer of the contemporary, Paul Rabinow, to suggest in his book *The Accompaniment: Assembling the Contemporary* (2011) that despite initial and powerful resistance at Bayreuth to Pierre Boulez, "one of the great formalist innovators in twentieth century music" (ibid., 200), his production of Wagner's *Ring* would come to be a consummate success, by dint of nothing less than repetition: "Five years of annual performances, however, gradually familiarized these faithful to what Boulez was attempting to do. In 1980, when Foucault witnessed the performance, there was one and one-half hours of applause at the end of the performance and more than one hundred curtain calls" (ibid., 200–201). On this account, Boulez effectively "covers" Wagner and the achievement thereby yields what can thus be defined as "a *contemporary* solution" (201).

Recall Adorno's reflection in *Quasi una fantasia* that Schoenberg himself, although lacking such recognition, would not have disdained such a crowning reception. Perhaps Adorno identifies with Schoenberg when he reflects in "Music and New Music" that:

> The new music suffers from the practised and the all-too-familiar, from which it differs so profoundly. It impotently takes up arms against the way of the world; its posture is aggressive. In its desire to submit only to its internal law and to mutiny against the law of demand, its subject, its potential being, which is concealed even from itself, expresses itself in highly concrete form. Its qualities become manifest in what it prohibits. This did not escape the notice of Schoenberg who would have been only too delighted to be a great composer like the predecessors he revered. (Adorno 1992, 256)

Adorno (ibid.) reports that Schoenberg "bit the hand" that would have fed him by reacting indignantly to a film mogul who "greeted him with a compliment about his '*lovely*' music.'" Insulted, the composer supposedly furiously shouted in reply, "My music is not lovely." Schoenberg lost the associated film contract thereby and Adorno points out that he regretted this loss. The same style of character was displayed by Luigi Nono, whose anger is often remarked upon; these days, he is retroactively diagnosed with Asperger's syndrome, as if only a kind of autism could explain this artistic pride.

---

52 The distinction Gadamer wishes to maintain is of course here translated as "genuine art" and this he argues depends, very Platonically, upon its capacity to communicate "to us by virtue of the power in its consummately wrought form" (Gadamer 1986, 52).

By invoking "the violence of surrealist onslaughts,"[53] Adorno (1992, 256) diagnoses the tonality of the "new music" as that "of menace." The menace is by no means incidental. Referring to Cage's "Piano Concerto" (i.e., Cage's *Concert for Piano and Orchestra*, 1957–58) as "catastrophe music," Adorno emphasises "Its gesture of menace is unmistakable when it discards its internal logic as a mere semblance [*Schein*] and throws itself on the mercy of chance" (ibid., 257).

If such violence "has its limitations," of course, it nonetheless attests to a transformation of "the nature of music" (Adorno 1992, 257). Here, on the futures of the contemporary, we can consider a contrast (reminiscent of Agamben's point regarding taste, high and low, pop and not), which Adorno makes reminding us of the same question Danto and others claim to be at the heart especially, most pronouncedly, of contemporary art: "Is that really music at all?" which Adorno slices through in advance saying "the only way to answer it is with an emphatic, Yes" (ibid.). If the music transformed by the new music was bourgeois by nature, Adorno's point is that bourgeois music was not only "decorative," as he puts it, but far more perniciously—and exactly in "its greatest achievements"—"made itself pleasant to people, not just directly, to its listeners, but objectively, going far beyond them by virtue of its affirmation of the ideas of humanism. It was given notice to quit because it had degenerated into ideology, because its reflection of the world in a positive light, its call for a better world, became a lie which legitimated evil" (ibid.). The music of "menace," catastrophe, choreographic sonic newness, counters bourgeois tonality.

Thus in the chapter "Commodity Music Analysed" Adorno (1992, 49) reflects on the famous "happy ending" cherished by the "culture industry" analysed by Adorno along with Max Horkheimer that haunts our genres at every level, and not only with respect to films (the metanoia in the pop performer Carly Rae Jepsen's music video for "Call Me Maybe" [2012] testifies to the persistence of this same filmic ideal in its one-joke subversion: the guy she is crushing on, literally plastering herself on the bonnet of a car she is washing in non-sublimated transfer, is gay, of course he's gay: or, so the maybe turns out—and: there goes happiness).

For Adorno, that the dream-machine of the filmic carries the dreamwork with it (Slavoj Žižek does not do this any better in his happily misogynistic, victim-blaming reading of James Cameron's *Titanic* [in Fiennes 2012]), induces Adorno's shop girl "to admit to herself what the entire organization of life normally prevents her from admitting: that this good fortune will not be hers. What is taken for the wish-fulfilment is the meagre liberation which consists in the realization that you do not have to deny yourself the most minimal degree of happiness, namely the knowledge that happiness is not for you, although it might be" (Adorno 1992, 49–50). The film is a Kafkaesque dream machine because: "The shop girl's experience is like that of the old mother who sheds tears at someone else's wedding, blissfully conscious of the happiness she herself has missed. Even the most stupid people have long since ceased to be

---

53 The full sentence is instructive: "The aggression which the new music directs against the established norms even now, after thirty years, an aggression in which something of the violence of surrealist onslaughts still survives, has its own specific tone; it is a tone of menace" (Adorno 1992, 256).

fooled by the belief that everyone will win the big prize" (ibid., 50). Hence, "The positive element of kitsch lies in the fact that it sets free for a moment the glimmering realization that you have wasted your life" (ibid.).

Conclusion

Our perspective on such questions, masculinist as it tends to be, offers a spectator's aesthetic but not an artist's aesthetic if only because it is the artist who games taste. Thus Nietzsche argued that the artist articulated a creative aesthetics. In this way, the Nietzsche who believed in the "force of age" (I am alluding with this phrase to Simone de Beauvoir's take on this notion [1960] as Nietzsche emphasises force for his own part) maintained that there were discrete periods of vitality: beyond the usual divisions of birth, childhood, youth, and maturity as ages of capacity. Thus in a section toward the close of *The Wanderer and His Shadow* entitled "*Lebensalter*," Nietzsche dismisses the notion that life has a winter, highlighting *only* the years of a man's 20s, 30s, *and* 40s as the unique decades of creative power (Nietzsche [1880] 1980, 668–69)—foregrounding the vitality that has no choice but to express itself and excluding the incapacity that is a prelude along with retrospective decadence and depletion, illness, and exhaustion, quite in addition to mortality. Similarly attuned to the *death* of an art form, Nietzsche writes on the *birth* of tragedy.

Tragedy on Viagra is Euripides: a dying art brought back to life, "forced" as Nietzsche writes, now to use a botanical metaphor, to bleed great gouts of blood drawn forth from dried-out flowers. At the hand of one of its poets, tragedy met with an especially gory suicide, committed in the aftermath of a mechanical resuscitation. Speaking above of Nietzsche's antipathy to theatrical effect, I also noted Nietzsche's argument that the artist could aspire to theatrical effect, like the female writers Nietzsche made fun of, authors who composed for "impact," and so that one would notice them. We routinely read Nietzsche's unpleasant comments as referring to actual female artists like George Sand and others but on the reading I am giving, Nietzsche is, for the most part, speaking of Wagner in his decline.

Expert on the tragic age of Greece, Nietzsche knew that an art form could outlive its era. In the same way, an artist can fail to die at the proper time. When this happens, the result, so Nietzsche contended, may be compared with *Parsifal*. Wagner fans will not agree with Nietzsche and it is not my project here to persuade them but only to review Nietzsche's organic conception of the birth—and death—of an art, for spectators, for artists, and all for the sake of the contemporary.

References

Adorno, Theodor W. [1975] 1991. "Culture Industry Reconsidered." Translated by Anson G. Rabinbach. In *The Culture Industry: Selected Essays on Mass Culture*, edited by J. M. Bernstein, 98–106.

London: Routledge. Essay written 1963; first published 1967 as "Résumé über Kulturindustrie" in Theodore W. Adorno, *Ohne Leitbild: Parva aesthetica* (Frankfurt am Main: Suhrkamp). Translation first published 1975 (*New German Critique* 6, Fall 1975: 12–19).

———. 1992. *Quasi una fantasia: Essays on Modern Music*. Translated by Rodney Livingstone. London: Verso. First published 1963 as *Quasi una fantasia: Musikalische Schriften II* (Frankfurt am Main: Suhrkamp).

———. (2006) 2009. *Current of Music*. Edited by Robert Hullot-Kentor. Cambridge: Polity. First published in German and English 2006 (Frankfurt am Main: Suhrkamp).

Adorno, Theodor W., and Hanns Eisler. (1947) 1994. *Composing for the Films*. London: Continuum. First published 1947 (New York: Oxford University Press).

Agamben, Giorgio. 1999. *The Man without Content*. Translated by Georgia Albert. Stanford, CA: Stanford University Press. First published 1994 as *L'uomo senza contenuto*, 2nd ed. (Macerata, Italy: Quodlibet).

———. 2009. "What Is the Contemporary?" In *What Is an Apparatus? and Other Essays*, translated by David Kishik and Stefan Pedatella, 39–54. Stanford, CA: Stanford University Press. Essay first published 2008 as *Che cos'è il contemporaneo?* (Rome: Nottetempo).

Anders, Günther. 1987. *Gewalt ja oder nein: Eine notwendige Diskussion*. Edited by Manfred Bissinger. Munich: Knaur.

Andina, Tiziana. 2010. *Arthur Danto: Un filosofo pop*. Rome: Carocci. Translated as *Arthur Danto: Philosopher of Pop* (Newcastle upon Tyne: Cambridge Scholars, 2011).

Andina, Tiziana, and Erica Onnis, eds. 2019. *The Philosophy and Art of Wang Guangyi*. London: Bloomsbury.

Armitage, John. 2003. "Art and Fear: An Introduction." In Virilio 2003, 1–13.

Augustine. 1961. *Confessions*. Translated by R. S. Pine-Coffin. London: Penguin.

Babich, Babette. 2010. "'Thus Spoke Zarathustra,' or Nietzsche and Hermeneutics in Gadamer, Lyotard, and Vattimo." In *Consequences of Hermeneutics: 50 Years after Gadamer's* Truth and Method, edited by Jeff Malpas and Santiago Zabala, 218–43. Evanston, IL: Northwestern University Press.

———. (2010) 2014. "Early Continental Philosophy of Science." In *The New Century: Bergsonism, Phenomenology, and Responses to Modern Science*, edited by Keith Ansell-Pearson and Alan D. Schrift, 263–86. London: Routledge. First published 2010 (Durham, UK: Acumen).

———. 2012. "Die Ästhetik des 'Dazwischen': Raum und Schönheit"/"The Aesthetics of the Between: Space and Beauty." In *Jeff Koons: The Sculptor*, edited by Vinzenz Brinkmann, Matthias Ulrich, and Joachim Pissarro, 50–69. Frankfurt: Schirn Kunsthalle Frankfurt.

———. 2013. "Nietzsche's Performative Phenomenology: Philology and Music." In *Nietzsche and Phenomenology: Power, Life, Subjectivity*, edited by Élodie Boubill and Christine Daigle, 117–40. Bloomington: Indiana University Press.

———. (2013) 2016. *The Hallelujah Effect: Philosophical Reflections on Music, Performance Practice, and Technology*. New York: Routledge. First published 2013 (Farnham, UK: Ashgate).

———. 2017a. "Nietzsches Lyrik: Archilochos, Musik, Metrik." In *Nietzsche und die Lyrik: Ein Kompendium*, edited by Christian Benne and Claus Zittel, 405–29. Frankfurt am Main: Metzler.

———. 2017b. "Winckelmann's Apollo, Nietzsche's Dionysus: Color and Music." *New Nietzsche Studies* 10 (3/4): 113–46.

———. 2018a. "Ivan Illich's *Medical Nemesis* and the 'Age of the Show': On the Expropriation of Death." *Nursing Philosophy* 19 (1). Accessed 28 January 2019. https://doi.org/10.1111/nup.12187.

———. 2018b. "Musical 'Covers' and the Culture Industry: From Antiquity to the Age of Digital Reproducibility." *Research in Phenomenology* 48 (3): 385–407.

———. 2018c. "On Günther Anders, Political Media Theory, and Nuclear Violence." *Philosophy and Social Criticism* 44 (10): 1110–26.

———. 2018d. "Solicitude: Towards a Heideggerian Care Ethics-of-Assistance." In *Relational Hermeneutics: Essays in Comparative Philosophy*, edited by Paul Fairfield and Saulius Geniusas, 9–28. London: Bloomsbury.

———. 2019a. *Reading David Hume's "Of the Standard of Taste."* Edited by Babette Babich. Berlin: De Gruyter.

———. 2019b. "Talking Weather from Ge-Rede to Ge-Stell." In *Sustainability in* the Anthropocene: Philosophical Essays on Renewable Technologies*, edited by Róisín Lally, 51–64. Lanham, MD: Rowman and Littlefield.

———. 2019c. "Wang Guangyi: On Contemporary Pop Art, 'Covers,' Remix, and Political Theology." In Andina and Onnis 2019, 111–146.

Benhamou-Huet, Judith. 2001. *Art Business: Le marché de l'art ou l'art du marché*. Paris: Assouline. Translated by Charles Penwarden as *The Worth of Art: Pricing the Priceless* (New York: Assouline).

Benjamin, Walter. (1968) 2007. "The Work of Art in the Age of Mechanical Reproduction." In *Illuminations: Essays and Reflections*, edited by Hannah Arendt, translated by Harry Zohn, 217–52. New York: Schocken Books. Essay first published 1936 as "L'œuvre d'art à l'époque de sa reproduction mécanisée" (*Zeitschrift für Sozialforschung* 5 [1]: 40–68). This edition first published 1968 (New York: Harcourt Brace Jovanovich).

Berger, John. (1972) 2008. *Ways of Seeing*. London: Penguin. First published 1972 (London: British Broadcasting Corporation and Penguin Books).

Bernhard, Eric. 2005. *Kunst als Kapitalanlage: Kunstmarktfonds als Verbindung zwischen Kunst- und Kapitalmärkten*. Frankfurt am Main: Deutscher Universitätsverlag.

Borschke, Margie. 2017. *This Is Not a Remix: Piracy, Authenticity and Popular Music*. London: Bloomsbury.

Bryson, Norman. 1984. *Tradition and Desire: From David to Delacroix*. Cambridge: Cambridge University Press.

Clair, Jean (Gérard Régnier). 2000a. "Duchamp at the Turn of the Centuries." Translated by Sarah Skinner Kilborne. *Tout Fait: The Marcel Duchamp Studies Online Journal*. Accessed 29 January 2019. https://www.toutfait.com/duchamp-at-the-turn-of-the-centuries. Essay first published as Clair 2000b.

———. 2000b. *Sur Marcel Duchamp et la fin de l'art*. Paris: Gallimard.

Cohen, Leonard. 1966. *Beautiful Losers*. Toronto: McClelland and Stewart. Translated into French by Michel Doury as Cohen 1972.

———. 1972. *Les perdants magnifiques*. Translated into French by Michel Doury. Paris: C. Bourgois. First published as

Cohen 1966.

Danto, Arthur. 1981. *The Transfiguration of the Commonplace: A Philosophy of Art*. Cambridge, MA: Harvard University Press.

———. 1997. *After the End of Art: Contemporary Art and the Pale of History*. Princeton, NJ: Princeton University Press.

———. 2000. "Marcel Duchamp and the End of Taste: A Defense of Contemporary Art." *Tout-Fait: The Marcel Duchamp Studies Online Journal* 1 (3). Accessed 29 January 2019. https://www.toutfait.com/issues/issue_3/News/Danto/danto.html.

———. 2013. *What Art Is*. New Haven, CT: Yale University Press.

de Beauvoir, Simone. 1960. *La force de l'âge*. Paris: Gallimard.

de Duve, Thierry. 1993. *Kant after Duchamp*. Cambridge, MA: MIT Press.

Diderot, Denis. 1966. *Rameau's Nephew*. In *Rameau's Nephew and D'Alembert's Dream*, translated by Leonard Tancock. New York: Penguin.

Edmonds, J. M., ed. and trans. 1931. *Elegy and Iambus: Being the Remains of All the Greek Elegiac and Iambic Poets from Callinus to Crates, with the* Anacreontea; *Volume II*. Loeb Classical Library. London: William Heinemann; New York: G. P. Putnam's Sons.

Eliot, T. S. (1933) 1964. *The Use of Poetry and the Use of Criticism: Studies in the Relation of Criticism to Poetry in England*. Cambridge: Harvard University Press. First published 1933 (Cambridge, MA: Harvard University Press).

Elkins, James. 1999. *Why Are Our Pictures Puzzles? On the Modern Origins of Pictorial Complexity*. London: Routledge.

Emmer, C. Edward. 1998. "Kitsch against Modernity." *Art Criticism* 13 (1): 53–80.

Enwezor, Okwui. 2007. "Best of 2007 (Part 1)." *Artforum* 46 (4) (December). Accessed 29 January 2019. https://www.artforum.com/print/200710/okwui-enwezor-42227.

Enzensberger, Hans Magnus. 1995. *La grande migration; suive de Vues sur la guerre civile*. Translated into French by Bernard Lortholary. Paris: Gallimard. First published as *Die grosse Wanderung* (Frankfurt am Main: Suhrkamp, 1992) and *Aussichten auf den Bürgerkrieg* (Frankfurt am Main: Suhrkamp, 1993). *Aussichten auf den Bürgerkrieg* translated into English by Piers Spence and Martin Chalmers as *Civil War* (London: Granta, 1994).

Felshin, Nina, ed. 1995. *But Is It Art? The Spirit of Art as Activism*. Seattle: Bay Press.

Fiennes, Sophie, dir. 2012. *The Pervert's Guide to Ideology*. London: P Guide Productions.

Freeland, Cynthia. 2001. *But Is It Art? An Introduction to Art Theory*. Oxford: Oxford University Press.

Fried, Michael. (1967) 1998. "Art and Objecthood." In *Art and Objecthood: Essays and Reviews, 148–72*. Chicago: University of Chicago Press. Essay first published 1967 (*Artforum* 5 [June]: 12–23).

Gadamer, Hans-Georg. 1986. "The Relevance of the Beautiful." In *The Relevance of the Beautiful and Other Essays*, edited by Robert Bernasconi, 1–56. Cambridge: Cambridge University Press. Essay first published 1977 as *Die Aktualität des Schönen* (Stuttgart: Reclam).

Godwin, William. 1794. *Things as They Are; or The Adventures of Caleb Williams*. London: B. Crosby.

Greenberg, Clement. (1967) 1993. "Recentness of Sculpture." In *The Collected Essays and Criticism, Volume 4: Modernism with a Vengeance, 1957–1969*, edited by John O'Brian, 250–56. Chicago: University of Chicago Press. Essay first published 1967 in *American Sculpture of the Sixties*, edited by Maurice Tuchman (Los Angeles: Los Angeles County Museum of Art), 24–26.

Gunkel, David J. 2016. *Of Remixology: Ethics and Aesthetics after Remix*. Cambridge, MA: MIT Press.

Heelan, Patrick A. 1972. "Toward a New Analysis of the Pictorial Space of Vincent Van Gogh." *Art Bulletin* 54: 478–92.

———. 1983. *Space Perception and the Philosophy of Science*. Berkeley: University of California Press.

Henderson, Linda Dalrymple. 1983. *The Fourth Dimension and Non-Euclidean Geometry in Modern Art*. Princeton, NJ: Princeton University Press.

Hölderlin, Friedrich. (1799) 1920. *Hyperion; oder, Der Eremit in Griechenland*. Potsdam: Kiepenheuer. First published 1799 as *Hyperion; oder, Der Eremit in Griechenland. Zweiter Band*. Tübingen: J.G. Cotta'schen Buchhandlung.

Huysmans, Joris-Karl. 1998. *Against Nature.* Translated by Margaret Mauldon. Oxford: Oxford University Press. First published 1884 as *À rebours* (Paris: G. Charpentier).

Irigaray, Luce. 1985. *This Sex Which Is Not One*. Translated by Catherine Porter. Ithaca, NY: Cornell University Press. First published 1977 as *Ce sexe qui n'en est pas un* (Paris: Minuit).

Jacques, Juliet. 2012. "Marina Abramović: 'The Artist is Present': The Legendary Performance Artist's Retrospective Is Lovingly Documented on DVD." *New Statesman*, 17 September. Accessed 12 February 2019. https://www. newstatesman.com/blogs/art-and-design/2012/09/marina-abramovic-artist-present.

Jepsen, Carly Rae. 2012. "Call Me Maybe." YouTube/Vevo video, 03:19, posted by "CarlyRaeMusic," 1 March 2012. Accessed 30 January 2019. https://www.youtube. com/watch?v=fWNaR-rxAic.

Kendrick, Anna. 2013. "Anna Kendrick—Cups (Pitch Perfect's 'When I'm Gone')." YouTube/Vevo video, 04:21, posted by "AnnaKendrickVEVO," 12 April 2013. Accessed 18 January 2019. https://www. youtube.com/watch?v=cmSbXsFE3l8.

Kramer, Jane. 1994. *Whose Art Is It?* Durham, NC: Duke University Press.

Kunze, Carsten. 2002. *Kunst als Kapitalanlage: Neue Perspektiven für Privatanleger*. Norderstedt, Germany: Books on Demand.

Kuspit, Donald. 1993. *The Cult of the Avant-Garde Artist*. Cambridge: Cambridge University Press.

———. 1995. "Marcel Duchamp, Imposter Artist." *New Art Examiner* (March): 17–21.

Lenain, Thierry. 2011. *Art Forgery: The History of a Modern Obsession*. London: Reaktion.

Lessing, Gotthold. 1772. *Emilia Galotti*. Berlin: Christian Friedrich Voß.

Lodge, Oliver W. F. 1927. *What Art Is*. New York: George H. Doran.

Lucian. 1915. "Κατάπλους ἢ Τύραννος. The Downward Journey, or The Tyrant." In *Lucian*, translated by A. M. Harmon, 7 vols, 2:1–57. Loeb Classical Library. London: William Heinemann; New York: G. P. Putnam's Sons.

Lulu and the Lampshades. 2009. "You're Gonna Miss Me." YouTube video, 01:37, posted by "LandShapes," 8 June 2009. Accessed 18 January 2019. https://www.

youtube.com/watch?v=DWCOYJg9ps4.

Mitchell, W. J. Thomas. 1994. *Picture Theory: Essays on Verbal and Visual Representation*. Chicago: University of Chicago Press.

Mortensen, Freben. 1997. *Art in the Social Order: The Making of the Modern Conception of Art*. Albany: State University of New York Press.

Nancy, Jean-Luc. 2010. "Art Today." Translated by Charlotte Mandell. *Journal of Visual Culture* 9 (1): 91–99. First delivered as a lecture, Milan, 2006.

Nehamas, Alexander. 2007. *Only a Promise of Happiness: The Place of Beauty in a World of Art*. Princeton, NJ: Princeton University Press.

Nietzsche, Friedrich. (1872) 1980. *Die Geburt der Tragödie* [*The Birth of Tragedy*]. In *Kritische Studienausgabe, Bd. 1*, edited by Giorgio Colli and Mazzino Montinari, 7–156. Berlin: De Gruyter. First published 1872 (Leipzig: Fritzsch).

———. (1874) 1980. "Vom Nutzen und Nachteil der Historie für das Leben" ["On the Uses and Disadvantages of History for Life"]. In *Kritische Studienausgabe, Bd. 1*, edited by Giorgio Colli and Mazzino Montinari, 245–334. Berlin: De Gruyter. Essay first published 1874 as in *Unzeitgemässe Betrachtungen* [*Untimely Meditations*] (Leipzig: Fritzsch, 1873–76).

———. (1878) 1980. *Menschliches, Allzumenschliches: Ein Buch für freie Geister* [*Human, All Too Human: A Book for Free Spirits*]. In *Kritische Studienausgabe, Bd. 2*, edited by Giorgio Colli and Mazzino Montinari, 9–363. Berlin: De Gruyter. First published 1878 (Chemnitz: Schmeitzner).

———. (1878–79) 1993. "Die griechischen Lyriker" ["The Greek Lyric Poets"]. In *Kritische Gesamtausgabe. II.2, Vorlesungsaufzeichnungen (SS 1869–WS 1869/70); Anhang: Nachschriften von Vorlesungen Nietzsches*, edited by Fritz Bornmann and Mario Carpitella, 107–182. Berlin: De Gruyter.

———. (1880) 1980. *Menschliches, Allzumenschliches II: Der Wanderer und sein Schatten* [*Human, All Too Human II: The Wanderer and His Shadow*]. In *Kritische Studienausgabe, Bd. 2*, edited by Giorgio Colli and Mazzino Montinari, 535–704. Berlin: De Gruyter. First published 1880 (Chemnitz: Schmeitzner).

———. (1882) 1980. *Die fröhliche Wissenschaft* [*The Gay Science*]. In *Kritische Studienausgabe, Bd. 3*, edited by Giorgio Colli and Mazzino Montinari, 343–651. Berlin: De Gruyter. First published 1882 (Chemnitz: Schmeitzner).

———. (1887) 1980. *Zur Genealogie der Moral* [*On the Genealogy of Morals*]. In *Kritische Studienausgabe, Bd. 5*, edited by Giorgio Colli and Mazzino Montinari, 245–412. Berlin: De Gruyter. First published 1887 (Leipzig: Naumann).

———. (1889) 1980a. *Der Fall Wagner: Ein Musikanten-Problem* [*The Case of Wagner: A Musician's Problem*]. In *Kritische Studienausgabe, Bd. 6*, edited by Giorgio Colli and Mazzino Montinari, 9–53. Berlin: De Gruyter. First published 1889 (Leipzig: Naumann).

———. (1889) 1980b. *Götzen-Dämmerung* [*Twilight of the Idols*]. In *Kritische Studienausgabe, Bd. 6*, edited by Giorgio Colli and Mazzino Montinari, 55–161. Berlin: De Gruyter. First published 1889 (Leipzig: Naumann).

———. (1920) 2016. "On the Theory of Quantitifying Rhythm." Translated by James W. Halporn. *New Nietzsche Studies* 10 (1/2): 69–78. First published 1920 in Friedrich Nietzsche, *Gesammelte Werke; Marionausgabe, Zweiter Band. Kleinere Schriften: 1869–1874*, edited by Richard Oehler and Friedrich Würzbach (Munchen: Musarion), 294–304.

Pater, Walter. (1893) 1998. *The Renaissance: Studies in Art and Poetry*. Edited by Adam Phillips. Oxford: Oxford University Press. Contains the text of the 4th ed. first published 1893 (London: Macmillan).

Poe, Edgar Allan. 1846. "The Philosophy of Composition." *Graham's Magazine* 28 (4) (April): 163–67.

Rabinow, Paul. 2011. *The Accompaniment: Assembling the Contemporary*. Chicago: University of Chicago Press.

Rampley, Matthew. 2000. *Nietzsche, Aesthetics and Modernity*. Cambridge: Cambridge University Press.

Richter, Simon. 1992. *Laocoon's Body and the Aesthetics of Pain: Winckelmann, Lessing, Herder, Moritz, Goethe*. Detroit, MI: Wayne State University Press.

Runtagh, Jordan. 2017. "John Cale on Transforming Leonard Cohen's

'Hallelujah' into a Modern Classic." *People*, 24 March. Accessed 17 January 2019. https://people.com/music/john-cale-leonard-cohen-hallelujah-arrangement-fragnments-of-a-rainy-season/.

Sassower, Raphael, and Louis Cicotello. 2000. *The Golden Avant-Garde: Idolatry, Commercialism, and Art*. Charlottesville: University of Richmond.

Schlegel, Friedrich. 1962. *Lucinde*. In *Kritische Friedrich-Schlegel-Ausgabe*, vol. 5, edited by Hans Eichner. Munich: Schöning. *Lucinde* first published 1799 (Berlin: Heinrich Frölich).

Shell, Marc. 1995. *Art and Money*. Chicago, IL: University of Chicago Press.

Smith, Terry. 2010. "The State of Art History: Contemporary Art." *Art Bulletin* 92 (4): 366–83.

Strong, Tracy Burr. 2017. "Authors and Authority: On Art, Objects, and Presence." Non-site.org., 1 November. Accessed 12 February 2019. https://nonsite.org/feature/authors-and-authority.

Taylor, Henry Osborn. 1911. *The Classical Heritage of the Middle Ages*. 3rd ed. New York: Macmillan.

Vasari, Giorgio. 2008. *The Lives of the Artists*. Oxford: Oxford University Press. Translated by Julia Conaway Bondanella and Peter Bondanella. First published 1550 as *Le Vite de' più eccellenti pittori, scultori, e architettori* (Florence: Lorenzo Torrentino).

Virilio, Paul. 2003. *Art and Fear*. Translated by Julie Rose. London: Continuum. First published 2000 as *La procédure silence* (Paris: Galilée).

Wagenführ, Horst. 1965. *Kunst als Kapitalanlage*. Stuttgart: Forkel.

Woodmansee, Martha. 1994. *The Author, Art, and the Market: Rereading the History of Aesthetics*. New York: Columbia University Press.

Part 2
Contemporary Practices

On Aesthetic Experience as Anachronic Experience

Heiner Goebbels
Composer and director

The concept of the *contemporary* matters to me as an artist as much as the question of what name I give the work I do. When I was invited to contribute to this publication, I admit I was a little uncomfortable with the discussion of the contemporary as a concept that "promotes or excludes things and practices according to their ability to diagnose previously unnoticed aspects of the present" (see the Introduction to this volume, 7). Rather than highlighting the present in the contemporary, one may actually need to counter the insistence on it in the performing arts (theatre, music theatre, time-based performance) that promotes the idea that the stage is a mirror of reality, which confirms and reinforces stereotypes, clichés, and existing gender roles. Venues are full of such performances. Due to the weight of their traditions, these art forms remain representative, not having developed away from their representational characters as they would have done in the visual arts. They are in constant danger of ambitiously diagnosing aspects of the present, which theatre directors proudly think they are the first to notice. Heiner Müller warned us not to reduce texts to making statements on reality—which would degrade them—but instead to consider texts as being realities of their own. We can generalise what we have just said about theatre to apply to any kind of performance: art forms should not be reduced to diagnosing the present (or the reality of the medium). Rather, a work of onstage art should be considered as a reality in itself; the richness of its artistic possibilities should be developed to raise questions and not to underestimate the audience—there should be a deep confidence that reality and the present are something spectators bring with them anyway. From an artistic perspective and from an artist's perspective, diagnosing the present is not our business. As artists, who do we think we are and what higher position do we think we have that allows us to look down on the so-called present?

Instead of answering such questions, I will try to explain my strategies to avoid and deal with the trap of the contemporary.

In the process of creating a radio composition, a piece of music, or a music theatre work my starting points come from a wide variety of rather remote inspirations: a picture (by Jacob van Ruisdael), a hundred-year-old documentary recording (by an ethnographer), or intriguing encounters with music (by Hanns Eisler), musicians (griots from Senegal), performers (such as André Wilms), spaces (such as the monuments of industrial culture at the Ruhrtriennale), or texts (by Adalbert Stifter, Søren Kierkegaard, Edgar Allan Poe, Gertrude Stein,

T. S. Eliot, Alain Robbe-Grillet, and Heiner Müller—I mention these names not "to only name a few" but because these are the main authors found in my works).

I admit that at first I often choose these sources unconsciously and instinctively. However, the topic of the present volume has made me think about this issue in more detail. The main sources of my work were always created in the past. I see myself more as reacting within a succession of traditions and I don't hide these sources. On the contrary, I insist on time being offset in this way, on having that distance. I try to resist the pretension of "actuality," except for the fact that it is present only as the actual time in which I try to reanimate those artefacts back into the light again.

I choose these artefacts initially to discover their potential for the stage. What I'm looking for are non-dramatic texts that have not been written for the theatre, texts that share questions with the reader/the audience rather than suggesting that they embody psychological confrontations. Maybe I choose them because I suspect they are capable of raising questions that can touch us from the past. Another motivation is to keep these sources from being forgotten, or at least from being underestimated in their potential for public interest. Nevertheless, this has consequences for the aesthetics of what goes on onstage. As Maurice Blanchot put it in *The Infinite Conversation* (1993, 342), "as soon as literature affirmed itself as a question, question of the world and question of itself, manifestly suspending any response, it had to break as well with all the habits of a rhetoric of development" (which neatly prepares us to speak of Gertrude Stein, but we'll return to her later . . .).

It wasn't intentional, but it turns out that I am attracted by previously ignored artefacts of the past and the possibility of discovering qualities that have been lost. I'll now turn to discussing some examples from my work.

Eraritjaritjaka, with texts by Elias Canetti, takes its title from a word I found in Canetti's anthropological studies (his book *Crowds and Power* [1962]).[1] The word was taken from the language of the Australian Aboriginal Arunta (Arrernte) tribe and means "desperately looking for something that has been lost." This is also true of the precious treasure to be found in Canetti's relatively unknown five or six notebooks.

The piece is actually not meant to be nostalgic at all—it includes many self-referential and political texts and various pieces for string quartet, which are all from the twentieth century, except for the piece with which the work ends, a contrapunctus from Bach's *Art of Fugue*, written for four voices but with a fifth voice added, that of the actor.

"Eraritjaritjaka" is a lost word. It became what it actually means: when we performed the work in Sydney we applied to the authority protecting the language of their ancestors for permission to use that word from the Arunta language; but the people we contacted in the community had difficulties because

---

1 https://www.heinergoebbels.com/en/archive/works/complete/view/11.

they could not reconstruct its meaning precisely. Is it an anachronism to bring this word back to where it came from?

In *Anachronic Renaissance*, two art historians, Alexander Nagel and Christopher S. Wood (2010), discuss a "plural temporality of the work of art" (chap. 1), which includes the potential of "artifacts" to "resist anchoring in time" (7), and works of art with the ability to bend time and "whose relation to time is plural. . . . backward to a remote ancestral origin . . . or to an origin outside of time. . . . [and also] forward to all its future recipients who will activate and reactivate it as a meaningful event" (9). This might be something I could claim for my work.

As Nagel and Wood (2010) suggest, *anachronism* is "a judgmental term that carries with it the historicist assumption that every event and every object has its proper location within objective and linear time" (13). "To describe a work of art as an 'anachronism' is to say that the work is best grasped not as art, but rather as witness to its times" (14). In contrast, "to describe the work of art as 'anachronic' . . . is to say what the artwork *does*, qua art" (14). As they conclude, "'Art' is the name of the possibility of a conversation across time, a conversation more meaningful than the present's merely forensic reconstruction of the past" (18).

But more interesting than simply showing that the sources that play key roles in my work are historical or mythological, or at any rate "outdated," is the fact that all of them carry obvious traces—or can be considered to be direct references—to even earlier periods of time. Let us take a tour through the "multiplicity of temporalities" that are evoked in my works, which might contribute to this conversation across time.

Edgar Allan Poe's parable "Shadow" is the dramaturgical spine in *Schwarz auf Weiss* (*Black on White*, 1996).[2] But Poe's writing strategy is to borrow the authority of the parable by pretending it is actually a document that was "graven with a stylus of iron" thousands of years ago by a Greek called Oinos after surviving a plague of pestilence in the ancient city of Ptolemais (Poe [1835] 2011).

Similarly, in 1990 Michael Simon and I were inspired by Heinrich Schliemann's diaries to create the theatre piece *Newton's Casino*.[3] Schliemann's diaries record the excavations he made attempting to find and reconstruct the long-submerged ruins of Troy, as passed on to us in Homer's *Iliad*. Nevertheless, two days before the premiere we erased all the texts completely; this liberated us from the intimidating heaviness of mythological rubble, turning the piece into an architectonic and performative construction through which sound and space could be discovered and the audience could have an aesthetic experience.

To untrained ears, the considerable influence of Hanns Eisler's music may be less obvious. Eisler reclaimed a strict distinction between "material" and a "method of working," and, although he was Arnold Schoenberg's student, he referred directly to Schubert (in his songs), Beethoven (in some compositional phrases), and Bach (in the architecture of his cantatas). His musical language makes frequent use of the tonal modes (the Gregorian modes: Aeolian, Dorian,

---

2   https://www.heinergoebbels.com/en/archive/works/complete/view/37. Recorded as Goebbels (1997).

3   https://www.heinergoebbels.com/en/archive/works/complete/view/254.

Lydian, etc.), which can be found in sacred music from the early Middle Ages up to the sixteenth century; and, for example, as detected by Jürgen Elsner, he used the cadences of the Phrygian mode in his *Solidarity Song*. I used an extract from this in instrumental form in *Eislermaterial* (1998),[4] a staged concert performed with Ensemble Modern where I tried to re-arrange my own experiences in the seventies with Eisler's music, which played a huge role in my life.

While I compiled and adapted Eisler's materials, I didn't actually compose much; instead, I reduced myself to a structural, choreographic role, turning the concert's programme into more of a *Lehrstück* (as Brecht would have put it) by installing several difficulties (improvisations, no fixed arrangements, no conductor, large distances between performers, an empty centre).

The responsibility and inner communication this work requires is an experience for the musicians as much as for the audience. It does not pretend to be a contemporary music concert, and does not try to identify the potential actuality of those texts and tunes that seem to be overcome; rather, it appears as an old, intriguing, and distant ritual, where the audience is not addressed visually and what is presented is purely acoustic. But the concert form in which the ritual appears is surprising. It is shy, cautious, reluctant—or as Hanns Eisler instructs us (but which is rarely respected), "with extreme discretion" (mit äußerster Diskretion) (Eisler 1976, 162).

Many texts by Heiner Müller are mythological adaptations, corrections, even rude deformations; they are exaggerated and polemical perspectives on history, and he insists "that theatre lives from anachronism" (Muller [1983] 2005, 259; Ich muß Dir nicht sagen, daß Theater vom Anachronismus lebt). I have realised nearly twenty projects with words by him, sometimes including his voice or inviting him personally as a reader onstage. One of the earliest was *Die Befreiung des Prometheus* (*The Liberation of Prometheus*, 1985).[5]

If we believe Müller, Prometheus was bound to the rock and nourished by the eagle for three thousand years; Heracles, repelled again and again by the horrible wall of stench of the eagle's and Prometheus' faeces, had to circle around that rock for another three thousand years. "At last, helped by a rain which lasted five hundred years, Herakles managed to approach within shooting range" (Müller 1994, [20]). It is highly visible how generously Müller creates unbelievable and fascinating dimensions of work and time, filth and stench, to push it as far away as possible, before he dared to finally turn this text into a political parable—in the GDR—which can then be discovered as the present.

Is that a conversation across time? Isn't it more a mask for a critical position from 1972 for the educated middle classes appearing as historicism?

Or we could consider another of Heracles's tasks, his second, fighting against the Hydra, which, in *Ou bien le débarquement désastreux* (*Or the Hapless Landing*, 1993),[6] Müller so brilliantly turned into a text-architecture that leaves behind

---

4 https://www.heinergoebbels.com/en/archive/works/complete/view/31. Recorded as Goebbels (2002).

5 A staged version was produced in 1993: https://www.heinergoebbels.com/en/archive/works/complete/view/51. Recorded as CD 1 of Goebbels (1994).

6 https://www.heinergoebbels.com/en/archive/works/complete/view/50. Recorded as Goebbels (1995).

not only Heracles—indistinguishable from his enemy in a bloody battle—but also the reader, struggling with the meaning of the text and lost in a forest of words, which sometimes are not even punctuated.

In this work I tried to translate this confrontation through a dialogue with Joseph Conrad's "Congo Diary" from 1890 (written ten years before *Heart of Darkness*) and in a musical counterpoint between three French musicians, who played my music, and two Senegalese griots, who sung and played musical material probably dating back to traditions from the thirteenth to the early seventeenth centuries, dealing with historical or mythological topics from the Mali empire.

As a reflection of a colonial encounter with the stranger/the unknown/the voice of the Other, this work is my attempt to translate these texts into a confrontation between all onstage elements (voices, instruments, bodies, sculpture, wind, hair, light) into a drama of the elements, a drama of perception—perhaps a drama of times—into an experience, for the performers as well as for the audience.

By invitation of the Hilliard Ensemble, a famous vocal quartet specialising in early a cappella music, I composed a music theatre piece with the title *I Went to the House but Did Not Enter*.[7] The work is a chain of failures: a failed story by Maurice Blanchot, the line "fail better" from *Worstward Ho*, one of Samuel Beckett's later texts, and a failed love song by T. S. Eliot. Of course, I did not go against the expertise of the members of the Hilliard Ensemble, who for many years have been dedicated to the music of Pérotin, Josquin des Prez, Guillaume Dufay, and Carlo Gesualdo—they've basically stood in churches for the last forty years (until the ensemble disbanded in 2014). But for the first time in their professional career, I put the members of the ensemble into the uneasy position of becoming performers in a music theatre piece with lots of texts. We heard the argument that the influence of the early music renaissance could be found even in Eisler's composition; it can also be heard in my work on Eliot's *The Love Song of J. Alfred Prufrock* at the culmination of the first act.

My point is that my work is not about continuing an existing tradition (e.g., directing an opera by Monteverdi) or reinterpreting it in a "new way" (e.g., Mozart with motorcycles); instead, free of the baggage of interpretations, I try on the basis of clear, transparent, independent sources to create a unique and peculiar "reality by itself" (sculpting time?). Or I try to compose combinations/confrontations of inconsistent, independent elements in a way that allows—through music and through art—a triangle of experiences to be offered in which spectators cannot necessarily identify or mirror themselves but find their own position. Such works build connections to these predecessors but in absolutely different and, though I say so myself, perhaps previously unnoticed ways.

Although seventeenth-century painter Nicolas Poussin's works are mostly based on mythological topics, the subject of his *Landscape with a Man Killed by a*

---

7 https://www.heinergoebbels.com/en/archive/works/complete/view/211.

Snake (1648) is not believed to have a literary source. I worked without a direct hint and was more interested in formal correspondences to his paintings and perspectives, but it inspired me to compose the opera *Landschaft mit entfernten Verwandten* (*Landscape with Distant Relatives*, 2002).[8] The project in fact was more concerned with my desire to compose an opera based first on a decentralised view.

In Poussin's painting there is an exceptional balance between horror and beauty. In my opera, the struggle for this balance provokes multiple perspectives, where the spectator is always invited or even forced to drift between left and right, foreground and background, between sound and words, between this scene and the next one, and so on. It tries to widen the spectator's view rather than narrow it. The opera consists of many uncommented upon, unmediated, and sudden clashes between rival images and sounds, cultures, religions, constellations, and times.

Ultimately, as Nagel and Wood (2010, 11) describe the anachronic character, the opera is a "chain of substitutions, one work standing in for the next, not as a historical reality but as a fiction that the artist and a viewing public create backward from present to past. The new work, the innovation, is legitimated by the chain of works leading back to an authoritative type. But the chain also needs the new work. It is the new work that selects the chain out of the debris of the past." Next to civilised criminals (or rude soldiers, etc.), we see saints or priests performing rituals, we see whirling dervishes, religious ceremonies, and so on. We are confronted with a re-enactment of Velázquez's *Las Meninas* at the end of the opera, and with T. S. Eliot's "Triumphal March," a poem on the Roman hero and general Coriolanus.

Counting the weapons during this parade wasn't meant to be a direct comment on UN weapons instructor Hans Blix who, two years after the opera premiered, gave the statement that "there were about 700 inspections, and in no case did we find weapons of mass destruction" (Powell 2004). My reasonable suspicion is that being political (or even being contemporary?) can only happen unintentionally and in the bodies and minds of spectators. Furthermore, the kneeling instrumentalists in white greatcoats turning sticks on the rims of temple bowls were not supposed to be a symbol for Guantanamo, nor for a laboratory for chemical weapons; they didn't even pretend to be real monks in a Japanese cloister, they were just kneeling instrumentalists in white greatcoats. There are no symbols.

In this work I tried also to translate Gertrude Stein's concept of landscape plays to the operatic stage. Operas belong to a genre, which traditionally is based on a linear narration, on protagonists in the centre and minor characters circling around them. In *Landschaft mit entfernten Verwandten* the stage is populated with groups—collectives, communities, and societies—in de-centralised images. As Gertrude Stein said—and now we touch more deeply on time relations in the perception of the performing arts—

---

8   https://www.heinergoebbels.com/en/archive/works/complete/view/3. Recorded as Goebbels (2007).

I felt that if a play was exactly like a landscape then there would be no difficulty about the emotion of the person looking on at the play being behind or ahead of the play because the landscape does not have to make acquaintance. You may have to make acquaintance with it, but it does not with you, it is there and so the play being written the relation between you at any time is so exactly that that it is of no importance unless you look at it. (Stein [1935] 1967, 75)

The landscape has its formation and as after all a play has to have formation and be in relation one thing to the other thing and as the story is not the thing as any one is always telling something then the landscape not moving but being always in relation, the trees to the hills the hills to the fields the trees to each other any piece of it to any sky and then any detail to any other detail, the story is only of importance if you like to tell or like to hear a story but the relation is there anyway. (Ibid., 77)

A landscape does not move nothing really moves in a landscape but things are there, and I put into the play the things that were there. (Ibid., 80)

We could also complete this idea of relations in a landscape, or in a landscape play, by adding the relation between this time and that time, the past and the present, or a more archaeological relation between the time of the performance, the time shown onstage, the time at the play's origin, the times when the play's sources were created, the times mentioned in the sources, the times the sources refer to, and so on. Each leaves its trace in the piece of art, which is a reality by itself. In turn, this directs our attention more and more from the artistic production towards perception, the aesthetic experience.

"Impact [*Wirkung*] awakens to a life of its own," says philosopher Bernhard Waldenfels (1999, 119), "if sight and speech and action"—and we can add hearing—"are no longer teleologically ordered towards a 'true whole thing' [*wahre Ganze*], when the things of the experience rival one another and want to dispute our view, which means when one way of seeing"—or hearing—"comes out on top of the other without the one being therefore more true than the other."[9] Or, in the words of Nagel and Wood (2010, 18), "The ability of the work of art to hold incompatible models in suspension without deciding is the key to art's anachronic quality, its ability really to 'fetch' a past, create a past, perhaps even fetch the future."

Finally, artists or directors who "decide" or (in Waldenfels's words) "show what is more true" assume the position of a hubris, and underestimate those who are to perceive, that is, the audience.

The danger and limitation of an aesthetic that aims for a representation of reality/the present is, as we said at the beginning, a reduction to falling back onto stereotypes, what we are used to seeing. But that's what theatre has been doing. Instead, theatre could be something utopic or traditional. In our "individual present," which has so many perspectives and "truths," the time gap between past and future is essential for us to make up our own minds.

---

9 "Wirkung erwacht ebenfalls zum Eigenleben, wenn Sehen, Reden und Tun nicht mehr teleologisch auf ein wahres Ganzes hingeordnet sind, wenn die Dinge der Erfahrung miteinander rivalisieren und einander unseren Blick streitig machen, . . . wenn also immer wieder eine Sehordnung und Sehweise sich gegen die andere durchsetzt ohne deshalb schlechthin wahrer zu sein als die andere."

Here is another of those "chains": In 1841 Kierkegaard travelled to Berlin. He then tried to repeat that trip two years later, which is reflected in his treatise *The Repetition*. This work (together with a song by Prince and dialogues from various novels by Alain Robbe-Grillet) inspired me in 1995 to create a music theatre play with the same title, *The Repetition*.[10] On the subject of chains of substitutions it is interesting to mention another piece of feedback: that Alain Robbe-Grillet, having not published a novel since 1981, finally in 2001 published a new book, titled *La Reprise*, which became a long overdue comeback for his career as one of the most influential French writers in the second half of the twentieth century—and he kindly mentioned that my production was one of the inspirations for him to do so.

Now we come to our final example, concerning my performative installation/music theatre work *Stifters Dinge* (*Stifter's Things*, 2007):[11] In 1841 Adalbert Stifter wrote his "Eisgeschichte" (Ice story), which the author included in *Die Mappe meines Urgroßvaters* (My great grandfather's folder), thus dating the setting of the story to easily another hundred years before. Distance—distance—distance. The beginning of Stifters's text, "I had never seen a thing like this before" (Goebbels 2012b, T5), is at the same time a definition of what an aesthetic experience is: an encounter with something we have no words for. Heidegger described it as follows:

> The story tells how the Doctor, driving with his servant on a winter's day to visit his sick patients, encounters an iced forest. Stifter calls the icing of the forest simply "the thing."
>
> Is what matters in the story based on the strangeness of the thing, which fascinates the reader? Or is the story's impact based on the art in which Stifter describes the thing, leaving the reader to be astonished? Or is the impact based on both: in the strangeness of the thing and in astonishment at what is presented? Or does the impact of the poetic word perhaps have something else in mind? (Heidegger [1964] 1983, 195, my translation)

The idea for this production was to create a work without human performers, and instead to enable the "things" or elements to become the main protagonists onstage: several pianos, light, sound, water, rain, fog, ice, metals, trees, and acousmatic voices. The working method was composing—and that too is not a new idea. In 1928, in his Breslau lecture on *Die glückliche Hand*, Arnold Schoenberg was already wishing he could "[make] music with the media of the stage":

> For a long time, a form had been in my mind which I believed to be the only one in which a musician might express himself in the theatre. I called it, in my own private expression: *making music with the media of the stage*. . . . In reality, tones, if viewed clearly and prosaically, are nothing else than a particular kind of vibrations of the air. As such they indeed make some sort of impression on the affected sense organ, the

---

ear. By being joined with each other in a special way, they bring about certain artistic, and, if one may say so, certain spiritual (emotional) impressions. Now since this capability is on no account present in the individual tone, it should also be possible, under certain conditions, to bring about such effects with other media; that is to say, if they were treated like *tones*. If, without denying their material meaning, but *independent* of this meaning, one understood how to combine them in forms and figures, after one had measured them, like tones, as to time, height, breadth, intensity, and many other dimensions. (As translated in Crawford 1974, 589–90)

According to the technical restrictions of his time, Arnold Schoenberg was not yet able to realise such a concept; but now, with the help of an interface—programmed in Max MSP by Hubert Machnik, a composer and friend—it was possible to create a MIDI keyboard, with which I could control all these elements: not only the pianos and all their stepper motors inside, but also the shutters of the lights, the movement of the stones, the rain, the fog, and so on.

One sound source in *Stifters Dinge* is the "traditional Greek song Kalimérisma—sung by Ekateríni Mangoúlia, recorded in 1930 by Samuel Baud-Bovy (1906–86), pioneer of musicology. The song belongs to the repertoire of the women from the island of Kalymnos; they sing this melody, reminiscent of a lament, while they work their hand mills. Instead of mourning laments they welcome the immigrants and offer good luck to the fishermen arriving from the Barbarian Coast (Maghreb)" (Goebbels 2012a, 12).

We could discuss standing still in time, to give a definition of *anachronic*. Really, our topic here is being out of date as a condition of aesthetic experience. One could speak about *deceleration*, a decelerated perception, since self-dependent autonomous discovery takes more time than a purely consuming perception. But suddenly even this slowness is no longer a problem, at least not of the kind that Gertrude Stein described as unease between one's own sense of time and the narrated time of the stage performance:

> Your sensation as one in the audience in relation to the play played before you your sensation I say your emotion concerning that play is always either behind or ahead of the play at which you are looking and to which you are listening. So your emotion as a member of the audience is never going on at the same time as the action of the play. This thing the fact that your emotional time as an audience is not the same as the emotional time of the play is what makes one endlessly troubled about a play. (Stein [1935] 1967, 58)

Just as in "excitement in real life" (ibid., 61) or "something really happening" (ibid., 63), which Stein contrasts with a theatrical scene in the theatre, in *Stifters Dinge* the idea of "trouble" is suddenly suspended as one watches shadows cast by rising and falling curtains, for instance, or reflections on the surface of an expanse of water, or a cloud of fog rising above several pianos, or rain disturbing the water's surface. Is that real time in theatre? "The work of art 'anachronizes.' . . . To anachronize is to be belated again, to linger. The work is late, first because it succeeds some reality that it re-presents, and then late again when that re-presentation is repeated for successive recipients. . . . [A] double postponement" (Nagel and Wood 2010, 13). Regarding the examples discussed here, we could easily discuss triple or multiple postponements.

Let's celebrate the "plural temporality of the work of art" (ibid., chap. 1) as an important space and source for the imagination of those who perceive it. After performances of *Stifters Dinge* I often hear people say with a certain relief, "Finally nobody onstage to tell me what to think." Maybe we can add, "Nobody onstage to tell me what time it is."

REFERENCES

Blanchot, Maurice. 1993. *The Infinite Conversation*. Translated by Susan Hanson. Minneapolis: University of Minnesota Press. First published 1969 as *L'entretien infini* (Paris: Gallimard).

Canetti, Elias. 1962. *Crowds and Power*. Translated by Carol Stewart. London: Victor Gollancz. First published 1960 as *Masse und Macht* (Hamburg: Claassen).

Crawford, John C. 1974. "*Die glückliche Hand*: Schoenberg's *Gesamtkunstwek*." *Musical Quarterly* 60 (4): 583–601.

Eisler, Hanns. 1976. *Gesammelte Werke, Serie I, Bd. 16: Lieder für eine Stingstimme und Klavier*. Edited by Stephanie Eisler and Manfred Grabs. Leipzig: Deutscher Verlag für Musik.

Goebbels, Heiner. 1994. *Hörstücke nach Texten von Heiner Müller*. Performed by David Bennent, Peter Brötzmann, Peter Hollinger, dem Kammerchor Horbach, Alexander Kluge, René Lussier, Megalomaniax, et al. ECM New Series, ECM 1452–54, 3 compact discs.

———. 1995. *Ou bien le débarquement désastreux*. Performed by André Wilms, Sira Djebate, Boubakar Djebate, Yves Robert, Alexandre Meyer, Xavier Garcia, Heiner Goebbels, and Moussa Sissoko. ECM New Series, ECM 1552, compact disc.

———. 1997. *Black on White*. Performed by Ensemble Modern. BMG Classics, 09026 68870 2, compact disc.

———. 2002. *Eislermaterial*. Performed by Ensemble Modern and Josef Bierbichler. ECM New Series, ECM 1779, compact disc.

———. 2007. *Landschaft mit entfernten Verwandten*. Performed by David Bennent, Georg Nigl, Ensemble Modern, Deutsche Kammerchor, and Frank Ollu. ECM New Series, ECM 1811, compact disc.

———. 2012a. Untitled liner note for Goebbels 2012b, 12.

———. 2012b. *Stifters Dinge*. ECM New Series, ECM 2216, compact disc.

Heidegger, Martin. (1964) 1983. "Adalbert Stifter's 'Eisgeschichte.'" In *Gesamtausgabe I. Abteilung: Veröffentlichte Schriften 1910–1976; Bd. 13: Aus der Erfahrung des Denkens*, 185–98. Frankfurt am Main: Klostermann. First delivered 26 January 1964 as a radio broadcast as part of the Radio Zürich series *Wirkendes Wort*.

Müller, Heiner. (1983) 2005. "Brief an den Regisseur der bulgarischen Erstaufführung von *Philoket* am Dramatischen Theater Sofia." In *Heiner Müller: Werke, Bd. 8*, edited by Frank Hörnigk, 259–69. First published 1983 in *Herzstück* (Berlin: Rotbuch), 102–10.

———. 1994. "The Liberation of Prometheus." Translated by Alan Miles. Libretto for *Die Befreiung des Prometheus* (1985) by Heiner Goebbels, in liner notes for Goebbels 1994, [20]. Müller's text first published 1974 as "Befreiung des Prometheus" in *Zement (nach Gladkow)* (Berlin: Henschel).

Nagel, Alexander, and Christopher S. Wood. 2010. *Anachronic Renaissance*. New York: Zone Books.

Poe, Edgar Allan. (1835) 2011. "Shadow." Edgar Allan Poe Society of Baltimore. Accessed 11 February 2019. https://www.eapoe.org/works/tales/shdwa.htm. First published 1835 (*Southern Literary Messenger* 1 [13]: 762–63).

Powell, Bonnie Azab. 2004. "U.N. Weapons Inspector Hans Blix Faults Bush Administration for Lack of 'Critical Thinking' in Iraq." UC Berkeley News. Accessed 14 February 2019. https://www.berkeley.edu/news/media/releases/2004/03/18_blix.shtml.

Stein, Gertrude. (1935) 1967. "Plays." In *Look at Me Now and Here I Am: Selected Works, 1911–1945* edited by Patricia Meyerowitz, 58–81. London: Peter Owen. Essay first published 1935 in *Lectures in America* (New York: Random House).

Waldenfels, Bernhard. 1999. *Sinnesschwellen: Studien zur Phänomenologie des Fremden 3.* Frankfurt am Main: Suhrkamp.

The Crackle of Contemporaneity

Geoff Cox, Andrew Prior, and Ryan Nolan
University of Plymouth

There comes a time to move beyond asking the broad question "What is contemporaneity?" to consider more acute ways in which this question can be traced and signalled. We consider the notion of *signal* to be particularly appropriate in the consideration of contemporaneity, since signals are a constitutive element of contemporary infrastructures and our experience of time even if they are relatively undetectable. They operate underneath human perceptual thresholds as carriers, controllers, and codes, while also surfacing into perceptual and semiotic registers, as signs across various media—textual, visual, and, of course, sonic—all the while accessible as traces. Perhaps in this way it is possible to experience contemporaneity at a range of different scales—from the microtemporal to the planetary—to register both our closeness and distance from it (Agamben 2009), and to exemplify how times come together disjunctively in the present.

Moreover, although contemporaneity has been widely theorised around visual culture and post-conceptual art, the role of sound within this discourse is almost entirely missing.[1] This is strange not only because, as Jacques Attali (1985) argued, changes in sound and music often pre-empt changes within visual, and indeed, political culture, but because sound and music are inherently temporal in character: made up of acoustic vibrations (and often electronic signals) that unfold dynamically, constructing and constituting important aspects of presence, while reflecting temporality in their material character. As such, sound perhaps offers a unique opportunity to understand the topologies and currents of contemporaneity. But attention to these material characteristics significantly alters Attali's idea of sound as an indicator of change, since for him it indicated change at a semiotic level that required a hermeneutic approach in its analysis. We argue that signals not only *represent* but *enact* control structures and temporal complexity, prompting a more materialist or archaeological analysis in order to be able to hear some of the nuances of temporal complexity.

Put simply, this chapter explores the idea of listening to contemporaneity, through an engagement with signals that operate both above and below the threshold of human perception. In particular, we explore *Detektors* (2010–12),

---

1 One notable exception to this is Peter Osborne's discussion of new music in *The Postconceptual Condition: Critical Essays* (2018). This is also the hypothesis for Ryan Nolan's PhD research, "What Does 'Contemporary Music' Mean Now?" (University of Plymouth), which we take as a point of departure for this essay.

an artistic research project by Martin Howse and Shintaro Miyazaki, in which workshop participants used bespoke circuits to demodulate and listen to the crackle of signal traffic within the electromagnetic spectrum. What is exposed is the materiality of signal traffic as well as the technical apparatus through which it is made perceivable. Our proposition is that this spectral realm of signals allows us to understand contemporaneity as a temporal complexity that operates between surface and depth, and through this we can begin to hear that "time is out of joint" (*Hamlet* 1.5, Shakespeare [1623] 2005, 691). Aside from Hamlet's response to the world, we make explicit reference here to Mark Fisher's essay "The Metaphysics of Crackle" (2013) to point to some of the material conditions for this temporal complexity, not least in registering the crackle of technology through which this particular experience of time is made possible at all: and through which we might experience the crackle of contemporaneity.

LISTENING TO CRACKLE

The chapter foregrounds the embedded research methods of *Detektors* to engage with the "techno-temporal" infrastructures and topologies of the contemporary infosphere. The project is understood as one contribution to, and indicative of, a wider set of critical and aesthetic practices that interrogate the underlying material and processual structures of contemporaneity. Engaging with *Detektors* allows us to try to draw together materialist analyses of sound with the discourse of contemporaneity. Additionally we discuss archaeological methods and then the concept of hauntology, along with Fisher, as a way to witness the forensic materiality (or what we here call crackle[2]) of the signals themselves.[3] Fisher discussed the crackle of vinyl records, explored as a reminder (or remainder) of the presence of the recording and production apparatus. He argued against the symptomatic privileging of live performance and its claim for authenticity over recorded and sampled forms (such as in the case of dub or hip hop)—which fail to account for texturality, mediation, or sound production and in doing so, miss what might be described as a *metaphysics of absence*. Similar to Fisher's exploration of *recorded* media and their associated artefacts, *Detektors* explores the forensic materiality of *live* electromagnetic emissions. In this case, the metaphysics of absence comes in the otherwise imperceptible materiality of such technological signals.

---

2 We refer to this as *crackle*, following Fisher's use of the term, but this is not the most prominent feature of these signals: they also squeal, chirp, fizz, and pulse.

3 "Forensic materiality" is a phrase taken from Matthew Kirschenbaum's *Mechanisms: New Media and the Forensic Imagination* (2007), in which he draws a distinction between "forensic materiality" and "formal materiality." Forensic materiality is based on what he calls "the principle of individualization" in which no two things can be said to be exactly alike and is thus the foundation of discriminatory investigation of traces, remains, debris, and any and all other material evidence in forensics (Kirschenbaum 2007, 10).

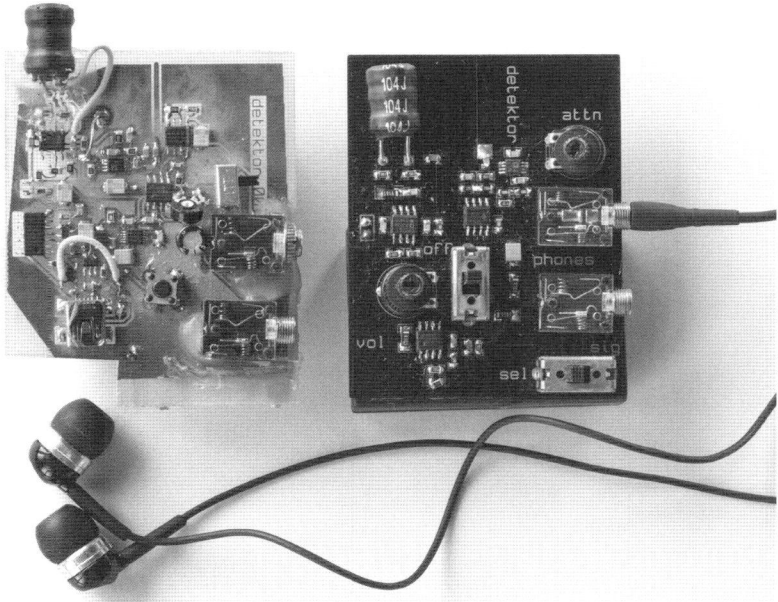

Figure 5.1.

All electronic technologies—from the transmissions of Wi-Fi and GSM tele-communications, to lighting, automatic teller machines (ATM), and security cameras—produce such emissions. Telecommunications even harness them: signals are mixed (modulated) with a carrier signal before they are transmitted, in order to make them suitable for transmission. Modulation allows transmissions to occupy particular areas of the electromagnetic frequency spectrum that are usable, and, by using carrier signals of different frequencies, it allows multiple channels of signal traffic to sit, side by side, within the frequency spectrum. *Detektors* centred on the use of circuits (see figure 5.1), designed by Howse and Miyazaki to demodulate electromagnetic signals between 100 megahertz and 3 gigahertz, and sonify these into an audible range of 20–20,000 hertz.[4] Using these devices, the project sought to develop a cartography of electromagnetic emissions: "conceived as a website (now offline) with a cartography of user-generated geolocational sound recordings, logs and walks, which reveal [the] hidden electromagnetic geographies, spaces and topologies of our urban areas; and a database and catalog of sonic studies of electromagnetic emissions produced by our everyday electronic devices" (Miyazaki 2018).

---

4   Television and radio occupy the megahertz region. Wi-Fi refers to the 2.4 gigahertz (ultra high frequency) and 5.8 gigahertz (super high frequency) region of the electromagnetic spectrum.

Figure 5.1. *Detektors* (2010–12), circuits built by Howse and Miyazaki. Image cour-   tesy of the artists.

In addition to its aesthetic and metaphysical aspects, *Detektors* also operates as a (geo)political project. Howse and Miyazaki's efforts to create a cartography of user-generated sound recordings, sonically mapping the geolocational "ghostly double" of towns and cities (Howse, 2018), had the potential to reveal differences in the materiality of electromagnetic activity on a planetary scale. Such a cartography would no doubt begin to reveal aspects of what the Marxist geographer David Harvey has called spaces of "uneven geographical development" (2006). In the case of *Detektors*, what would be revealed sonically is the uneven development of networked infrastructures that were partially visualised in 2012 by Carna, a botnet that collected and mapped the location of every IPv4 address on the internet network.[5] This mapping is directly related to the subjective experience of the historical present, which in Peter Osborne's terms is a geopolitical fiction. In *Anywhere or Not at All*, Osborne (2013, 25) argues that the contemporary cannot be perceived as a whole and differs to a remarkable degree depending on one's global location. Global network maps provided by internet service providers illustrate one way in which otherwise disjunctive localities are becoming interconnected in time, but they also evidence huge inequality in terms of the material reality of digital infrastructure.

In addition to geopolitics, we might read *Detektors* in line with an aesthetic tradition of sonifying the hidden electromagnetic realm: *Drive-in Music* (1967) by Max Neuhaus, Joyce Hinterding's *Aeriology* (1995), Alan Lamb's *Primal Image* (1995), and Christina Kubisch's *Electrical Walks* (2004–present), among others, or various "signal-sniffing" compositions such as Nicolas Collins's *El Loop* (2002), David First's *Tell Tale 2.1* (2004), and Andy Keep's *My Laptop Colony* (2009). In these projects, the drones, squeaks, and crackles of electromagnetic phenomena emerge from a variety of different contexts, from the cosmic microwave background and other sources of background radiation (such as rocks, soil, and plants), to signals produced by electronic devices. In most projects though, the sounds are a kind of waste (although less so with Neuhaus): the inadvertent by-product or excess of other processes, whether natural or technological. While *Detektors* shares some of the aesthetic characteristics of these works, and some of the motivations to sonify electromagnetic signals, Howse and Miyazaki shift their focus away from the electromagnetic character of the natural world, or by-products of technology, to the sonification of digital traffic that courses through contemporary informational infrastructures. Detecting and demodulating signals into a frequency range and acoustic form audible to humans highlights a tension at the heart of their project. As in the work of Kubisch, human participants walking and listening become an affective means to understand the hidden realm of microwave activity.

---

5 Similar to the intentions of Howse and Miyazaki, the creator(s) of the Carna botnet used the Nmap Scripting Engine (NSE) to gather geolocational information on all IP addresses that responded to an ICMP message (Carna botnet 2018).

The methodological approach of *Detektors* is also broadly in line with "media archaeology" as a way of practising media criticism from a *nonhuman* perspective—"epistemological reverse engineering" as Wolfgang Ernst (2011, 239) puts it—revealing how media (and not just humans) become active archaeologists of knowledge (Miyazaki 2013b, 514). Ernst's example of this is Fourier analysis, in which the technical device demonstrates its analytical precision over the human sensory apparatus in its analysis of complex soundwaves. As such, "Only by the application of such medial-technological tools can we explain the microtemporal level of such events," as Ernst puts it (2011, 245). Unlike in sonic *arts* approaches, in which such signals become expressive or somewhat compositional, Howse and Miyazaki instead investigate the sonic *aesthetics* (whether directly perceivable or not) of contemporary urban infrastructures, using the capture and documentation of signals as an archaeological research method to "make audible the hidden infoscapes of *our time*" (Miyazaki 2018, our emphasis).

Central to this approach is the idea of listening as an embodied research tool, and sound as a form of knowledge that is particularly appropriate to understanding the intangibility and temporality of network infrastructures. As Jonathan Sterne and others make clear, forms of auditory knowledge have a long history, from "mediate auscultation" (Sterne 2003, 99–136)—that is, the practice of listening to the body (in particular by use of a stethoscope to diagnose illness) and deep listening of sonar operators—to car repair (the purr, wheeze, or rattle of specific engine parts are often the quickest way to diagnose an issue). Unlike the "cool gaze" of visual research or the incorporeal quality of argumentation, such approaches foreground embodiment (beyond visuality), pattern recognition, and other affective encounters.

In sonifying electromagnetic signals, and placing emphasis on humans listening to and negotiating signaletic spaces, *Detektors* challenges the implied objectivity of media archaeology and additionally foregrounds aesthetic practice and subjective experience. But then again—and setting aside Ernst's potential over-emphasis of signals over semantics—perhaps all archaeology does just this whether overtly or not, as it oscillates between the presence and absence of humans in order to assemble previously hidden phenomena to grant access to the present. Suffice to say that it is through the bringing together of a materialist, archaeological approach and the discourse on contemporaneity (Ebeling 2017)[6] that human and machine witnesses—or "detectors"—begin to uncover some of the conditions of contemporaneity that otherwise remain inaccessible (see figure 5.2).

6　This "archaeology of contemporaneity" is explored in depth by Ebeling (2017).

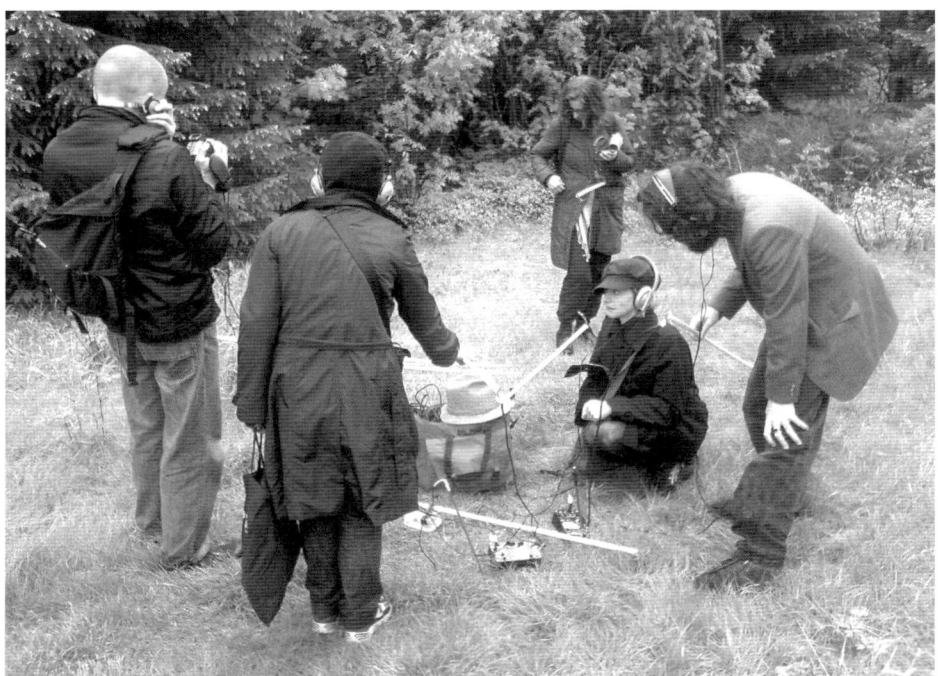

Figure 5.2.

Detektors makes a good analytical object in this way because we want to high-light the importance of signals and microtemporality, and their deep involve-ment in wider planetary-scale assemblages on the one hand—what Benjamin Bratton refers to as "the stack"[7]—and more localised affective experience on the other, embodied in the user of the technical device not least. We argue that this layering of scales and interconnection of technological and social enti-ties can be seen as a key feature of the contemporary—evoking Boris Groys's "Comrades of Time" (2009), in which he explains how we collaborate with time and demonstrate solidarity with it. Once entangled in planetary-scale technical infrastructures, time can be seen to be nonlinear and multidimensional, layered and relational, thus bringing together not only people from past and future times into the present but also technology that contributes to our collective experience of it. To emphasise this point, Groys invokes Jacques Derrida, who, in his critique of what he calls the "metaphysics of presence," has demonstrated "that the present is originally corrupted by past and future, that there is always absence at the heart of presence" (Groys 2009, 1).

---

7   We take this term from Benjamin Bratton (2016). "The Stack" is a layered technical mega-structure that operates on a planetary scale, comprising "Earth, Cloud, City, Address, Interface, User."

102

Figure 5.2. In 2008, Howse tested early ver-sions of the Detektor hardware in his Maxwell City Workshop, Oslo, in conjunction with Erich Berger.

The importance of an archaeological approach in tracing and signalling contemporaneity, alongside the affective and embodied subjectivity of aesthetic encounters involved in *Detektors*, helps offset the reductive pragmatism of the data produced through such means. To stress the point once more, we therefore argue that Howse and Miyazaki's project—and the exigencies of understanding contemporaneity from a material and techno-temporal point of view—are as much about the human experience of signal-traffic, as they are about microtemporality and archaeological data-mining.

This is very different to other approaches to understanding contemporaneity rooted in a humanist tradition such as, to name one key example, Peter Osborne's conception of the contemporary as the defining historical temporality of the present, which is firmly situated in the times of human lives, demonstrated by his assertion that there exists no *socially shared subject position* from which the totality of the present can be perceived (Osborne 2013, 23). Our intention is to nuance these ideas with the profusion of machinic and techno-temporalities in the constitution of contemporaneity, while, at the same time, maintaining the importance and sensibility of the social realm. As such, *Detektors* allows us to narrow our analysis to signals, *and* allows us to trace fragments of the contemporary through the spectral materiality of electromagnetism and the transmission of coded messages to human sensory perception through the affective act of listening to demodulated signals. Here we are highlighting the interconnections of objective and subjective registers of the contemporary (Cox and Lund 2016), as both a mode of being in time, a particular relationship to the historical present, and as a sort of shared historical periodisation, as in "our" contemporaneity. Moreover if we can speak of "our" contemporaneity in a collective sense, it is because ours is markedly different than other "present times" throughout history—owing largely not only the proliferation of digital network ecologies and planetary computation, but also the emergent politics that arise when these networks interface with human worlds and nonhuman ecologies.

SIGNAL HAUNTOLOGY

A spectre is haunting the spectrum: the spectre of contemporaneity.[8] Parody aside, the spectral quality arises because signals occupy parts of the electromagnetic spectrum outside human perception, and because they are temporal—capable of decay, and surges, spikes, and troughs. Signals express a material-temporal ambiguity for humans as they are imperceptible to our sensory apparatus but ever present. These comments derive from what Derrida has called *hauntology*, a term from *Specters of Marx* (1994), further developed in the context of sound by Fisher (2012, 2013, 2014) and Simon Reynolds (2010), among others. Indicated not least by his essay title "The Metaphysics of Crackle," Fisher is referring not only to Derrida's concept of hauntology but

---

8   Making reference, like Derrida, to the infamous opening lines of *The Communist Manifesto*, "A spectre is haunting Europe. . . ." (Marx and Engels [1888] 1985, 78).

also to his *metaphysics of presence* to examine the tension between the "authentic" live voice and its recording (Fisher 2013, 44). By drawing a neat parallel to voice and writing in Derrida, it can be seen that when it comes to music, there has been a symptomatic privileging of live performance over recorded forms as if they were somehow less authentic or significant. Presence is revealed to be an illusion maybe, but our interest is less metaphysical and more rooted in the lack of recognition of the material pre-conditions of the sounds.

Indeed hauntology is a concept that has repeatedly emphasised that presence can only ever be perceived in fragmentary form. *Fragmentary* is here understood in two ways: both as incomplete or partial, and as broken or out of joint. Addressing these different understandings of fragmentation in order, first, the sounds and signals encountered in *Detektors*—or indeed, in any strategy for engaging with contemporaneity—will always be incomplete, pointing to the wider conditions of its production, without ever fully capturing it. As such, *Detektors* is perhaps less an attempt at the exhaustive and empirical logging of data, than an example of praxis geared to the adjustment of one's *habitus*—Pierre Bourdieu's notion of the ways in which one understands the world and reacts to it (1990, 52)—through affectively confronting a spectral world of electromagnetic emissions. The second understanding of fragmentation found in contemporaneity, and expressed hauntologically, refers to the notion that the complexity and multiplicity of the present must necessarily be experienced as loss, or absence. It remains broken because it is bewildering and excluding, in the sense that so much of contemporary experience is not for us—as individuals, groups, societies, even as humans so it would appear. Mediation plays a part here too, since, "the broken-time proper to hauntology" (Fisher 2013, 47) diverts the presence of a present moment via a re-presentation or re-enactment of that which is absent, a return of the past (or commingling of different locations, different presents) and subsequent lost futures. This re-mediation is important because "when the present has given up on the future, we must listen for the relics of the future in the unactivated potential of the past" (ibid., 53). Here, not least, the spectre of historical (or dialectical) materialism can be detected.[9]

Written soon after the dissolution of the communist bloc in 1989, Derrida's *Specters of Marx* developed a set of ideas around spirit or spectre, and the hauntological, in order to counter claims of the "end of history" (Fukuyama 1992), and to consider the continued legacy of Marxism: reawakening the so-called "spirit of Marx" (Derrida 1994, 2). Indeed, Derrida used the uncanniness and untimeliness of the spectre to articulate this critique—ghosts, after all, don't belong to a particular time or place; they are present but not quite—since it allowed him to critique homogeneous and teleological conceptions of time that underpin the end of history and the perceived impasse of Marxism set against a triumphant capitalism, as if there was no alternative future imaginable. His thinking on temporality has since been revisited for its ability to shed

9 As in the media archaeology of Walter Benjamin, for example "On the Concept of History" (2003), in which the past enters into a constellation with the present, interrupting the mechanical temporal process of historicism.

light on heterogeneous understandings of time; it is interesting too since the rhetorical trope of the spectre introduces a subjective and speculative register, yet one offset by the dislocated, asynchronous, and often intangible presences of informational capitalism and the gross inequalities that it perpetuates.[10] In Marx's alleged favourite Shakespeare play, *Timon of Athens*, the question arises, "How goes the world?—It wears, sir, as it grows" (as quoted in Derrida 1994, 77). Derrida takes this as the nature of growth in the context of global expansion, and we might add how time expands in the present and in turn "is out of joint," under capitalist conditions (ibid.). For, "As that which is and is not, the specter represents temporalities that cannot be grasped adequately in terms of present time" (Postone 1998, 371). The logic of past times haunts the present and renders it spectral and uncertain.[11]

It should be stressed at this point that although we discuss hauntology in relation to sound, our use of the term is not specifically intended to invoke what has become known as the musical genre of sonic hauntology (Born, Fisher, Reynolds et al.[12]), which was characterised by nostalgia, appropriating and mixing past cultural artefacts—such as sampling vinyl recordings—as an exercise in "transtemporal invention" (Born 2015, 379). Reynolds (2012, 328) describes the sensibility of sonic hauntological practices clearly when he writes that they "captur[e] the sense of a collective unconscious, the ghosts of our life coming back to haunt us." Fisher's use of the term applies to recorded music and how what is past appears in the present like a spectre of the material mode of production, for instance; it also applies to unacknowledged past influences (such as the way in which white culture is unable to escape the influence of black music[13]). In the spirit of Afrofuturism, he explains: "It is, in other words, a *technologised* time, in which past and future are subject to ceaseless de- and re-composition" (Fisher 2013, 47). Thus temporal complexity and its inherent disjunctions can be clearly heard in the ways that sounds are recomposed in the present through sampling or decolonisation (Mbembe 2001), and the like. Everything appears to be here and now,[14] or as part of a cyberpunk imaginary. We can also detect this disjunctive tendency in Howse's other projects, which operate in the tradition of what he calls "psychogeophysics," observing other realities such as the earth's physical properties and its interaction with local

---

10 The notion of *spectre* might also be argued to counter platitudes of impersonal capital, and of disinterested neo-conservative power. "Moreover, the current world situation is characterised by an enormous inequality of techno-scientific, military, and economic development, with the result that 'never have violence, inequality, exclusion, famine, and . . . economic oppression affected as many human beings' (85). This situation undermines any teleological understanding of history (53–54, 63–64, 78)" (Postone 1998, 373, citing Derrida 1994).

11 And being; as Hamlet famously describes: "'to be or not to be,' but nothing is less certain" (Derrida 1994, 10).

12 We also refer here to artists such as Burial, The Caretaker, and Belbury Poly, and the record label Ghost Box. These examples each foreground the sounds of surface crackle, some emphasising retro-aesthetics of a lost future.

13 To Fisher, black experience has always been out of joint with any universal notion of the contemporary and in this respect, and as an aside, he points to Afrofuturism, as a way to understand this condition of the contemporary and its disjunctions.

14 As well as "anywhere, or not all" (Osborne 2013). Decolonialised time is clearly an important intervention here, such as in the work of Achille Mbembe (2001).

signal ecologies[15]—engaged as much with pataphysics as metaphysics (see, for example, Howse's essay "The Aether and Its Double" [2008], which combines models of theoretical physics with the literary writings of Lewis Carroll).

Despite allusions to science fiction, *Detektors* was not a decolonial or compositional project, and has little to do with aesthetic and semiotic motifs of this or that musical genre, or arguably their stated concerns. Yet, there are clear connections to the project under discussion: music of sonic hauntology, and the writings that discuss it, emphasise a sense of fragmentation, the "technical uncanny" and atemporality—the experience of time out of joint. Nevertheless it should be emphasised here that Fisher's writing on the subject goes much further than a straightforward analysis of sonic hauntology as a musical genre, and already encapsulates such temporal complexity. To Fisher, sonic hauntology "blurs contemporaneity' with elements from the past" (2013, 46).

The concept of the spectre suggests a virtual, insubstantial state of being, a simulacrum, a ghostly presence that signifies absence. As we have already stated, Derrida utilises this "non-identical, non-presentist temporality of spectrality" (Postone 1998, 371) to markedly extend his critique of "presence" as the most authentic state of being, which was important to the broader project of deconstruction and was framed most famously by the opposition between the embodied voice and textual writing (see Derrida 1997). The implications of Derrida's critique of the metaphysics of presence necessarily problematises the concept of linear history—and deeper structures of historical time—by foregrounding the heterogeneity of time's multiplicity inherent in the temporal logic of "haunting": "Haunting is historical, to be sure, but it is not *dated*, it is never docilely given a date in the chain of presents, day after day, according to the instituted order of a calendar" (Derrida 1994, 3).

Fisher takes this haunting as symptomatic of what he referred to as a paradoxical shift in historical temporality, which occurred with the passing of modernity to the pastiche time of postmodernity (and we might add the contemporary as a further periodisation if we accept this logic). The paradox that Fisher is pointing to is that artworks created by those working under the rubric of sonic hauntology were not only haunted by ghostly relics of the past, but were also mourning the loss of once conceivable futures that will no longer be realised. The distinction here is important, Fisher (2012, 16) notes, explaining that the hauntological emphasis on lost futures isn't so much about the future as historical actuality as it is the loss of a social imaginary capable of conceiving an alternative future to contemporary capitalism.

Referring to Fredric Jameson's discussion of Lawrence Kasdan's 1981 film *Body Heat*, Fisher (2013, 45–46) highlights a key difference between the artworks to which he simply refers as "*postmodernism*" and the work produced by hauntological artists. In his analysis, Jameson (1991, 20) explains how Kasdan actively sought to engage the viewer in a "'nostalgia' mode of reception," enacting a number of directorial and cinematographic decisions which ultimately "dis-

---

15   See Howse's website http://www.1010.co.uk/org/. For more on psychogeophysics, see http://www.psychogeophysics.org/wiki/doku.php.

tance the officially contemporary image from us in time."[16] To Fisher (2013, 46), this describes the distancing of the contemporary image as an act of "*gloss*[ing] *over* the temporal disjunctures," while pointing out the material difference of the "hauntological artists [who] foreground them." The disjunctive aspect is crucially important as it highlights a key similarity between the internal structural logic of hauntology and the concept of the contemporary, in both its art-critical and philosophical-historical sense. That is, albeit differently, both hauntology and the contemporary register the existence, or "coming together" to use Osborne's phrase (2013, 17), of multiple temporalities and different types of time in the historical present.

In one of his earlier blogs on the concept, Fisher (2006) introduces the phrase "technological uncanny" to encompass a number of tenets of sonic hauntology. Most prominently, and as we have discussed throughout this chapter at length, it foregrounds the "noise" produced by the technological apparatus itself—what Fisher refers to as crackle: the effect of which unsettles the distinction between surface and depth, and through which we begin to hear that time is out of joint. Thus the illusion of presence is unsettled in two ways, according to Fisher: temporally, as we realise we are listening to a "phonographic revenant"; and ontologically, by "introducing the technical frame, the material pre-condition of the recording, on the level of the content" (Fisher 2013, 48–49). This is part of his response to the problem of postmodernism's terminal temporality (its endgame). Here again he is drawing upon Jameson's nostalgia mode, which isn't necessarily a state of wistful affection for the past or of a specific historical moment, but what Jameson (1991, xvii) describes as "a depersonalised visual [and we would add, sonic] curiosity and a 'return of the repressed'" separate from particularly personal or affective qualities. The difference with *contemporary* art is that it is concerned less with reclaiming lost histories or unimaginable futures, and more with deeply examining the temporal complexity that follows from bringing together different times in the same historical present. It follows that *Detektors* can be said to be contemporary—even an example of contemporary art although perhaps not intended to be—in this sense as it permits an examination of the multiplicity of different times, human and nonhuman, coming together in the same present.

Temporalities of crackle

"The crackle . . . reminds us of the technological means by which this capturing of time was made possible" (Fisher 2013, 49) and seems to offer a critique of an inert presentism. Just as the surface crackle and acoustic depth of recorded media indicate a temporal palimpsest—problematising totalising understandings of time—the spectral quality of live electromagnetic emissions similarly

---

16 The historical present has been colonised by "pastness" displacing "real" history in Jameson's critique of postmodernism, and thereby displacing politics (1991, 20). This is why Jameson prefers the phrase "late-capitalism" to "postmodernism" in order to reject the view that new social formations no longer obey the laws of industrial production, and thereby to stress relations of production and the continued importance of class struggle.

challenge such notions. Materially present and perceptually absent, they orchestrate the command and control of network processes that go relatively unnoticed day-to-day, but play a determining factor in all manner of contemporary experience. The technical detail here is important and helps us substantiate what might otherwise seem to be rather speculative claims.

While digital computation operates at a symbolic level of code, and beneath this as binary information, it is articulated by time-based electronic signals and physical hardware states. Electronic signals are fundamentally temporal in their character: impulses, fluctuations, and waves that propagate through a medium (like a wire, or a circuit). The orchestration of such signals—their ordering such that messages and state-changes happen in correct sequences—is therefore "time-critical" (to use Wolfgang Ernst's term). Across digital networks and even within individual digital devices, small timing errors can have dramatic effects. Two key drivers of the field of information theory—in which the concepts and techniques of digital technologies were first developed—concerned finding ways to encode, optimise, and decode signals for transmission, either through networks or within a device (in time and through space); and, in relation to this, overcoming the inherent technical challenges of electromagnetic noise during transmission. Such research was developed at sites like Bell Laboratories to meet the challenges of reliable transmission of information across telecommunications networks. In this context, noise in transcontinental networks was considered a big problem—rather than a creative opportunity as with our examples from sonic arts—as this text from Bell Canada Archives explains:

> There was sputtering and bubbling, jerking and rasping, whistling and screaming. There was the rustling of leaves, the croaking of frogs, the hissing of steam, the flapping of bird's wings. There were clicks from telegraph wires, scraps of talk from other telephones, curious little squeals that were unlike any known sound. . . . The night was noisier than the day, and at the ghostly hour of midnight, for what strange reasons no one knows, the babel was at its height. (Quoted in Gleick 2012, 197)

At a material level, digital information is the time-based modulation of electromagnetic signal into mathematically calculated patterns, sufficiently repetitive to overcome the noise-floor of given hardware, yet with sufficient difference and articulation to communicate messages with minimum time and energy.[17] Through such encoding, and optimisation against noise, messages become unintelligible to humans: even if they were within a perceptible frequency range, they are no longer an analogue of an acoustic waveform. Nevertheless, such emissions do display pattern and rhythm, texture, pitch, and dynamics, that when demodulated to an appropriate frequency range, and transduced from signal into sound, are formally legible, though not humanly decipherable. As Miyazaki asserts (2012), the temporal quality of such signals lends them to listening—itself a mode in which rhythms and textures are easily apparent. Listening to such signals has the potential to reveal patterns and features that

---

17   While the efficiency of such hardware has increased wildly (and therefore the issues of atmospheric noise decreased), the vast increase in communications continues to drive attempts to optimise communication signals (to fit more information through), even while bandwidth is increased.

other modes of investigation do not. Not least, one reason for media theories to shift focus from visual studies to "acoustic space" (to use McLuhan's term) is that the human ear is especially sensitive to microtemporal changes of pattern and rhythm (Ernst 2016).

This approach is made apparent in Miyazaki's concept of algorhythmic analysis as a means to examine these signals, as material instantiations of symbolic step-wise instructions. He explains that algorhythms "occur when real matter is controlled by symbolic and logic structures like instructions written as code. 'Algorhythms' let us hear that our digital culture is not immaterial, but lively, rhythmical, performative, tactile and physical, and, most importantly, that 'algorhythms' are not just normal rhythms" (Miyazaki 2013a, 135). Such rhythms remind us that machines run sequences and processes that are carefully orchestrated. Machines can thus be seen to manipulate time in particular ways, rendering the algorhythmic "an epistemic model of a machine that makes time itself logically controllable and, while operating, produces measurable time effects and rhythms" (Miyazaki 2012). "Understanding computation means doing epistemic reverse-engineering of their inbound and outbound processes, signals and rhythms," Miyazaki explains while paying attention to "its audible, tactile, vibrational, more dynamic and ephemeral aspects" (ibid.).

This technique of deep listening[18] to analyse computer operations has a longer history that intersects with information theory and the identification of noise as an inherent quality of communication. This further resonates with Howse's other experiments with noise, such as *Demons in the Aether* (2008), which also involved workshop participants sonifying the surrounding electromagnetic activity and was instructive to the development of the hardware used in *Detektors*. In playing various streams of data, the "noise probe" could indicate a fault from its change of tone by tuning into the rhythm of the machine or by the identification of a particular pattern. The temporal dimension of this emphasises that signals are not stable and always changing. They are subject to very particular kinds of temporality, the temporality of material infrastructures and of the data itself as well as the changing algorithm.

Yet signals also occupy space.[19] In video documentation of *Detektors*, we see a point-of-view camera perspective of the researcher—moving around half-

---

18 *Deep listening* is a term associated with Pauline Oliveros to describe an aesthetics of listening that responds to environmental conditions on the basis of principles of improvisation, ritual, teaching, and meditation.

19 The measurement of wavelength specifically refers to the signal's occupation of space. Higher frequencies (i.e., shorter wavelengths) take up less space while low frequencies propagate over longer distances. In the same way as the visible section of the electromagnetic spectrum (light) occupies and transforms a space so do Wi-Fi, Bluetooth, and GSM signals. The *Wifi Camera* project (2010) by Adam Somlai-Fischer Usman Haque, and Bengt Sjölén (http://wificamera.propositions.org.uk/) makes a good example of this, through which physical objects are "illuminated" by Wi-Fi energy (even though human eyes can't see this), and similarly such objects cause "shadows" in Wi-Fi beams. For a moment, it seems it's the spatiality, rather than temporality, of these signals that becomes important. They remain physical instantiations of symbolic patterns, but their materiality is affected by space and surface. Temporality returns however in two clear ways: first, spatial features diffract, resonate, reflect, absorb, and otherwise modulate these signals, dynamically changing them, as they travel, in time. Second, the incredibly high speed of signal transmission and its ability to cover long distances mean that signal transmission has the effect of folding space, and cutting time.

empty university buildings and empty labs, travelling bus routes, and finding areas of electromagnetic intensity in what often feel like visually and spatially insignificant locations. These clips emphasise that the signals detected by the equipment—the protocols and transmissions—are part of huge invisible infrastructures, spread out in topologies distinct from the physical structures. The "landmarks" of the infosphere, the points of intensity and interchange, are only sometimes coincident with visual, urban topologies. Human presence does haunt these spaces, but at one remove, in the structural forms of the network, in protological decisions, and of course as communications; furthermore, at a material level of sound and signal, they remain encrypted and impenetrable. Also key, is the sense that the command and control of the stack, which such signals flow from and through, happens elsewhere. These signals knit together, but also divide out, time and space according to informational logics unbounded by human notions of scale and orientation.

Communications networks stretch across and around the whole planet, but more fundamentally than this, the planet's atmosphere constitutes the medium electromagnetic transmissions occupy as energy. Transmissions have to contend with the properties and noise-floor of this planetary medium. The optimisation techniques of information theory were designed precisely to overcome the challenges of such conditions, and the tendency—summed up in the second law of thermodynamics—for patterns and structures to err towards entropy and disorganisation over time. Listening to noise within the electromagnetic spectrum, at particular times of day, and in particular places, emphasises this point: "Lightning produces a wide range of radio waves. Some of the VLF waves are bent by the atmosphere and follow the earth's magnetic fields. The ionosphere acts as a prism, in that the higher frequency radio waves travel faster through the ionosphere than do the lower frequency ones. That seems to explain why one hears the whistler's high-frequency tones first" (Fox 1990, 107–8).[20] The rounding and filtering of such emissions through space, and in time, emphasises the material character—alien though it is to us—of radio energy. While such atmospheric effects are less of an issue above the VLF range, they are indicative of the material forces at issue. As such, wireless digital transmissions also have to contend with such challenges—much of their characteristic patterns when sonified are a product of optimisation of the signal to maximise power and ward against errors.

Howse and Miyazaki's project extends the phenomenological experience of physical urban space to the unseen energies of the techno-temporal. They offset imperceptible infrastructures of electromagnetic networks against the relatively fixed infrastructures and architecture of services, buildings, and roadways (Miyazaki 2013, 520): presenting a displacement of the visual to the aural. Of course, as Shannon Mattern argues in *Code and Clay, Data and Dirt* (2017, xxvi), the infrastructural systems of both media communications and architecture are not mutually exclusive, but are rather "mutually constructed." By con-

---

20 Whistlers are descending tones heard within the very low frequency (VLF) electromagnetic range of 3–30khz (just below the broadcast radio range), caused by lightning at a "geomagnetic conjugate point" (that is, a point on the same geographic longitude, but the opposite hemisphere) (Fox 1990, 107).

sidering the "city-as-media-infrastructure," she demonstrates the myriad ways in which the materiality of the built city, and other urban centres, reinforce and support the hidden or imperceptible infrastructures of signal communication (ibid.). The signals and digital infrastructures made known by *Detektors* are only perceptible to the human sensory apparatus through processes of demodulation and transduction. Prior to this technological process electromagnetic signals can be understood in terms of their implicit *sonicity*, which Ernst (2016, 23) describes as the epistemological "message" of sound signals that addresses humans on the temporal level (for the sense of hearing permits the clearest resolution of microtemporal processes[21]). This is the "essential temporal nature" of sound separate from its affective qualities (ibid.) and thus, for Ernst, provides its analytical precision. To breach the surface and enter into the realm of signification requires "a temporalizing medium like the record player to make it *explicit* through time-sequential unfolding" (ibid., 22). This is a techno-temporal process where *effects* of microtemporal operations in digital media surface to become an *affective* experience—either through visually perceiving changing data as a continuous stream on a computer screen or audibly, as is the case with *Detektors*, by transposing hidden data into the audible frequency range of the human sensory apparatus.

How we register the disjunctive temporalities of contemporaneity when mediation has become immediation—when material processes are, on the surface, immaterial—becomes centrally important. *Detektors* makes knowable what appear to be relatively instantaneous technological processes (sending and receiving an email; the constant refreshing of pixels perceived as a continuous picture; facetime calls) and foregrounds the production, or productive forces (signal traffic) of these processes. It (re)introduces what Fisher called the "grainy materiality" (2013, 44) of digital communications through demodulating messages carrying signals (the medium), rendering the medium itself audible and sensible. And this is an important point, which further echoes Marshall McLuhan: *Detektors* deals with the medium of communication through signals, not the message itself.[22] (In any case, humans could not perceive the message being carried by the signal, which is intended for Wi-Fi routers, mobile phones, and other modem/networked devices.)

In the same way that proponents of sonic hauntology reclaimed the uncanny effects of technologised time by situating the crackle and hiss of technical production at the centre of their compositions, with *Detektors*, Howse and Miyazaki restore a sense of the uncanny by uncovering the textual reality of immaterial communication synonymous with contemporaneity. Further to this, as we have attempted to demonstrate throughout this chapter, the onto-epistemological message (see Prior 2015) of the *Detektors* project is twofold: first, through the

---

21 According to the experiments of Ruth Litovsky and H. Steven Colburn, whose research is an extension of Helmut Haas's work on the precedence effect, humans can aurally detect an echo threshold down to approximately four or five milliseconds. That is not to say, however, that two sound sources are heard as clearly divisible auditory events; however, they are nonetheless perceivable as what could be called a microtemporal process (see Litovsky et al. 1999).

22 Marshall McLuhan famously indicates how the form of a medium embeds itself in any message it transmits.

demodulation of ghostly electromagnetic signals, it provides insight into what is in the world, by sonifying that which is otherwise imperceptible to humans; second, and most pertinent to the experience of historical contemporaneity, the project actively foregrounds notions of spatio-temporal disjunction and interconnection. We maintain that to deeply examine the conditions of the historical present, emphasis must be placed on what we have called the techno-temporalities of contemporaneity. Like Miyazaki's concept of the algorhythm, which invokes rhythmical qualities of both analogue and digital processes, our emphasis on techno-temporalities is intended to synthesise the discursive and non-discursive realms of the contemporary. In this we are echoing Mattern's contention that material and media archaeological analyses often diminish the function of people, cities, and buildings—the analogue network within which these technological media exist and operate (Mattern 2017, 24). *Detektors* encapsulates this sensibility to the fullest extent, as it operates as both the techno-archaeologist *and* the time-sequential device through which affective experience for the human is generated.

Contemporaneity is increasingly defined by complex relationships and registers of time: from the microprocesses of delay lines to spatio-temporal evolutions in planetary history. Under the conditions of contemporary capitalism, coupled with the ubiquity and immediacy of digital communication methods, it could be argued that temporal disjunction has never been more detectable. Algorithms both pre-empt risk in global financial markets[23] and prioritise yesterday's posts on our social platforms,[24] just as network technologies granularise communications, simultaneously fragmenting existing relations and creating new ones. A material remainder can be found in the signal: and it becomes possible to hear the crackle of contemporaneity. The crackle signals the disjunctive aspects of presence, while ontologically reflecting temporal complexity in its material character in the present.

REFERENCES

Agamben, Giorgio. 2009. "What Is the Contemporary?" In *What is an Apparatus? and Other Essays*, 39–54. Translated by David Kishik and Stefan Pedatella. Stanford, CA: Stanford University Press. Essay first published 2008 as *Che cos'è il contemporaneo?* (Rome: Nottetempo).

Attali, Jacques. 1985. *Noise: The Political Economy of Music*. Translated by Brian Massumi. Minneapolis: University of Minnesota Press. First published 1977 as *Bruits: Essai sur l'économie politique de la musique* (Paris: Presses universitaires de France).

Avanessian, Armen, and Suhail Malik. 2016. "The Time Complex: Postcontemporary." *Dis Magazine*. Accessed 28 September 2018. http://dismagazine.com/discussion/81924/the-time-complexpostcontemporary/.

23 The notion of pre-emption is central to the concept of what has come to be called the post-contemporary, an alternative historico-temporal argument that best describes the historical present largely explicated by theorists Armen Avanessian and Suhail Malik. The basic premise here is that the experience of the historical present is pre-produced, through pre-emptive acts: "the future happens before the present, time arrives from the future" (Avanessian and Malik 2016).

24 In a recent paper on algorithmic music, Geoff Cox and Morten Riis (2018) have discussed the ways in which algorithms operate across multiple temporalities at both micro and macro scales.

Benjamin, Walter. 2003. "On the Concept of History." In *Selected Writings, Volume 4, 1938–1940*, translated by Edmund Jephcott and others, edited by Howard Eiland and Michael W. Jennings, 389–400. Cambridge, MA: Belknap Press of Harvard University Press. Essay first published in 1942 as "Geschichtsphilosophische Reflexionen," in *Walter Benjamin zum Gedächtnis*, edited by Max Horkheimer and Theodor Wiesengrund Adorno (Los Angeles, CA: Institut für Sozialforschung).

Born, Georgina. 2015. "Making Time: Temporality, History, and the Cultural Object." *New Literary History* 46 (3): 361–86.

Bourdieu, Pierre. 1990. *The Logic of Practice*. Translated by Richard Nice. Cambridge: Polity. First published 1980 as *Le sens pratique* (Paris: Minuit).

Bratton, Benjamin H. 2016. *The Stack: On Software and Sovereignty*. Cambridge, MA: MIT Press.

Carna botnet. "Internet Census 2012: Port Scanning /0 Using Insecure Embedded Devices." Accessed 21 September 2018. http://census2012.sourceforge.net/paper.html.

Cox, Geoff, and Jacob Lund. 2016. *The Contemporary Condition: Introductory Thoughts on Contemporaneity and Contemporary Art*. Berlin: Sternberg Press.

Cox, Geoff, and Morten Riis. 2018. "(Micro) Politics of Algorithmic Music: Towards a Tactical Media Archaeology." In *The Oxford Handbook of Algorithmic Music*, edited by Alex McLean and Roger T. Dean, 603–26. Oxford: Oxford University Press.

Derrida, Jacques. 1994. *Specters of Marx: The State of the Debt, the Work of Mourning and the New International*. Translated by Peggy Kamuf. London: Routledge. First published 1993 as *Spectres de Marx: L'état de la dette, le travail du deuil et la nouvelle Internationale* (Paris: Galileé).

———. 1997. *Of Grammatology*. Translated by Gayatri Chakravorty Spivak. Corrected ed. Baltimore: Johns Hopkins University Press. First published 1967 as *De la grammatologie* (Paris: Minuit).

Ebeling, Knut. 2017. *There Is No Now: An Archaeology of Contemporaneity*. The Contemporary Condition 7. Berlin: Sternberg Press.

Ernst, Wolfgang. 2011. "Media Archaeography: Method and Machine versus History and Narrative of Media." In *Media Archaeology: Approaches, Applications, and Implications*, edited by Erkki Huhtamo and Jussi Parikka, 239–55. Berkeley: University of California Press.

———. 2016. *Sonic Time Machines: Explicit Sound, Sirenic Voices, and Implicit Sonicity*. Amsterdam: Amsterdam University Press.

Fisher, Mark. 2006. "Phonograph Blues." K-punk, 19 October. Accessed 20 September 2018. http://k-punk.abstractdynamics.org/archives/008535.html.

———. 2012. "What Is Hauntology?" *Film Quarterly* 66 (1): 16–24.

———. 2013. "The Metaphysics of Crackle: Afrofuturism and Hauntology." *Dancecult: Journal of Electronic Dance Music Culture* 5 (2): 42–55.

———. 2014. *Ghosts of My Life: Writings on Depression, Hauntology and Lost Futures*. Winchester: Zero Books.

Fox, Tom. 1990. "Build the 'Whistler' VLF Receiver." *Electronic Hobbyists Handbook 1990*, 107–111. New York: Gernsback.

Fukuyama, Francis. 1992. *The End of History and the Last Man*. London: Penguin.

Gleick, James. 2012. *The Information: A History, a Theory, a Flood*. London: Harper Collins.

Groys, Boris. 2009. "Comrades of Time." *E-flux* 11. Accessed 1 March 2019. https://www.e-flux.com/journal/11/61345/comrades-of-time. Page numbers refer to the PDF available at http://worker01.e-flux.com/pdf/article_99.pdf.

Harvey, David. 2006. *Spaces of Global Capitalism: Towards a Theory of Uneven Geographical Development*. London: Verso.

Howse, Martin. 2008. "The Aether and Its Double." *Acoustic Space* 7. Riga: RIXC.

———. 2018. "Mapping the Electromagnetism: Detektors by Martin Howse and Shintaro Miyazaki." *Digicult*. Accessed 21 September 2018. http://digicult.it/news/mapping-the-electromagnetism-detektors-by-martin-howse-and-shintaro-miyazaki/.

Jameson, Fredric. 1991. *Postmodernism; or, The Cultural Logic of Late Capitalism*. London: Verso.

Kirschenbaum, Matthew G. 2007. *Mechanisms: New Media and the Forensic Imagination*. Cambridge, MA: MIT Press.

Litovsky, Ruth Y., H. Steven Colburn, William A. Yost, and Sandra J. Guzman. 1999. "The Precedence Effect." *Journal of the Acoustical Society of America* 106 (4): 1633–54.

Marx, Karl, and Friedrich Engels. (1888) 1985. *The Communist Manifesto*. Translated by Samuel Moore. London: Penguin. First published 1848 as *Manifest der Kommunistischen Partei* (London: J. E. Burghard). This translation first published 1888 (London: W. Reeves).

Mattern, Shannon. 2017. *Code and Clay, Data and Dirt: Five Thousand Years of Urban Media*. Minneapolis: University of Minnesota Press.

Mbembe, Achille. 2001. *On the Postcolony*. Translated by A. M. Berrett, Janet Roitman, Murray Last, and Steven Rendall. Berkeley: University of California Press. First published 2000 as *De la postcolonie: Essai sur l'imagination politique dans l'Afrique contemporaine* (Paris: Karthala).

Miyazaki, Shintaro. 2012. "Algorhythmics: Understanding Micro-temporality in Computational Cultures." *Computational Culture: A Journal of Software Studies* 2. Accessed 2 August 2018. http://computationalculture.net/page/62/?issue.

———. 2013a. "AlgoRHYTHMS Everywhere: A Heuristic Approach to Everyday Technologies." *Off Beat* 26: 135–48.

———. 2013b. "Urban Sounds Unheard-Of: A Media Archaeology of Ubiquitous Infospheres." *Continuum* 27 (4): 514–22.

———. 2018. "*Detektors.*" Accessed 26 July 2018. http://shintaro-miyazaki.com/?work=detektors.

Osborne, Peter. 2013. *Anywhere or Not at All: Philosophy of Contemporary Art*. London: Verso.

———. 2018. *The Postconceptual Condition: Critical Essays*. London: Verso.

Postone, Moishe. 1998. "Deconstruction as Social Critique: Derrida on Marx and the New World Order," review of *Specters of Marx: The State of the Debt, the Work of Mourning, and the New International*, by Jacques Derrida. *History and Theory* 37 (3): 370–87.

Prior, Andrew. 2015. "Mediality is Noise: The Onto-epistemology of Noise, Media Archaeology and Post-digital Aesthetics." PhD thesis, Aarhus University.

Reynolds, Simon. 2012. *Retromania: Pop Culture's Addiction to Its Own Past*. London: Faber and Faber.

Shakespeare, William. (1623) 2005. *Hamlet*. In *The Oxford Shakespeare: The Complete Works*, edited by John Jowett, William Montgomery, Gary Taylor, and Stanley Wells, 2nd ed., 681–718. Oxford: Oxford University Press. Text based on the folio edition first published 1623 (London: Jaggard and Blount).

Sterne, Jonathan. 2003. *The Audible Past: Cultural Origins of Sound Reproduction*. Durham, NC: Duke University Press.

Aporetic Temporalisations and Postconceptual Realism

Pol Capdevila

Pompeu Fabra University

We live in complex times.[1] The multiple and contradictory versions that describe our epoch are a symptom of this. One of the aspects of our contemporaneity that generates a large number of studies and that reflects this complexity refers precisely to the temporal characteristics of our epoch. This is no accident, since it also refers to the conceptual nucleus of the term *contemporary*. The working hypothesis that I present at the outset consists of gathering the different aspects of the temporality of our epoch into three groups of problems. In the second section, I relate these three problematics to the three aporias of time described by Paul Ricœur. According to him, these aporias are three types of problems without a philosophical solution that nevertheless can be articulated in practical experience by way of narrative. My second thesis affirms that part of contemporary art, by transgressing narrative conventions, reveals the conflicts among the temporal aporias and thus casts a critical look at reality. It does so starting from artistic practices like appropriation, performance, and participation, whose idiosyncrasy has also to be analysed. In the last section, I discuss two aesthetic projects that reveal the aporias of the artistic contemporary. We will see that their way of articulating the temporal paradoxes consists of introducing initiatives of a social character into their practices.

PROBLEMATICS OF CONTEMPORARY TEMPORALITY

1. The first group of questions concerning the temporality of our epoch refers to everyday experience. Philosophy and sociology have studied the imposition of a unique chronological temporality, structured by the abstract time of the clock and the calendar, in all aspects of life. According to these studies, the rhythm of life is being regulated to such an extent by the benchmark of productivity that time for rest is decreasing enormously and "dead times" have come to be a taboo in our society (Attali 1982; Crary 2014). This thesis is confronted by opposed analyses. These analyses affirm that our epoch offers a wide range of temporal experiences, which are essentially different from one another. This large repertory is supposed to have been made possible thanks to the technological mediation of our experience (Keightley 2012). Other studies affirm that the plurality of temporal experiences—or heterochronicity—is

---

1   This paper has been developed as part of the research project "Generating Knowledge in Artistic Research: Towards an Alternative Account. A Meeting Point of Philosophy, Art and Design" (2016–18), funded by the Spanish Ministry of Economy and Competitiveness.

115

provided by creative activities like art or cinema as a critique of the standardisation of chronological time (Hernández 2016; Speranza 2017). More generally, a
defence has been made of the need to construct niches of alternative experience in which appear necessary modes of living like taking one's time, slowing
down, doing nothing, being bored, or the search for the most propitious, most
relevant, or most complete moment (*kairós*) (Rosa 2016).

2. Other problematics related to the temporality of the contemporary concern
the level of historical and social time. Koselleck ([1985] 2004) has explained
how, in modernity, the overvaluation of the horizon of expectations—excessive
attention paid to the next new thing—has made us lose our attentiveness to
the experience of the past and has progressively reduced the space available for
experiences of the present. In this way, the present has been shrinking and is
projecting us toward the future in a movement that is getting faster and faster.
The lack of presence of our times has also been mentioned by other theorists
of speed (Virilio 1991). Other analyses—not always acknowledged inheritors
of the postmodern theses of the end of history and of times—emphasise the
immobility of the present, which extends into the future and into the past. In
this slow present or regime of presentism, all change remains on the surface
of a history that already no longer advances and that, hence, is no longer history (Gumbrecht 2010; Hartog 2015). Attempts have also been made to combine the thesis of futurism and that of presentism. According to this suggestion, the force of progress and accelerated transformations would dominate in
some social spheres in such a way that other spheres, especially the ideological
sphere and that of relations of power, would remain stable (Rosa 2005). These
models of historical and social consciousness are characterised by the fact that
they identify the invasion by one form of time—future or present—of the other
two forms of time: present and past.

  Other critics pronounce, along with Hamlet, that time "is out of joint"
(Shakespeare [1623] 2005, 691). From this perspective, the experience of past,
present, and future is possible, but the problem consists of articulating them in
a whole. The capacity for investing time with meaning has been lost, which is as
if time were dead (Han 2017). As a solution, some have called for the recuperation of history: the revival of past political struggles as a mode of resistance to
the end of times (Foster 1983). Others extol memory and its ability to generate
productive anachronisms, which can activate suppressed potentialities in the
past and open new possibilities for the future (Rancière 1996; Didi-Huberman
2000; Bal 2016).

3. The third group of problems is epistemological in nature and is expressed
in each approach's claim to represent the essential idea or image of the contemporary. There are essentialist approaches in which this "together in time"
is defined as progress toward the globalisation of one or more sectors of our
society: the economic, the technological, the chronological, the scientific, the
media sector, the leisure industry, and so on. Globalisation can acquire very
concrete forms on the basis of fantastic exercises in synecdoche: the society

of the spectacle, of surveillance, of risk, of insecurity, the fluid society, global terrorism. . . . Against the visionaries of essences of contemporaneity, other observers insist on complexity and present themselves as defenders of the multiplicity of perspectives. There then appear characterisations of tendencies such as postcolonialism, cosmopolitanism, heterochronicity, and the plurality of narratives: tendencies that represent values of unquestionable alterities, which resist standardising globalisation (Said 1978; Moxey 2013; Smith 2009; Giunta and Diez Fischer, 2014). It is interesting to note how, according to their respective opponents, both simplifying globalisation and increasing its complexity are supposed to be responsible for an indomitable epistemological atmosphere: the perfect breeding ground for relativism and fake news.

Various characteristics discussed here are included in highly diverse theories of contemporaneity. I have juxtaposed them in these three groups without having the least intention of proposing a new theory or even an ideal typology. I have suggested this schema, because it helps us understand what sort of philosophical problems are posed by the analysis of contemporary temporality and, hence, what sort of solutions are proposed. By way of the schema, we comprehend that these three problematics are analogous to the three aporias regarding time that Ricœur presents in *Time and Narrative*. In the next section, I will relate each of Ricœur's aporias to the three problematics regarding contemporary time.

THE APORETICS OF TIME AND OF THE CONTEMPORARY

In his magnum opus, *Time and Narrative* (first published between 1983 and 1985), Ricœur provided an in-depth analysis of the major reflections on time of Aristotle, Augustine of Hippo, Kant, Husserl, and Heidegger, and he concluded that, in developing its different aspects, they all ran into theoretical problems that they were not able to resolve. Either they fell into considerations that contradicted their initial postulates or they introduced opaque metaphors with no referent. Ricœur gathered these sets of problems into a triple aporetics of time. As abstract as these reflections may appear, they try to give an account of the reality of time and hence can be used as models for understanding the temporal problematics of our epoch. In the following paragraphs, I will categorise the problems regarding contemporaneity raised above as particular forms of the aporias of time. There are many fascinating issues related to each aporia, but I will have to confine myself to being as schematic as possible.[2]

1. In the first group of problems, I have referred to the level of everyday experience, in order to contrast the imposition of a single time—chronological temporality, which is external, abstract, and uniform—to the experience of multiple temporalities, which are different in intensity, extension, and so on.

---

2 For an extensive and detailed discussion of the aporias regarding time, see Ricœur (1988, part 4 and "Conclusions"). In an article, I have summarised the aporias of time and have applied them to concrete spheres of human experience, in such a way that they serve as a theoretical tool for analysing the different aspects of temporal experience, especially in the artistic sphere (Capdevila, 2015).

This contrast is analogous to the first aporia, which appears when philosophy reflects on time, adopting either the cosmological perspective or the phenomenological perspective.

The first perspective takes natural phenomena as its starting point and examines the time of the cosmos. Following the metaphor that Aristotle gave us, it thinks this time as a line: a homogeneous elapsing of which the points are successive moments that measure a before and an after, that is, an order and a direction. This is a time that is external to the subject: immense and regular and thus serving as a measure of movement in nature.

It is important to bear in mind that the time of nature, considered from a cosmological perspective, is not the same as the time of the clock and the calendar—what is commonly called chronological time. The time produced by these apparatuses is based on natural forces and astronomical cycles, but they are human inventions that possess different characteristics than natural temporality. Nonetheless, one of the principal ideas of theorists like Crary and Attali is that the apparatuses of the clock and the calendar have come to govern human life to such an extent that chronological time has become second nature. It is no longer natural cycles that set the rhythm of our lives, but rather the clock and the calendar, and the problem in this process of naturalisation is that there are already no refuges left—or hardly any—for other forms of temporal experience.

The cosmological perspective is opposed to the phenomenological one. The latter takes the life of consciousness as its point of reference. Every experience becomes conscious in the present. This present extends in two directions: into the past in the form of memory and into the future in the form of expectation. Its extension is imagined as a continuous duration of a consciousness that links together a chain of experiences. As Augustine of Hippo already observed, whether this present is experienced as more punctual and intense or more ample and homogeneous depends on a dialectic between the attention and distension of our consciousness.

The phenomenological perspective affirms the irreducible subjectivity of the feeling of the passage of time in each given situation. Moreover, as Benjamin showed, attention and distension can even condition technological media. In this way, for different technical media providing access to reality, there are different temporalisations of experience: slower or faster, direct, frozen, repetitive, interrupted, placed or not placed within a meaningful structure, and so on. That is why those who defend heterochronicity as a paradigm for our epoch—whether thanks to technological apparatuses or in the sphere of aesthetic practices—mainly adopt a phenomenological perspective.

2. Second, I have grouped together questions referring to the historical consciousness of our epoch starting from two divergent general positions, which are not always opposed in practice: on the one hand, those that defend the colonisation by one form of time—future, present, or past—of the others; on the other, that which consists of affirming the fragmentation of time into three sorts of experience—present, past, and future—which, however, are already

cut off from one another and incapable of being articulated in a unitary sense, whether on the individual or the collective level.

These problems can be considered as current forms of the paradoxes that appear in the second aporia. The latter contrasts the usual manner of thinking and speaking about time as unitary with the clear differentiation of its three modes of being: the past, the present, and the future. Whereas time is always unitary for us, the qualities of memory, perception, and expectations—the forms of the three "ecstases of time," as Ricœur (1988) puts it—are radically different. So too, in an analogous manner, are the three social times: history, current events, and the future.

In general, the thesis of the colonisation of the other forms of time by one form of time—especially that of presentism, in which the experience of the past and of the future become diffuse in the present—would appear to be a current version, setting aside the important differences, of the model of a unitary time. On the other hand, the problems of articulation between the three ecstases of time reflect the theoretical problems that philosophers like Husserl have had in trying to address its unity.

3. In the third group of problems, I have mentioned those theoretical approaches that posit an essence of the contemporary as against those that defend a multiplicity of perspectives and temporal aspects. In particular, I have pointed to the contrast between, on the one hand, the standardising tendency of the different models of globalisation and, on the other, the forces that give rise to an increase in difference and plurality. Where is/are our society/ies heading?

A profound epistemological problem appears in this question: a problem that Ricœur categorised as the third aporia of time or that of inscrutability. In analysing how each philosopher developed the concept of time, he noted that each ended up presupposing characteristics deriving from prior traditions. This is to say that what one is trying to constitute—time—"reveals itself as belonging to a constituted order always already presupposed by the work of constitution" (Ricœur 1988, 261). Time thus shows itself to be inscrutable and unrepresentable. According to Ricœur, this is what explains that multiple figurations of human time appear: for "the unrepresentable can only be projected, it seems, in terms of fragmentary representations" (ibid., 264).

Pursuing the parallelism of Ricœur further, the multiplication of versions of contemporaneity, whether essentialist or pluralist, demonstrates rather that the contemporary as a unitary idea is inscrutable. It is perhaps to this aporetic character of the contemporary that paradoxical definitions like "temporal unity in disjunction and disjunctive unity of present times" (Osborne 2013, 17) are pointing.[3] Is it possible that the contemporary can only be characterised on the basis of paradoxes and images that are contradictory but complementary?

---

3 Osborne's (2013, 21) proposal to consider the contemporary as a regulative idea in the Kantian sense has certain similarities to what is shown by Ricœur's third aporia as applied to this concept.

PHILOSOPHICAL PROBLEMS RELATED TO TIME AND THEIR ARTICULATION IN NARRATIVE

To answer the above question, we need to add another aspect of Ricœur's study of time: namely, the function of narrative. His main and most general thesis is that if it is indeed impossible to think time without falling into unresolvable contradictions, there is nevertheless a human experience in which temporal experience is complete and consistent. This form of experience is narrative in the largest sense, which characterises history and everyday life as much as literature and art. Narrative is, then, our common form of temporal experience. As he argues in *Time and Narrative*, "time becomes human to the extent that it is articulated through a narrative mode, and narrative attains its full meaning when it becomes a condition of temporal existence" (Ricœur 1984, 52). What is important is to consider that narrative, in articulating the different paradoxes of time, also provides a practical articulation—not a theoretical solution—to the philosophical problems that hinge on time. Narrative articulates a vision of human life via a temporal structure: in a coherent whole, it thus includes considerations about reality and about the self, about our manner of knowing reality, about moral life and about modes of representing it. It articulates questions of ontology, epistemology, ethics, and aesthetics.

In this section, I will relate each temporal aporia to one of the philosophical problems that are associated with it. We will also see the sort of solutions that poetics can provide. Further on, we will see how aesthetic practices destabilise these relations, in order to reveal their conflicts.

1. The contradictions between the phenomenological and the cosmological perspectives point to a problem of articulation between the time of the world and that of the subject—both individual and collective. In contemporary terms, one of the fundamental problems that is at stake in this debate on temporality is the development of subjectivities. As a solution to the aporia, Ricœur argues that narrative theory proposes the configuration of the plot, which is constructed by the actions of the subjects. Narrative plot offers a practical solution to the antinomy of identity, since it represents it as identical with itself, but different on the subjective level (Ricœur 1988).

2. The second aporia highlights the conflict between the singularity and the plurality of time and hence the possibility of past, present, and future—as differentiated experiences—getting articulated into a unitary and meaningful whole (biography, community, etc.). One of the most active contemporary debates in this regard concerns the possibility of intervening in the sense of history, in the capacity of a community to propose futures and influence historical development.

Ricœur offers two limited solutions. The first consists of the mediation of historical narrative, which has humanity as its regulative idea and universal history as its desirable, but unattainable, horizon—universal history as a result of an interpretation of the past against a unitary future horizon. The second solution is merely indicated in *Time and Narrative*, but it is fundamental in the context of certain contemporary aesthetic practices, as I will show further on. This solution consists of salvaging the Nietzschean concept of the *force of the present* and applying it to the idea of *initiative*. It aims, then, more at practice than narrative—even if narrating is a practice. An initiative is a moment of the present of an action, which articulates past and future. Moreover, it goes beyond the vision of the historian, adding greater power to the present moment, since it moves the present from the category of seeing to the category of doing. In doing so, it introduces aspects of the theory of action, like the concept of intervention (G. H. von Wright) and of promise, and it develops the relationship between the physical level (the body) and the mental level (intentions).[4]

3. As concerns the solution that poetics is supposed to provide to the third aporia of time, Ricœur recognises, at the end of his long investigation, that there is not any single narrative or total representation of time. As we indicated earlier, "not even narrative exhausts the power of the speaking that refigures time" (Ricœur, 1988, 261). The plurality of representations of time that our culture is producing constitutes a growing awareness—which has come about in postmodernism—of this limitation.

THE TEMPORALITY OF CONTEMPORARY ARTISTIC STRATEGIES

Confronted by the vast universe of current visual culture, are there aesthetic forms that represent our epoch or that could be called contemporary? I will refer briefly to Agamben's text—which is discussed more extensively in another part of the present book[5]—to provide a basis for critical reflection on the contemporary and a selection criterion. The Italian philosopher recuperates the untimely spirit of Nietzsche (*Unzeitgemässe Betrachtungen*): "those who are truly contemporary, who truly belong to their time, are those who neither coincide with it nor adjust themselves to its demands" (Agamben 2009, 40). By virtue of this maladaptation, the contemporary individual is able to see, in the *intimate darkness* of his or her epoch, what is not obvious about the present. To look into the dark signifies turning one's attention toward that which one generally does not want to see: the conflictual aspects of a society. But the contemporary individual is able to do this not only with the intention of criticising, but also to furnish that which enriches the present. For this reason, he or she perceives what has been sown and will grow in the future. According to Agamben, the future does not always have the form of something new: "there is a secret affinity between the archaic and the modern" (ibid., 51), since sometimes what is novel is to be found hidden in the forgotten past, in prehistory. Therefore, to be

---

4   Alfredo Martinez Sánchez (1999) has emphasised the importance of the concept of *force of the present* and of *initiative* in the pragmatic resolution of the second aporia, which Ricœur himself still had not sufficiently appreciated in *Time and Narrative*. A detailed analysis of the evolution of Ricœur's thinking on the function of the concept of initiative demonstrates that, ultimately, "the announced *reply* to the second aporia is more practical than poetic" (ibid., 133).

5   See Chapter 3 by Babette Babich.

contemporary means to be anachronistic: to introduce fissures and cuts in time that generate the possibility of a rearticulation of past, present, and future.

If we combine Agamben's characterisation of the contemporary individual and Ricœur's narrative theory, we establish a selection criterion. From a critical perspective, contemporary phenomena will not be those that reconcile the paradoxical aspects of our epoch, but rather those that confront the dark aspects and its conflicts. What is of interest to us, then, are those aesthetic forms that, by subverting narrativity, make the temporal aporias appear and reveal the deep conflicts of our world.[6] I will now introduce the three typical strategies on the basis of which they succeed in so doing and their temporal characteristics. These strategies are appropriation, performance, and participation. As these strategies have gained wide acceptance in contemporary art, there will be no need to characterise them generally.

The appropriation of motifs, forms, and styles from other artworks or from other spheres of visual culture became established as a legitimate artistic practice starting in the 1970s, despite already having an extensive history at the time. As appropriation of elements of the past, some art critics identified it as an abandonment of the modern project and a return of the tradition in its different forms and imaginaries (Bonito Oliva 2000; Joachimides 2000). Other critics provided an immediate reply to this conservative position. Starting from progressive positions, they defended appropriation as the possibility of completing the suppressed project of the avant-garde and hence as a way of maintaining a resistance struggle for modern historical meaning (Foster 1996). Be that is it may, both positions revealed a certain exhaustion of the modern project and of its capacity to push toward the future.

Currently, the appropriative strategy is reformulating its critical recovery of the past. Appropriation may introduce anachronisms in the work, in order, in the first place, to subvert the chronological model of time, understood as the foundation of an ideology that transforms the unfolding of events into a causal chain in which no profound change is possible (Rancière 1996). In the second place, anachronism can salvage from the past futures that have been buried in oblivion and can give them the power of renewal. See, for example, Bal's interesting study (2016) on Stan Douglas's photography project *Midcentury Studio*, which was created in 2010. The artist simulates the work of a photographer from 1946 and the different genres that such a photographer could use. He thus introduces different temporal layers in one and the same work—heterochronicities—something that generates an intimate relationship between that past and the present. But Bal's detailed analysis identifies the critical aspects of the work, which subtly questions the US social history represented in the photos and thus posits the possibility of thinking social relations in a different way.

Despite the foregoing and the praise that is being showered on it today, it is important to recognise that anachronism does not possess an inherently

6   The idea that contemporary art transgresses narrative conventions and that it thereby encourages paradoxical temporal aesthetic experiences and problematises fundamental questions of our world is deserving of a more detailed argument. I have developed this idea in another article, in which I bring together current aspects of narrative theory and of counter-narrativity (Capdevila 2015).

destabilising potential. Anachronism is in itself aporetic, because it reveals the conflicts between the different approaches to temporality: between a current identity and a desired one (first aporia) and between the meaning of history and a society's capacity to influence it (second aporia). Hence, it can serve to found as much an essentialist model of identity as a constructivist one or it can serve as the basis for the postmodern theory of the end of history or as part of a critical approach to the established order.

The performative dimension starts appearing in art to the extent that it abandons its representational paradigm and invades the space and physical time of the public: first, by way of the objecthood of the work with its presence and then with the action of the artists themselves. I will highlight just three particular temporary qualities.

First, the work emphasises its processual nature. Whether it is an action (direct or recorded) or an object (an image or an abstract object), the work, as something perfectly finished, has to abandon classical virtual atemporality, in order to participate in the time of the public. Rather than transporting it to an ideal temporality, it occupies its time as duration and interpolates the public in its present situation.

Second, the processual nature of the work obstructs the development of a semantic structure. As Adorno was already able to see, "the constitutive insufficiency" of art emphasises, above all, the perception of materiality and of the components (Adorno 1997, 128). This breaks the teleological structure of the construction of sense and reveals the conventions and structures of the creation of meanings (Menke 1998).

Without being able to determine a semantic *telos* for the work, the present of the aesthetic experience is able to extend indefinitely. This type of temporality, which emphasises the present over the past and the future, introduces a third semantic-narrative problem. Amelia Jones (2013) has analysed how, by virtue of its performativity, the work or action resists being incorporated into general narratives—histories of art, for example—and also leaves its projection into the future on an ambiguous level. But what, to paraphrase Adorno, we could call *metanarrative insufficiency* is precisely what allows performance to open up an indeterminate space of participation: a space for new relations among the members of the public (ibid.). In this way, the performative character of art, which emphasises the experience of the present, introduces the possibility of other strategies, which strengthen the collective initiative and, as such, the dimension of the future.

The performative element is, then, intimately related to the participatory. Christine Ross has brilliantly analysed the temporal mechanisms of aesthetic experience that push the spectator to adopt a participatory attitude. Some of Melik Ohanian's video works appropriate and mix different registers of a common reality: the audio recording of Salvador Allende's final speech and the aerial bombing of the Palacio de la Moneda on 11 June 1973 with images of Santiago de Chile today taken by Ohanian himself. Following Ross, the anachronic editing produces a desynchronised perceptual experience of the work that breaks the continuity of history with the present. To achieve a unity of the work, which is a primary cognitive disposition, she or he must adopt a role analogous to that of the witness, something analogous to the history maker (Ross 2008, 145, citing Ricœur). Being confronted with past events as a witness and reinterpreting them through the keys of her or his own present means also opening up possible new unfoldings for history and, "in short, is more about the conditions of possibility of futurity than its noticeable actualization" (Ross 2008, 147–48).

If, thanks to its performativity, the participatory aspect is part of any work of art, it is especially so in so-called relational art. It is surely true that the degree of participation is overestimated in many insubstantial relational projects, but it is also certainly the case that relational art has created a qualitatively different space for participation. In addition to being intersubjective, its reception is also collective and thus opens up the possibility of exercising initiative.[7] This affects the temporal quality of the aesthetic. Whereas, as we have just seen, the anachronistic visual work is able to make its public engage with the *conditions of futurity* the relational work introduces a project for action with respect to a near future. Its temporal essence is not so much characterised by a utopian ideal (Bourriaud 2002) as by a collective artistic action.

Currently, many artistic institutions are trying to bring artistic action beyond their own frontiers and to transform it into a practical initiative. As Möntmann explains, especially as propelled by biennials and other global artistic events, art has adopted methods of production and distribution of the global economy, and with them, it has come to occupy other public spheres: art has plunged into the world (Möntmann 2017, 124, citing Lee 2012, 5). Along with this development, its willingness to influence society has also changed. Möntmann notes that in the panorama of the major artistic events, art that takes up the past, does not do so to preserve its memory: it "pluralizes the temporality of the contemporary moment and endows it with the potential to think alternative presents" (Möntmann 2017, 128). I would like to retain the idea of this intimate relationship of art with the world surrounding it, although I would qualify the temporal aspect. As we will see in the next section, rather than thinking alternative presents, art, by performatively activating pasts by way of a collective initiative, moves toward changing the course of the future.

Temporalisations of the aporias in contemporary art

In the last section, I discussed some typical strategies of current art, by way of which some of the temporal aspects of contemporaneity are materialised. In what follows, I will discuss how two current projects confront the problematics of the contemporary presented in this article. The first case, Antonio Vega Macotela's *The Mill of Blood*, consists of an artistic investigation that brings into play the different elements of the aporias without managing to articulate them in practice—although it does indicate a way out. The second case is based on

---

7   Here, we are treading on a complex problem. I will confine myself to defining aesthetic experience as intersubjective by virtue of the fact that every spectator, when confronted by a work, takes others into account: the spectator looks at the work as subject of a community (KdU §40, Kant 1987, 159–62). Aesthetic experience is collective when a group of people participate jointly in the work.

the practice of Forensic Architecture: an agency that is dedicated to investigating incidents of institutional violence, is characterised by its aesthetic methods, and has a significant presence in artistic spaces.

The Mill of Blood was shown at documenta 14, which took place in 2017, and, in my view, is representative of a series of projects at this important exposition-event. The work was the product of a long investigation of exhaustion by Antonio Vega Macotela. It involves a full-scale replica, nine metres across, of the mill at the Cerro Rico mine (Bolivia), one of three mills of this type that were in operation in Latin America during the colonial period. These mills were set up at the exits of high-altitude mines to mint coins with the metal extracted by the miners. They worked with an aboriginal slave labour force, either because it was too expensive to transport animals or because the animals died quickly due to the harshness of the conditions. The title refers to the blood of the slaves who moved the mill, with which it remained stained.

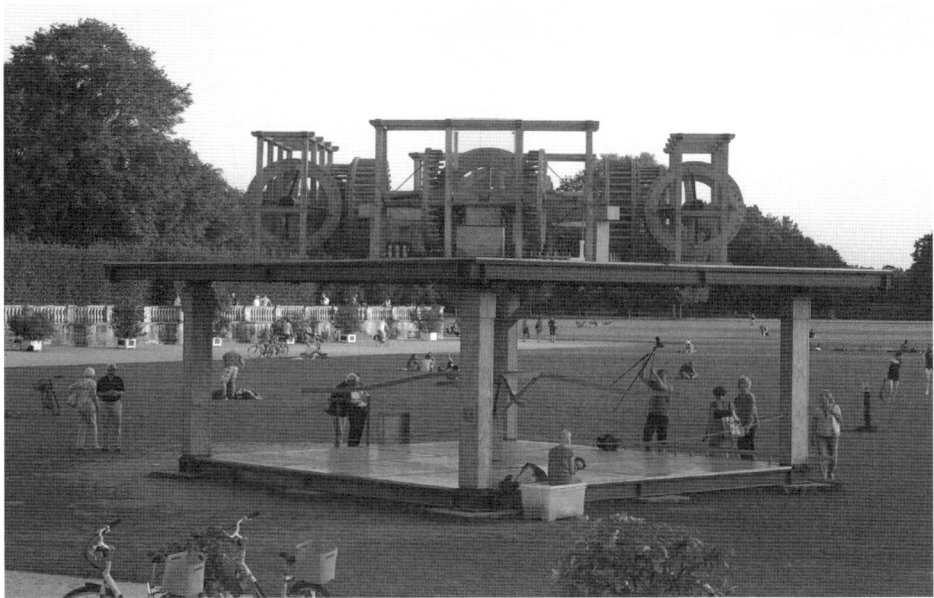

Figure 6.1.

Instead of the efforts and the slave blood of the aboriginal people of Latin America, the documenta mill used the efforts of the—mostly white and middle- or upper-class—visitors to produce the coins, which the artist baptised *teios*: a fusion of the Greek word *theos* (god) and *tio* (the protector-god of the Bolivian miners). The minted coin fell into a safe and activated an apparatus that created a *crypto-teio*: a virtual currency like bitcoin. According to the description of the project, during the third week of the exposition in Kassel, an ICO (initial coin offer) was supposed to be launched, which would give the

Figure 6.1. Antonio Vega Macotela's *Mill of Blood* at documenta 14, Kassel, 2017.

crypto-teios their definitive value. Trade in the latter was supposed to begin when documenta 14 ended, at which point the mill and the plates for the coins would be destroyed and, thereby, the possibility of minting new teios would be destroyed as well. The physical teios were supposed to be kept in a bank and the profit obtained by selling crypto-teios would be used to finance the project itself and a public debate in Mexico City on alternatives to the mechanisms of the capitalist production of value. Despite having tried to contact the artist and his gallery by different means, nonetheless, I do not know whether this initiative was brought to fruition.

By way of appropriative, performative, and participatory strategies, Macotela's mill reveals the contemporary problematics that I presented at the outset and that I classified using Ricœur's aporias. With respect to the first group of temporal problems, the circular movement of the mill serves as an allegory—as if it were a clock (it was in fact built by a clock or watch-making company)—for the model of chronological history: it recuperates the infamous history of the enrichment of the Spanish imperial capital and makes us aware of how collective identities—Latin American and European—are dependent on the historical relations between power and the means of production. On the other side of the aporia, the mill also temporalises the phenomenological model of time. In an act of appropriation, the artist uses it as an anachronism that inverts the meaning of the past. Inverting the master–slave relationship, visitors push the mill, but they will not receive compensation for their efforts in the form of a coin-souvenir. The mill thus opens up a temporality to the visitor that is critical of Ben Franklin's "time is money" on which capitalism is founded. The mill allows the two temporalities to be experienced, without offering the visitor a narrative with which to articulate the two temporalities into a whole.

The *Mill of Blood* also reveals the problems of the second aporia: the performative activation of a historical apparatus constructs an anachronism in which the boundaries between past and present become blurred. We have, then, before us a typical phenomenon of presentism: the contemporary version of the unicity of the time. Nonetheless, the critical character of the mill's interpellation of the visitor—by virtue of its performativity—leads him or her to establish a discontinuity between a past of oppression and a present in which we become aware of that oppression.

Finally, the third aporia is manifest in Macotela's work, inasmuch as the mill of blood functions hermeneutically as an allegory of the relations of domination of colonial history and their continuation in the present. It thus sets itself up as a critical symbol for the epoch in which we live. On the other hand, by being destroyed, it avoids the typical reification whereby museum institutions, by making works enter the dead time of the display case, convert them into pieces of those economic mechanisms of power. It thus resists begin reified as an image of our epoch.

I have argued that Macotela's project presents the contradictions of the three aporias without resolving them. In fact, this is not entirely the case. The project does not simply present itself as a work to be contemplated or with which to play at spinning around and minting valueless coins—which would be a sort of *kitsch* of artistic participation. As a project, it essentially includes a productive dimension. It presents itself as an initiative, in the sense discussed earlier in connection with Ricœur: the possibility of participating in a productive structure of economic value—trading in bitcoins—and of thinking alternatives to the neo-liberal productive system. In present practice, this initiative articulates an anachronistic re-reading of the past and a search for new futures.

That this initiative has not shown signs of success appears to be a symptom of the depth of contemporary temporal paradoxes, the resistance of the system, and the difficulty of finding a practical and viable way out of them. Nonetheless, as a project that exemplifies a certain sort of current artistic and curatorial practice, it points to a path that can be taken more often. Documenta 14 also illustrates the conflicts that underlie this sort of practice: its transfer to Athens, its Public Program, and a significant part of the projects that it housed aspired to have a direct impact on social collectives, on the construction of cultural practices transcending the institution itself, and on the configuration of new ideological and epistemic discourses.[8] Documenta 14—with its capacity to represent and consolidate contemporary tendencies—was a clear example of how a large part of contemporary art cannot be understood apart from this vocation to head outside the world of art and to participate in social reality. Of course, all this generated tremendous controversy, enormous expectations, disagreements, misunderstandings, and extraordinary disappointments.

This increasing permeability between the artistic and the mundane spheres motivates the artistic institution to host other sorts of cultural and social practices, which were not originally artistic. We need to observe how these sorts of practices acquire a different status within the institution of art and how they reflect contemporary temporal problematics. From this perspective, I will now analyse the sort of work done by the Forensic Architecture agency.

Forensic Architecture (FA) is not an artists' collective. It is an investigative agency founded in 2010 at Goldsmith College by Eyal Weizman and a group of architects, artists, investigative journalists, film-makers, and lawyers. They investigate state violence and violence by major corporations—particularly when it affects the architectural environment—either on their own initiative or as commissioned by international lawyers and NGOs. The immediate objective of their investigations is to clarify the account of certain events or to denounce an abuse of power, and the results are presented in international tribunals and civil courts, in the media, and in truth commissions. In a world that constantly produces more primary sources documenting episodes of violence—making such violations all the more visible—institutional attacks are also directed at denying the veracity of and at the provenance of these sources. In this context, FA's work consists of examining sources, geolocating them, and reconstructing a version of the events. FA thus breaks the monopoly of control of forensic medicine by the state and puts it at the service of other entities.

FA also sets a long-term objective for itself: it configures political strategies of civil defence vis-à-vis atrocities committed by power and it collaborates in

---

8   See Szymczyck (2017) and the statement on documenta 14's Public Program by Paul B. Preciado (2017).

the transformation of the epistemological construction of reality. In this sense, its practice has been characterised as a "forensic aesthetics" (Keenan and Weizman 2012) and an "investigative aesthetics" (Forensic Architecture 2017); adopting Rancière's idea, it could also be defined as a distribution of the sensible (Rancière 2000). FA promotes, then, a "collective exercise of imagination" (Forensic Architecture 2017) that implies, on the one hand, the construction of evidence—not its invention—and the most effective ways of presenting it; and, on the other, critical reflection on the nature of the latter and its relation to truth, ways of understanding human rights, the relations of power inherent in today's societies, and so on. This reflexive and deeply critical dimension is more commonly exhibited in books and in expositions in institutions like documenta, MACBA, the Haus der Kulturen der Welt, and so on.

Let us look at an example. FA's presence inside arts institutions tests the usefulness of the model of temporal aporias that I have used to interpret contemporary aesthetics; its activity in the practical world—that is, as an initiative aimed at social reality—dialectically articulates some of the contradictions.

Documenta 14 hosted an FA project, which was undertaken in collaboration with The Society of Friends of Halit and which had already been exhibited in the Haus der Kulturen der Welt. The project attempted to elucidate the death of Halit Yozgat in the context of murders with possible racist motivations, which may have been covered up by German law enforcement and the German judicial system. In addition to the audiovisual documents collected and produced by FA, documenta 14 also created spaces for debate and a workshop on the racial coding of sound technologies.[9] By way of all this, FA, on the one hand, called into question the official narrative concerning certain events and, on the other, provided tools of reflection and production of forensic evidence, pointing to a context of racist culture that persists in the structures of power in Germany. The investigation's project manager, Christina Varvia, stated: "we want to show another possibility of art—one that can confront doubt, and uses aesthetic techniques in order to interrogate" (quoted in Perlson 2017).

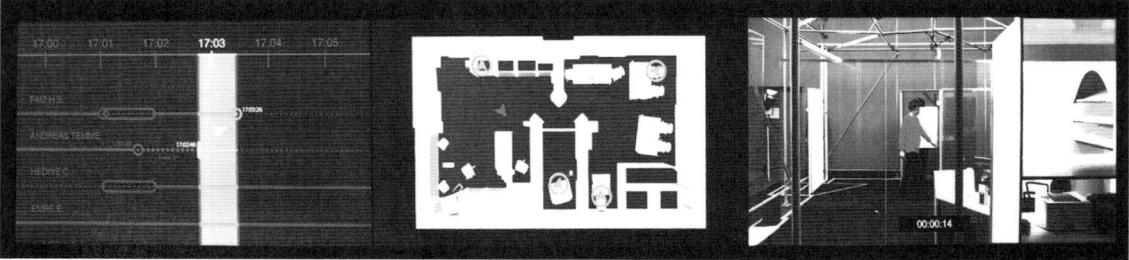

Figure 6.2.

9 "Sonic Segregations: A Critique of Racism and Audio Technologies," 30 May 2017, Kassel (see https://www.documenta14.de/en/calendar/21264/sonic-segregations-a-critique-of-racism-and-audio-technologies).

Figure 6.2. Forensic Architecture at documenta 17. Timeline reconstruction of the events of the day of Halit's murder.

How does FA display contemporary temporal problematics in its projects? First, FA calls into question the official accounts: not as a rejection of the chronological model that underlies every narrative, but rather as more or less open possibilities of re-narrating events. Sometimes it offers a spatial, geolocated perspective on the facts and leaves the final reconstruction of what occurred to the viewer; sometimes it suggests alternative narratives; and on other occasions, it offers its own finished version. If it is sure that narrativity determines its works to various degrees, they hide neither the lacunae nor the instability of the plots. The narrative thus shows itself to be more fragile and provisional, with ambiguous zones of heterochronicity.

With respect to the problems associated with the second aporia, the sort of forensic investigation done by FA consists of a restitution of the past; as such, it is opposed to the model of global presentism. It could seem, then, that it situates itself on the other side of the aporia: prima facie, the partial investigations that it conducts are presented as a multiplicity of fragmentary narratives on situations of conflict in different parts of the globe—such as Pakistan, Palestine, Syria, and Mexico. Nonetheless, despite the apparent heterogeneity of the local temporalities, a basic unity can be glimpsed: there is a regulative idea—in the Kantian sense—of human and natural rights that imparts an enlightened futuristic vision to its project (Forensic Architecture 2017). These horizons orient the investigations and are redefined by the results obtained. But the most important thing is that both these general ideas and the particular investigations concerning recent history have legal and political objectives in the broadest possible sense. They are, therefore, practical initiatives that, in the present, articulate the past with a transformation of the future. Here, Ricœur's concept of *initiative* again appears as a practical articulation of the problems of the second aporia.

Finally, the third aporia raises the question of whether FA's set of investigative projects can be understood as a general view of the time in which we live or whether they are determined by the historical context that precedes them. In this regard, the latter seems unquestionable: their debt to the Enlightenment tradition, elements of the Frankfurt School, and biopolitics is clear, as is their debt to historiographical postulates of reconstructions of the past and of combating fake news using empirical evidence. On the other hand, after postmodernity, the attitude of political engagement and social investigation has—in Agamben's sense—an anachronistic feel, which allows precisely for transcending the limits of the modern toward the contemporary. Examples of this are the transgression of methodological boundaries, the coordination of transdisciplinary teams, the invention of new epistemic methods of interpretation of reality and of production of evidence, and so on. Moreover, their presence in artistic institutions and museums also reveals a strong desire to be exposed to the critical gaze of theorists and artists and, therefore, to play an active role in the debate on new epistemologies.

In the end, we see again that the works of FA move on the terrain of the temporal aporias and of their philosophical implications—in ontological, epistemological, ethical, and aesthetic terms. Nonetheless, their narrative dimension and their socio-political initiative permit the articulation of the elements within a common practical horizon—even if it does not always resolve the aporias. For its part, the institution of art itself also goes deeper into its own contradictions by expounding the aporias. In doing so, it invests the aesthetic with notions like empirical truth, ethics, and social commitment, without ceasing to exercise its critical and self-reflexive role.

Conclusion

Both projects that we have analysed reflect aporetic aspects of the contemporary. Nonetheless, they both possess programmes and certain objectives that are very different. Hence, whereas the *Mill of Blood* presents conflicts without resolving them, FA produces narratives in which these elements find a practical articulation. Despite the obvious differences, there is a very important common element, which, in light of what has been seen in recent artistic events, acquires a significant presence. These projects suggest a practical initiative going beyond the classical autonomous sphere of the aesthetic and of the art world. They fracture the autonomous temporality of the institution of art, introduce mundane concerns into it, and impose the rhythms of the latter upon it. As initiatives, they impose a discontinuity in the inertia of becoming, articulate past, present, and future, and attempt to construct a time with other collectives.

This is why, rather than a being together in the same time or at the same time, we can define the contemporary using the synthetic proposition—not analytic, since we deduce it by way of this empirical exploration—as those actions that *construct* a common time: as constructing a time together. In light of their critical and self-reflexive gaze, as well as the pathos and engagement exhibited by these initiatives for changing the future, these contemporary aesthetic practices can be characterised as postconceptual realism.

References

Adorno, Theodor. 1997. *Aesthetic Theory*. Translated by Robert Hullot-Kentor. London: Continuum. First published 1970 as *Ästhetische Theorie: Gesammelte Schriften 7*, edited by Gretel Adorno and Rolf Tiedemann (Frankfurt am Main: Suhrkamp).

Agamben, Giorgio. 2009. "What Is the Contemporary?" In *What Is an Apparatus? And Other Essays*, translated by David Kishik and Stefan Pedatella, 39–54. Stanford, CA: Stanford University Press. Essay first published 2008 as *Che cos'è il contemporaneo?* (Rome: Nottetempo).

Attali, Jacques. 1982. *Histoires du temps*. Paris: Fayard.

Bal, Mieke. 2016. *Tiempos Trastornados: Análisis, historias y políticas de la mirada*. Madrid: Akal.

Bonito Oliva, Achille. 2000. "Avanguardia/Transavanguardia 1968–1977." In *Los manifiestos del arte posmoderno: Textos de exposiciones, 1980–1995*, edited by Anna Maria Guasch, translated by César Palma, 10–16. Madrid: Akal. Essay first published 1983 in *Avanguardia transavanguardia* (Milan: Electra).

Bourriaud, Nicolas. 2002. *Relational Aesthetics*. Translated by Simon Pleasance and Fronza Woods with Mathieu Copeland. Dijon: Presses du réel. First published 1998 as *Esthétique relationnelle* (Dijon: Presses du réel).

Capdevila, Pol. 2015. "Aporetic Experiences

of Time in Anti-Narrative Art." *Journal of Aesthetics and Culture* 7 (1): 1–14.

Crary, Jonathan. 2014. *24/7: Late Capitalism and the Ends of Sleep*. London: Verso.

Didi-Huberman, Georges. 2000. *Devant Le Temps: Histoire de l'art et anachronisme des images*. Paris: Minuit.

Forensic Architecture. 2017. *Forensic Architecture: Hacia una estética investigativa*. Edited by Ekaterina Álvarez Romero and Clara Plasencia. Barcelona: RM Verlag. Published in conjunction with the exhibition of the same name, shown at MACBA Museu d'art Contemporani de Barcelona and MUAC Museo Univseritario Arte Contemporáneo, Mexico City.

Foster, Hal. 1983. *The Anti-Aesthetic: Essays on Postmodern Culture*. Port Townsend, WA: Bay Press.

———. 1996. *The Return of the Real: The Avant-Garde at the End of the Century*. Cambridge, MA: MIT Press.

Giunta, Andrea, and Agustín Diez Fischer. 2014. *¿Cuándo empieza el arte contemporáneo?/When Does Contemporary Art Begin?* Translated by Tamara Stuby. Buenos Aires: ArteBA.

Gumbrecht, Hans Ulrich. 2010. *Lento Presente: Sintomatología Del Nuevo Tiempo Histórico*. Translated by Lucía Relanzón Briones. Madrid: Escolar y Mayo.

Han, Byung-Chul. 2017. *The Scent of Time: A Philosophical Essay on the Art of Lingering*. New York: Wiley. First published 2015 as *Duft der Zeit: Ein philosophischer Essay zur Kunst des Verweilens* (Bielefeld: Transcript Verlag).

Hartog, François. 2015. *Regimes of Historicity: Presentism and Experiences of Time*. Translated by Saskia Brown. New York: Columbia University Press. First published 2003 as *Régimes d'historicité. Présentisme et expériences du temps* (Paris: Seuil).

Hernández, Miguel Ángel. 2016. "Contratiempos del arte contemporáneo." In *Contratiempos: Gramáticas de la temporalidad en el arte reciente*, edited by Isabel Durante Asensio, Ana García Alarcón, and Miguel Ángel Hernández, 19–28. Murcia: CENDEAC.

Joachimides, Christos M. 2000. "Los expresionismos y el nuevo espíritu de los tiempos." In *Los manifiestos del arte posmoderno: Textos de exposiciones, 1980–1995*, edited by Anna Maria Guasch, translated by César Palma, 13–17. Madrid: Akal. Essay first published 1981 as "A New Spirit in Painting," in *A New Spirit in Painting*, edited by Christos M. Joachimides, Norman Rosenthal, and Nicolas Serota (London: Royal Academy of Arts), 14–16.

Jones, Amelia. 2013. "Unpredictable Temporalities: The Body and Performance in (Art) History." In *Performing Archives/Archives of Performance*, edited by Gunhild Borggreen and Rune Gade, 53–72. Copenhagen: Museum Tusculanum Press.

Kant, Immanuel. 1987. *Critique of Judgment*. Translated by Werner S. Pluhar. Indianapolis: Hackett. First published 1790 as *Kritik der Urteilskraft* (Berlin: Lagarde und Friederich).

Keenan, Thomas, and Eyal Weizman. 2012. *Mengele's Skull: The Advent of a Forensic Aesthetics*. Frankfurt am Main: Sternberg Press.

Keightley, Emily. 2012. "Conclusion: Making Time—The Social Temporalities of Mediated Experience." In *Time, Media and Modernity*, edited by Emily Keightley, 201–23. London: Palgrave Macmillan.

Koselleck, Reinhart. (1985) 2004. *Futures Past: On the Semantics of Historical Time*. Translated by Keith Tribe. New York: Columbia University Press. First published 1979 as *Vergangene Zukunft: Zur Semantik geschichtlicher Zeiten* (Frankfurt am Main: Suhrkamp). This translation first published 1985 (Cambridge, MA: Cambridge University Press).

Lee, Pamela M. 2012. *Forgetting the Artworld*. Cambridge, MA: MIT Press.

Martínez Sánchez, Alfredo. 1999. "Tiempo, historia y acción: Condiciones prácticas de la réplica de Paul Ricoeur a las aporías de la temporalidad." *Daimon: Revista de Filosofía* 18: 123–34.

Menke, Christoph. 1998. *The Sovereignty of Art: Aesthetic Negativity in Adorno and Derrida*. Translated by Neil Solomon. Cambridge, MA: MIT Press. First published 1988 as *Die Souveränität der Kunst: Ästhetische Erfahrung nach Adorno und Derrida* (Frankfurt am Main: Athenäum).

Möntmann, Nina. 2017. "Plunging

into the World: On the Potential of Periodic Exhibitions to Reconfigure the Contemporary Moment." In "Documenta: Curating the History of the Present," edited by Nanne Buurman and Dorothee Richter, special issue, *Oncurating* 33: 122–31.

Moxey, Keith. 2013. *Visual Time: The Image in History*. Durham, NC: Duke University Press.

Osborne, Peter. 2013. *Anywhere or Not at All: Philosophy of Contemporary Art*. London: Verso.

Perlson, Hill. 2017. "The Most Important Piece at documenta 14 in Kassel Is Not an Artwork. It's Evidence." *Artnet Worldwide*, 8 June. Accessed 11 March 2019. https://news.artnet.com/exhibitions/documenta-14-kassel-forensic-nsu-trial-984701.

Preciado, Paul B. 2017. "The Parliament of Bodies." documenta 14. Accessed 11 March 2019. https://www.documenta14.de/en/public-programs/.

Rancière, Jacques. 1996. "Le concept d'anachronisme et la vérité de l'historien." *L'inactuel* 6: 53–68. Translated as "The Concept of Anachronism and the Historian's Truth" (*In/Print* 3 [1], article 3).

———. 2004. *The Politics of Aesthetics: The Distribution of the Sensible*. Edited and translated by Gabriel Rockhill. London: Bloomsbury. First published 2000 as *Le partage du sensible: Esthétique et politique* (Paris: La Fabrique).

Ricœur, Paul. 1984. *Time and Narrative, Volume 1*. Translated by Kathleen McLaughlin and David Pellauer. Chicago: University of Chicago Press. First published 1983 as *Temps et récit 1* (Paris: Seuil).

———. 1988. *Time and Narrative, Volume 3*. Translated by Kathleen Blamey and David Pellauer. Chicago: University of Chicago Press. First published 1985 as *Temps et récit 3* (Paris: Seuil).

Rosa, Hartmut. 2005. *Beschleunigung: Die Veränderung Der Zeitstrukturen in Der Moderne*. Frankfurt am Main: Suhrkamp.

———. 2016. *Resonanz: Eine Soziologie Der Weltbeziehung*. Berlin: Suhrkamp.

Ross, Christine. 2008. "The Suspension of History in Contemporary Media Arts." *Intermédialités* 11: 125–48.

Said, Edward. 1978. *Orientalism*. London: Routledge and Kegan Paul.

Shakespeare, William. (1623) 2005. *Hamlet*. In *The Oxford Shakespeare: The Complete Works*, edited by John Jowett, William Montgomery, Gary Taylor, and Stanley Wells, 2nd ed., 681–718. Oxford: Oxford University Press. Text based on the folio edition first published 1623 (London: Jaggard and Blount).

Smith, Terry. 2009. *What Is Contemporary Art?* Chicago: University of Chicago Press.

Speranza, Graciela. 2017. *Cronografías: Arte y ficciones de un tiempo sin tiempo*. Barcelona: Editorial Anagrama.

Szymczyk, Adam. 2017. "14: Iterability and Otherness: Learning and Working in Athens." In *The Documenta 14 Reader*, edited by Quinn Latimer and Adam Szymczyk, 17–42. Kassel: Documenta.

Virilio, Paul. 1991. *The Aesthetics of Disappearance*. Translated by Philip Beitchman. New York: Semiotext(e). First published 1980 as *Esthétique de la disparition* (Paris: Balland).

Part 3
Problematising the Contemporary

Working the Contemporary

History as a Project of Crisis, Today

Peter Osborne

Centre for Research in Modern European Philosophy, Kingston University London

It is a somewhat disquieting but also an invigorating experience to have one's ideas placed into a musical context when one has so little academic background in that area. I have started to think about some of the implications of such an operation elsewhere (Osborne 2018b). I shall not further those particular reflections here. Instead, this essay approaches the critical issue of the contemporary in another, more theoretically expansive way: on the one hand, *methodologically* and, on the other, as a *thematic extension* of what is already (relative to most other literature on the topic) a conceptually extended position. It focuses on the ongoing expansion of the domain of the contemporary as a structure of historical temporality on a global scale.[1] In this respect, the "future of the contemporary" posited here is not a new "content" of some sort—it is not "new contemporaries," as they say in the artworld, where in the UK the phrase names an annual exhibition of young artists sponsored by Bloomberg, the New York financial, data, and media corporation. Rather, the future of the contemporary posited here is one of extended spatial diffusion and thereby temporal intensification of its basic form of temporal disjunctive conjunction. The connection to music lies buried in the concept of temporalisation, as an active production and organisation of temporal relations—which is one way of describing music itself, of course. The gap between this extended conception of the contemporary and the still relatively closed discourses of "music" represents a challenge, issued to music by the generic concept of art and vice versa.

The dual methodological and thematic extension at stake here draws upon two somewhat disparate sources: Georges Canguilhem's famous account of what it means to "work" a concept, from his 1963 essay "Dialectique et philosophie du non chez Gaston Bachelard" ("Gaston Bachelard's Dialectics and Philosophy of No") and Manfredo Tafuri's account of what he calls "the historical 'project,'" in the introduction, of that title, to his collection of essays

---

1   Earlier versions of parts of this essay were presented in talks at the Academy of Fine Arts Nuremberg, École Normale Supérieure Paris, and the Architecture programme of the Royal Institute of Art Stockholm, prior to the 14th International Orpheus Academy for Music and Theory in May 2017. I am grateful to all who participated in the discussions on each of those occasions.

The Sphere and the Labyrinth: Avant-Gardes and Architecture from Piranesi to the 1970s (Tafuri 1987).

It might seem strange to take one text by a French philosopher of science from the early 1960s, and another by an Italian historian of architecture from the late 1970s, as the way in to a discussion of the concept of the contemporary today, since "contemporary" emerges as a *critical* category, within a transnational discourse of "theory," only in the course of the 1990s, in the wake of the rapid collapse in the plausibility of the concept of the postmodern after "1989"—a collapse almost as sudden as that of the Berlin Wall itself; although the basis of the former collapse was, of course, immanent within the concept of the postmodern itself from its beginnings. Yet, as I hope to show, these two texts address issues that are central to current theoretical debates about "the contemporary": namely, *transdisciplinary concept construction and critique*, on the one hand, and *historical criticism*, on the other, respectively.

So, it is not Tafuri's history of architecture that I am concerned with here, although there are clearly connections to it, as there are to his account of the historical destruction of architecture in his 1973 *Architecture and Utopia: Design and Capitalist Development* (Tafuri 1976). (We might ask whether anything comparable is currently happening to the concept of music.) Rather, it is Tafuri's contribution to the philosophy of history: specifically, (1) the philosophy of history as the philosophy of *historical time* (where "history" names the speculative totalisation of historical time—including all present futures), and (2) the philosophy of historical time *today*, that is, under the conditions of capital as a globalising process, viewed from the phenomenological standpoint of the present as history (*der Gegenwart als Geschichte*), or the standpoint of the construction of historical experience, to evoke the Benjaminian trope central to Tafuri's thinking.

I will be using Tafuri as a starting point to construct an argument that goes beyond anything that he wrote, but which nonetheless aims to remain true to the spirit of what I take to be his central concept in this field, first formulated in 1977: namely, not merely "history as a project," but "history as a *project of crisis*." It is this grammatically awkward construction—*project of crisis/progetto di crisi*—in particular, which I am interested in, with regard to the temporality of contemporaneity. However, there are only certain aspects of it that I will have the opportunity to discuss here.

I shall proceed via the exposition of a series of loosely related premises and theses, which I shall summarise, highly schematically, as I go along, and attempt to explain, very broadly, in their loose logical interconnections. So, this is as much an exercise or an experiment in a certain *method of construction* as it is an interpretation of Tafuri. This construction, I want to suggest, gives a new, living meaning to Tafuri's proposition, which, as I have said, appears in its definitive version in the introduction to *The Sphere and the Labyrinth*. This is the proposition, that "The historical 'project' [*il "progetto storico"*] is always the 'project of a crisis'" (Tafuri 1987, 3). Note that these two phrases are accompanied by inverted commas, as a sign of both their technical philosophical meaning and the self-consciousness of the irony they carry with them. This is an irony that is ineliminable from any post-Hegelian philosophy of history, even when—indeed, especially when—such a philosophy of history has been *existentially*, *temporally*, and *geo-politically* problematised and transformed by being converted from a narrative meta-genre into a philosophy of historical time, or better (to deploy an early Heideggerian concept in a new context), an account of historical *temporalisation*.

Furthermore, when one hears the key mediating term "project" here, in English—Tafuri's *progetto*—one should bear in mind not only its existential-ontological connotations (the translational shadow of Heidegger's *Entwurf* that became Sartre's *projet*), as mediated in Tafuri via Massimo Cacciari, and his parallel readings of Heidegger and Benjamin, but also the architectural connotations of *progetto* as "design" and "plan." Indeed, some would argue, one may detect the connotation of "architecture" itself. History is an *architecture of crisis*, we might say. Or, in the spirit of Tafuri's own architectural writings: *history has the architecture of the crisis of architecture*. For, in Tafuri, the concept of the "project of crisis" is a product of his perception of the so-called *crisis of architecture*—a formulation he actually rejected, since it suggests that "architecture," in its conventional meaning, might survive. For Tafuri, it cannot/has not. "Project of crisis," then, we might say, is an *architecture of crisis writ large*—writ large because it is addressed to the source of the crisis of architecture in history itself, that is, in the history of capitalism: in the subjection of architecture (i.e., the primacy of the project, design, or plan) to a capitalistic form of urban planning, in which the capital functions of building have primacy over all "architectural" form. Indeed, we might even say, extending a genealogical argument in Marx about the historical status of certain general concepts: "History" in the collective singular simply is the history, pre-history, and imaginary post-history of capitalism, since history is a process unified—constructed—at the level of actuality only by the movements of the alienated universalities of the forms of value, in their complex relations to the disarticulating or disassembling resistances to this unity, which these alienated universalities both provoke (in their relations to other, non-commodified forms of life) and immanently produce, as conditions of their own self-development.

I am going to take Tafuri's proposition, read as a *speculative* proposition—"History is a 'project of crisis'"—out of its original context as the philosophical ground of the historical criticism of architecture and insert it into a process of "working" the concept of the contemporary into a historical concept, in Canguilhem's famous sense of "working a concept." This sense is famous ever since the passage in question appeared on the inside cover of all nine volumes of the French structuralist journal *Cahiers pour l'analyse*, published in 1966–69. I will come back to the quotation itself, shortly.

There are two methodological matters to note here, then: (1) the idea of a speculative proposition (in its broadly Hegelian meaning), and (2) the idea of "working a concept." In brief, a "speculative proposition," in Hegel's technical sense, is a special kind of proposition that expresses an absolute identity (the self-identity of the absolute) and hence violates or exceeds the standard propositional structure of subject and predicate—here, for example, "history" would be the subject and "project of crisis" would be the predicate—since the predicate is equally the subject and the subject is equally the predicate. "The project of crisis is history." Neither is a mere attribute of the other; and neither is reducible to the substantial form of a grammatical subject either. In a speculative proposition the two are interchangeable, that is, reversible; an infinite process of reflection between the two sides is produced and condensed, never stabilising into a simple identity, but driven on by the difference between the aspects that are identified. One thus understands each through its difference from, in identity with, the other, in the context of a specific experience of each of the terms, in each instance.

Regarding the idea of "working a concept," the most recent translation of the passage in Canguilhem reads: "to work a concept . . . is [1] to vary its extension and comprehension, [2] to generalize it through the incorporation of exceptional traits, [3] to export it beyond its region of origin, [4] to take it as a model or on the contrary to seek a model for it—to work a concept, in short, is progressively to confer upon it, through regulated transformations, the function of a form" (Canguilhem 1963, 452, as translated in Miller 2012, 70). I want to "work" the concept of the contemporary in this way, primarily by inserting it into the discourse of the philosophy of history, and the philosophy of historical temporalisation in particular—thereby *varying* its extension and comprehension, *generalising* it through the incorporation of exceptional traits (specifically, its constitutively disjunctive structure), *exporting* it beyond its region of origin (which was art, design, and architecture), and *taking it as a model*, in order to *import it back* into the region of its origin (art), theoretically transformed, as the basis of a renewed "historical criticism" of art—and hence also of music. Such a circuit of exportation/reimportation would be one way of describing the function of philosophical discourse in the conceptual movement of my book *Anywhere or Not at All: Philosophy of Contemporary Art* (2013). In the present context, of course, the domain into which an extensive concept of "the contemporary" is to be reimported is "music"—a category the unity and hence status of which is challenged by the very demand made upon it by "contemporaneity" as a temporal form.

Here, I am as interested in the method and movement of this process of "working a concept" (crossing Canguilhem with Tafuri) as I am in the details of its particular results, since, following Tafuri, historical analysis and criticism are understood here as an endless dialectical process of construction and dismantling, in which—and this is the important bit—*criticism transgresses the limits it itself sets for analysis, thereby putting itself into crisis*, as an essential part of its attempt not simply to grasp, but also to produce, the historical process as crisis. To quote Tafuri (1987) again: "The real problem is how to project a criticism capable of constantly putting itself into crisis by putting into crisis the real" (9) since "criticism speaks only if the doubt with which it attacks the real turns back on itself as well" (12). One can detect the shadow of Hegel's phenomenological critique of transcendental philosophy here, lurking beneath the allusion to Lacan.

What we have here in this extraordinary text (revived but in no way explicated by Marco Biraghi's recent book on Tafuri, *Project of Crisis* [2013], the virtue of which is to send us back to Tafuri's own text) is a sketch for a kind of post-Foucauldian "phenomenology of the spirit of criticism"—a phenomenological dialectic of critical consciousness—in which the self-transformative aspect of dialectical reflection, the "turning back on itself" of criticism, appears in its *unresolved historical openness* as a putting into crisis of the critical subject, which projects it beyond itself and its self-legislated limits into a newly speculative historical space. This is what I call the "fiction" of the contemporary. To quote Tafuri (1987, 13) once more: "inasmuch as it [historical analysis] is social practice—a socializing practice—it is . . . obliged to enter into a struggle that puts into question its own characteristic features. Within this struggle, history must be ready to risk: to risk, ultimately, a temporary 'inactuality.'" This is the classically Hegelian phenomenological gamble, displaced from the stately progression of "shapes of spirit" in Hegel's *Phenomenology of the Spirit* (Hegel 2018) into the murky waters of the dialectical interplay of the mutual "putting into crisis" of history and criticism. "History *as* a 'project of crisis,' then," as Tafuri concludes after setting out what were for him the premises of a properly historical criticism of architecture.

Working the concept of the contemporary in this way (crossing Canguilhem and Tafuri) leads to a series of premises, theses, and conclusions, which may be summarily expressed as part of a quasi-deductive structure of philosophico-historical thinking, as follows.

> Premise 1: *History in the collective singular is the history, pre-history, and imaginary post-history of capitalism.*

This is the intellectual product of the materialist critique of the Enlightenment critique of religion: the product of successive displacements of the unity of history from divine exteriority, to providential reason, to a rationality immanent in the history of spirit, to the profane universalising dynamic of the capital relation. The Hegelian transformation of the concept of spirit from a metaphysical concept to a historical succession of social structures of recognition—albeit still within an onto-theological framework—is the key mediating moment.

This is history in the collective singular (which encompasses a massive multiplicity of histories within itself) in the sense in which Reinhart Koselleck wrote the early semantic history of the term, *Geschichte*, but to which (contra Koselleck) the concept in no way remains constrained today. Tafuri's methodological point is that critiques of the unity of this "history" cannot but establish new provisional, speculative forms of unity in their wake. He is in line here with Adorno's famous dictum from *Negative Dialectics*: "Universal history must be constructed and denied" (Adorno 1966, 312, my translation). In other words, the critical "provincialisation of universalism" that we find in texts like Dipesh Chakrabarty's *Provincializing Europe* (2000) can only ever be a passing critical moment in the recognition of the particularity of historically specific universals, since universalising the critique of the provincialism of historically particular universals poses anew the problem of the construction of the unity, or relationality, of multiple histories beyond the restricted logical forms of universality inherited from the philosophical tradition. This is the transdisciplinary aspect of constructions of "history" in the collective singular. Post-Hegelian theoretical forms of dialectical unity—be they based on the romantic fragment, the Benjaminian constellation, or the Deleuzian concatenation of singularities—necessarily encompass and cross a wide variety of disciplinary divides and forms of positivity.

Furthermore, this imperative to pose anew the problem of unity as the problem of the unity of relations, after each and every critical-analytical dismembering of historical unity, is not a *merely* methodological imperative but derives from the historical process itself. This is my second premise.

> Premise 2: *The unity of our current historical present is constituted by the uneven "globalisation" of the social relations of capital itself—specifically, by the relative denationalisation of the regulation of markets in finance capital after the passing of state communism in Eastern European ("1989") and China's entry into the World Trade Organisation ("2001").*

The mobility of financial capital, it would seem, is more important in this moment than the mobility of variable capital (migration) that drove post-war accumulation; although, increasingly regulated and policed forms of such mobility remain crucial (as the construction sites of the museums and football stadiums in Abu Dhabi and Qatar show, and as the Gulf Labor project is dedicated to exposing.)

I take the first two premises to be relatively uncontroversial. I shall combine them with my first two theses. These are:

> Thesis 1: *Contemporaneity is the temporality of globalisation (that is, the globalisation of capital and its temporal consequences).*[2]
>
> Thesis 2: *The temporality of globalisation (global contemporaneity) is a temporality of crisis— the temporality of a crisis of crisis, in fact.*

These need a little more explaining. The first point about *Thesis 1* is that in so far as globalisation involves a fundamental change in the spatio-temporal matrix of possible experience (to use a Kantian formulation in a historical way), these changes are not simply happening "within" historical time, in the famous "homogenous empty" sense of time diagnosed by Heidegger, Benjamin, and Althusser alike as "historicism." Rather, they represent a new form of historical temporalisation, opening up the space of new temporalisations of "history." The second point is that the specific form of temporality produced by the "globalisation" of the social processes dictating the historical temporality of modernity is best grasped by the *term* "con-temporaneity," as an internally temporally *dis*junctive historical-temporal form: a "total" (but *not* thereby abso-

---

2 See Appendix, below.

lute), radically disjunctive, contemporaneity, which modifies and renders internally more complex the still-insistent *temporality of the modern or the new*—what Adorno (1997, 21) called "the aesthetic seal of expanded reproduction," that is, the temporality of the accumulation of capital. These new spatial forms have made the mutually implicated temporal rhythms of accumulation and social dependency more complicated and intense.

You can see, then, that I do not accept the common argument that globalisation is a "homogenisation"—a reduction to spatio-temporal homogeneity—but rather the opposite: *globalisation involves an intensification of differential relations* within an always tenuous process of unification through synchronisation. Within this process, homogenisation operates at three levels: (1) the various abstract determinations of the value form (commodity, money, capital); (2) the internationalisation of regulatory frameworks (such as the European Court of Justice, for example, which is primarily a court of economic/contractual justice, as the UK is belatedly waking up to, at its cost), and (3) the communicational meta-medium of the internet and other satellite-based communication systems.

The first two of these are not new (so-called globalisation merely extends them spatially). The third provides the technological basis for new kinds of simultaneity that *produce disjunctions*—disjunctions between different temporalities—as much as they produce any kind of spatio-temporal unification.

Unification is not necessarily homogenisation. Antipathy to homogenisation is generally antipathy to capital and its effects, displaced onto its geo-political dynamic—globalisation—which is not actually itself primarily "homogenising" but rather productive of new differentials. It is these new differentials that are currently causing havoc with the still essentially nineteenth-century political forms of European states.

Regarding Thesis 2 (*the temporality of globalisation [global contemporaneity] is a temporality of crisis—the temporality of a crisis of crisis, in fact*): this follows from the meaning taken on by multiple temporal disjunctions within social processes that depend upon the synchronisation of these processes for their functioning. These are primarily processes of expanded reproduction across different sectors of the economy, regulatory frameworks of various sorts, and the temporalities of culturally specific practices and modes of life. The claim here is that there is a convergence between the disjunctive temporal structures of a global contemporaneity and the temporality of crisis itself, which changes the historico-philosophical structure of the concept of crisis, and hence our practical relations to it. This is manifested in a growing structural disjunction between the "objective" and "subjective" sides of the concept of crisis, corresponding to the poles of the difference constitutive of the process of globalisation: namely, the difference between "globality" as objective process and its subjectively "worldly" appropriation. After all, what is called "globalisation" is actually, philosophically, the "worlding" of the global (Osborne 2018a).

In its most extended sense, *contemporaneity* is thus the overarching temporal form of global crisis—it carries the temporality of crisis immanently within itself—because crises are principally expressions of forms of temporal disjunction. All structural crises of capitalism, for example, are at root crises of the realisation of value (or the over-production of value) grounded in *disjunctions between moments in the circuit of money-capital*, of one sort or another: grounded in a lack of balance, or *unbalancing*, as they now say, between the circuits of different kinds of capital, between sectors, or between regions of the system. These disjunctions each have specific temporal expressions or modes of existence the relational totality of which constitute any particular crisis.

A global contemporaneity creates a crisis in the temporality of crisis because it suggests a permanent crisis. This destroys the conceptual core of crisis itself as a moment of decision within a process of transition. Of the "objective," modern meaning of the term *crisis*, Koselleck, for example, writes, the "only certainty" is that the crisis will eventually end. Capitalist economic crises are periodic or cyclical, but, as Marx insisted (contra Adam Smith), "permanent crises do not exist" (Osborne 2010, 20). The "permanent transition" of the time-consciousness of modernity (the permanence of the new) is thus *not* a temporality of crisis. Their confusion, however, is commonplace.

Empirically, the socio-spatial—and hence temporal—presuppositions that previously rendered the aspiration to a general historical mediation credible, if tenuous, for a certain period, broadly the 1860s–1960s (namely, national capitals and national labour aligned to nation states, and socialist internationalism), no longer hold. Rather, economic crises are increasingly the product of the global markets in finance capital, structuring a global contemporaneity. There is thus now, simultaneously, both an apparent *convergence* between the temporal structures of crisis and contemporaneity (with their common basis in transnational and global capital), and an ever-greater disjunction between economic and political temporalities (between "events" and "acts," one might say), since the global mobility and speed of capital transactions has no equivalent at the level of the political management or transformative exploitation of crises, by inter- and transnational institutions and movements.

On the one hand, this gap reinforces the tendency to naturalise economic crises; on the other hand, however, because of the perceived source of the crisis in quite specific forms of economic and financial practice and mechanisms, it is re-politicising the perception of economic crisis, if only in a negative, reactive manner. Hence the current political situation: anti-capitalism without a post-capitalist imaginary—a series of abstract ideas (freedom, equality, communism) severed from historical meanings rooted in particular social relations.

At this point, let me introduce my final premise, of an early Heideggerian lineage, but displaced here from its existential-ontological basis in *Dasein*, into a more formally structuralist mode.

Premise 3: *Temporalisation is subjectivation.*

The "subjects" of historical temporalisation are not necessarily human individuals or even groups, collectives, or classes, as such.

This leads to Conclusion 1, as the product of Premises 1–3.

Conclusion 1: *Capital is the subject of history.*

Subject names the empty place/"utopic point" of the "action of the structure" of history. This is Tafuri's point of crisis. This is a "structuralist" thesis, to be sure, but it is not restricted to the French, "hyperformalist" structuralism from which this particular formulation derives (Miller 2012). Compare, for example, a sentence from Walter Benjamin of which Tafuri was particularly fond: "History is the subject of a construction [*Konstruktion*] whose site is . . . time filled full by now-time [*Jetztzeit*]" (Benjamin 2003, 395). This leads to Conclusion 2, as the product of Theses 1 and 2, Premise 3, and Conclusion 1.

Conclusion 2: *Global contemporaneity, as a temporalisation of crisis, is a new mode of subjectivation of history (albeit without a socially actual single subject).*

Rather, individual and social processes of subjectivation/de-subjectivation/re-subjectivation are articulated by this globally disjunctive subjectivation of contemporaneity. Hence, to return to Tafuri's notion of history as project, we finally reach Conclusion 3 (as product of all the above).

Conclusion 3: *History as a project is the negativity of the unity of global crisis; that is, the negativity of the unity of the disjunctions constitutive of global contemporaneity.*

This is a negativity that cannot be appropriated (other than imaginarily) by human individuals, groups, collectives, or classes, but to which any historically plausible political project must be *related and articulated*, as both its most general condition and the condition of its own generality. This raises the questions: How might such a contemporaneity be musically constructed? How might it be made to sound? (Osborne 2018b, 199).

Appendix: The word *contemporary*

The English word *contemporary* (like its French equivalent, *contemporain*), in its basic meaning of the "coming together in time" of two or more *lives* (and by extension objects or things) has a reasonably long history. Derived from the medieval Latin *contemporarius*, and the late Latin *contemporalis*, it dates from around the mid-seventeenth century. However, the philosophical thinking of contemporaneity is a distinctively post-Hegelian phenomenon, associated in the first instance with the thinking of same-timeness [*samtidighed*] in Kierkegaard's existential theology; and it emerges as a critical concept only in the course of the 1990s, in the wake of postmodernism as a category for periodising the present (which eventually went the way of its theoretical predecessor, postformalism: its abstract negation engendered only a chaotic multiplicity of particular forms.) The structure of what would become a philosophical concept of contemporaneity emerges in Kierkegaard's *Philosophical Fragments* (Kierkegaard 1985), in opposition to the everyday historicist meaning of the contemporary as living, existing, or occurring together in the same chronological time. Instead, it denotes the coming together of lives as a unity in disjunction, or constructively produced disjunctive unity of times. As Gadamer puts it in *Truth and Method*, in his ontological deployment of the Kierkegaardian notion against the idea of the "simultaneity of aesthetic consciousness": "for Kierkegaard, same-timeness [*Gleichzeitigkeit*[3]] does not mean 'existing at the same time'" (Gadamer [1989] 2004, 124, translation adjusted). It is "not a mode of givenness in consciousness, but a task for consciousness and an achievement that is demanded of it" (ibid., 123–24). More specifically, for Kierkegaard, contemporaneity "names the task that confronts the believer: to *bring together* two moments that are not concurrent, namely one's own present and the redeeming act of Christ, and yet so totally to mediate them that the latter is experienced and taken seriously as present (and not as something in a distant past)" (ibid., 124, my emphasis). It thus consists in "holding on to the thing in such a way that . . . all mediation is superseded in total presence." This appears, superficially, to be similar to the simultaneity of aesthetic consciousness. However, Gadamer argues, "aesthetic consciousness . . . is based on *covering up and concealing* the task set by [same-timeness/]contemporaneity" (ibid., my emphasis), while Kierkegaardian same-timeness or contemporaneity, despite its dissolution of mediation, nonetheless understands this immediacy, paradoxically, as an achievement, and not as a given—hence, its own proto-Hegelianism (cf. Kierkegaard 1985, chap. 4).

This philosophical notion of same-timeness as a task and achievement of temporal combination (of past and present within the present)—grasped in German perhaps only in *Zeitgenössenschaftlichkeit*, of all the awkward words used as translations of "contemporary" (this is the "time" in Boris Groys's "Comrades of Time" [2009])—largely remained confined to religious existentialism and the lived experience of vanguard politics until, in the immediate aftermath of the Second World War, the term *contemporary* began to acquire a historical meaning, through its use to denote a new epochal periodication in contrast to *the modern*.[4] The immediate post-war years saw new uses of *contemporary* in English to denote both an emergent style of design ("contemporary design") and the artistic present more generally ("contemporary arts"), in their differences from the preceding period. This is the source of that sense of up-to-dateness with which the term remains predominantly identified in popular usage.

However, the separating out of "modern" and "contemporary," which this notion of contemporary arts involves, in no way dominated the historical consciousness of the institutional field of art at that time. In fact, it has been only

---

3 *Gleichzeitigkeit* is Gadamer's German translation of *samtidighed*, misleadingly translated into English as "contemporaneity" in Gadamer ([1989] 2004, 123).

4 The remainder of this Appendix draws upon Osborne (2011a); see also Osborne (2013, chap. 1, section 1).

with the decisive discrediting of postmodernism as a coherent critical concept, in the last ten years or so, that "contemporary" began to emerge into the critical daylight from beneath its commonplace function as a label denoting what is current or up-to-date. At the same time, the structure of contemporaneity is itself changing. Indeed, the very idea of contemporaneity as a *condition* is new (see Osborne 2018a). At the same time, the widespread diffusion of the term has placed it in danger of being emptied of its increasingly complex temporal-existential, social, and political meanings, by being treated as a simple label or periodising category. Yet what seems distinctive and important about the changing temporal quality of the historical present over the last few decades is best expressed through the distinctive conceptual grammar of con-temporaneity, a coming together not simply "in" time, but *of* times: we do not just live or exist together "in time" with our contemporaries—as if time itself were indifferent to this existing together—but rather the present is increasingly characterised by a coming together of *different, but equally "co-present"* temporalities or "times," a temporal unity in disjunction, or the production of a *disjunctive unity of present times*.[5] This is a unity of a geo-politically diffuse multiplicity of social times, combined within a historical present that cannot be *experienced*, directly, as such, in its unity, but only engaged via the construction of constitutively problematic, speculative, or fictional collective subject-positions. In this regard, the competition between different periodisations of the contemporary (1945, 1960, 1989), from different social and historical standpoints, registers both the layered and the *epistemologically constructive* and *politically overdetermined* character of the term.

REFERENCES

Adorno, Theodor W. 1966. *Negative Dialektik*. Frankfurt am Main: Suhrkamp.
———. 1997. *Aesthetic Theory*. Translated by Robert Hullot-Kentor. Minneapolis: University of Minnesota Press. First published 1970 as *Ästhetische Theorie*, edited by Gretel Adorno and Rolf Tiedemann (Frankfurt am Main: Suhrkamp).
Benjamin, Walter. 2003. "On the Concept of History." In *Selected Writings, Volume 4: 1938–1940*, translated by Edmund Jephcott and others, edited by Howard Eiland and Michael W. Jennings, 389–400. Cambridge, MA: Belknap Press of Harvard University Press. Essay first published in 1942 as "Geschichtsphilosophische Reflexionen," in *Walter Benjamin zum Gedächtnis*, edited by Max Horkheimer and Theodor Wiesengrund Adorno (Los Angeles, CA: Institut für Sozialforschung).
Biraghi, Marco. 2013. *Project of Crisis: Manfredo Tafuri and Contemporary Architecture*. Translated by Alta Price. Cambridge, MA: MIT Press. First published 2005 as *Progetto di crisi: Manfredo Tafuri e l'architettura contemporanea* (Milan: C. Marinotti).
Canguilhem, Georges. 1963. "Dialectique et philosophie du non chez Gaston Bachelard." *Revue Internationale de Philosophie* 17 (66): 441–52.
Chakrabarty, Dipesh. 2000. *Provincializing Europe: Postcolonial Thought and Historical Difference*. Princeton, NJ: Princeton University Press.

5 In this respect, the temporality of the contemporary seems to involve something like a social actualisation of the insights of Heidegger's (1962, 456–72) critique of the "ordinary" time consciousness of "within-timeness" and Fabian's (1983, 156–65) critique of anthropology's denial of the coeval, respectively. See also, Osborne (2011b, 17, 28, 62–68).

Fabian, Johannes. 1983. *Time and the Other: How Anthropology Makes its Object*. New York: Columbia University Press.

Gadamer, Hans-Georg. (1989) 2004. *Truth and Method*. 2nd ed. Translation revised by Joel Weinsheimer and Donald G. Marshall. London: Continuum. First published 1960 as *Wahrheit und Methode: Grundzüge einer philosophischen Hermeneutik* (Tübingen: Mohr). 2nd ed. of translation first published 1989 (London: Sheed and Ward).

Groys, Boris. 2009. "Comrades of Time." *e-flux* 11. Accessed 12 December 2018. https://www.e-flux.com/journal/11/61345/comrades-of-time.

Hegel, Georg Wilhelm Friedrich. 2018. *The Phenomenology of Spirit*. Translated by Terry Pinkard. Cambridge: Cambridge University Press. First published 1807 as *Phänomenologie des Geistes* (Bamberg: Goebhardt).

Heidegger, Martin. 1962. *Being and Time*. Translated by John Macquarrie and Edward Robinson. Oxford: Blackwell. First published 1927 as *Sein und Zeit* (Halle an der Saale: Niemeyer).

Kierkegaard, Søren. 1985. *Philosophical Fragments; or, A Fragment of Philosophy*. In *Philosophical Fragments; Johannes Climacus*, edited and translated by Howard V. Hong and Edna H. Hong, 1–112. Kierkegaard's Writings 7. Princeton, NJ: Princeton University Press. *Philosophical Fragments* first published 1844 as *Philosophiske Smuler eller En Smule Philosophi* (Copenhagen: C. A. Reitzel).

Miller, Jacques-Alain. 2012. "Action of the Structure." Translated by Christian Kerslake, revised by Peter Hallward. In *Concept and Form, Volume 1: Key Texts from the* Cahiers pour l'Analyse, edited by Peter Hallward and Knox Peden, 69–84. London: Verso. Chapter first published 1968 as "Action de la structure" (*Cahiers pour l'Analyse* 9 [6]: 93–105).

Osborne, Peter. 2010. "A Sudden Topicality: Marx, Nietzsche and the Politics of Crisis." *Radical Philosophy* 160 (March/April): 19–26.

———. 2011a. "Look Beneath the Label: Notes on the Contemporary." In *Bloomberg New Contemporaries 2011*, edited by Eileeen Daly and Rebecca Heald, 4–8. London: New Contemporaries.

———. 2011b. *The Politics of Time: Modernity and Avant-Garde*. 2nd ed. London: Verso.

———. 2013. *Anywhere or Not at All: Philosophy of Contemporary Art*. London: Verso.

———. 2018a. "The Postconceptual Condition: Or, the Cultural Logic of High Capitalism Today'." In *The Postconceptual Condition: Critical Essays*, 3–23. London: Verso. An earlier version was published in *Radical Philosophy* 184 (March/April 2014): 19–27.

———. 2018b. "The Terminology in Crisis: Postconceptual Art and New Music." In *The Postconceptual Condition: Critical Essays*, 184–99. London: Verso. First published in German translation as "Die Idee der postkonzeptuellen Kunst (und Musik)" (*MusikTexte: Zeitschrift für neue Musik* 151 [November 2016]: 40–50).

Tafuri, Manfredo. 1976. *Architecture and Utopia: Design and Capitalist Development*. Translated by Barbara Luigia La Penta. Cambridge, MA: MIT Press. First published 1973 as *Progetto e utopia: Architettura e sviluppo capitalistico* (Bari: Laterza).

———. 1987. *The Sphere and the Labyrinth: Avant-Gardes and Architecture from Piranesi to the 1970s*. Translated by Pellegrino d'Acierno and Robert Connolly. Cambridge, MA: MIT Press. First published 1980 as *La sfera e il labirinto: Avanguardie e architettura da Piranesi agli anni '70* (Turin: G. Einaudi).

Untimeliness
in Contemporary Times

Jacob Lund

Aarhus University

No contretemps . . . without the promise of a now in common, . . .
the desired sharing of a living present.

—Jacques Derrida (1992, 421)

"Today, we are stuck in the present as it reproduces itself without leading to any future," philosopher and cultural critic Boris Groys remarks (2011, 90). Sharing the concern of Groys and a number of other thinkers that we have lost the future as a political object, this chapter discusses the temporal complexity of our current situation—to which extent it even makes sense to speak of *our* situation. The loss of a futural moment and thus of another temporal horizon than the present one is connected to a sense of an ever-expanding present, a present defined by a capacity only for a short-term perspective. The present is no longer a hinge between the past and the future but has rather—in the felicitous phrasing of historian François Hartog (2015)—become omnipresent. Such presentism, the sense that only the present exists, is a crisis of time.

The loss of the future as a political object has been theorised by—among many others—cultural critic Fredric Jameson who famously sees the postmodern as a weakness in our imagination, as it is easier for us today (Jameson lectured on this in 1991) to imagine the deterioration of the earth and of nature than the breakdown of capitalism (Jameson 1994, xi–xii). More recently it has been analysed by philosopher Peter Osborne. Rather than investigating when the present—the omnipresent present, which in fact, when the present is all there is, is a lack of a present—began, Osborne (2015, 186) calls for the present to begin again, the present as the time of action and the time of the production of a qualitatively different future.

Against this background, the aim of this chapter is to provide a critical reading of the notion of *untimeliness*, particularly in Giorgio Agamben's influential text "What Is the Contemporary?" (2009), as a decisive aspect of being contemporary. In an often-quoted passage, Agamben makes the Nietzschean claim that:

> Those who are truly contemporary, who truly belong to their time, are those who neither perfectly coincide with it nor adjust themselves to its demands. They are thus in this sense irrelevant. But precisely because of this condition, precisely through this disconnection and this anachronism, they are more capable than others of perceiving and grasping their own time. . . .

> Contemporariness is, then, a singular relationship with one's own time, which adheres to it and, at the same time, keeps a distance from it. More precisely, it is *that relationship with time that adheres to it through a disjunction and an anachronism.* Those who coincide too well with the epoch, those who are perfectly tied to it in every respect, are not contemporaries, precisely because they do not manage to see it; they are not able to firmly hold their gaze on it. (Agamben 2009, 40–41)

Untimeliness is about temporal disjunction and anachronism. Agamben writes of "their time," "their own time," "the epoch," but what is *our* own time and *our* epoch? Who in the post- or decolonial situation actually does take part in the possessive determiner "our"? I will argue that it is becoming increasingly difficult to identify a hegemonic "cultural" time in relation to which one can be untimely; that the current contemporaneity—understood with Peter Osborne as a technical term designating the coming together of different times in the same historical present (see Osborne 2013, 17)—makes it practically impossible to be untimely and thus avant-garde in the traditional sense. Claiming that under contemporary conditions of an intensified global interconnection of different times and social narratives it is no longer useful to employ Agamben's conception of *untimeliness* when trying to engage with the present in order to reinstall a futural moment—or to install other temporal horizons than the one in which we live—this chapter will try to indicate how a contemporary kind of untimeliness, characterised by operating in relation to several times at once and thus differentiating the presentist present, may be seen to appear in the poetics and artistic practice of Kader Attia.

1

Today it seems redundant to criticise the linearly progressive and teleological understanding of history that is often associated with Western modernity. As indicated above, however, the farewell to this idea of history also has consequences for the ways we may conceive critical relationships with the times in which we now live and thus for what it might mean to be untimely when (the idea of) linear unified homogeneous history has become obsolete. These consequences seem less clarified and therefore worth pursuing.

To get a sense of what we have left behind let us nonetheless begin by returning to the concept of untimeliness—or what Jacques Derrida (1992) might call *contretemps* or counter-time—and what it can be seen to criticise. As indicated above, Agamben takes his cue from Friedrich Nietzsche and reads the latter's second *Untimely Meditation,* "On the Uses and Disadvantages of History for Life" (Nietzsche 1997), as a claim for contemporary relevance based on a disconnection from his own time, on an out-of-jointness (Agamben 2009, 40). One might say that Nietzsche's contemporariness is due not only to his thinking simply being independent and out-of-joint with the dominant thinking of his time but also to the content of his thinking, which was an explicit critique of the then dominating historicist understanding of time and history. Without wanting to go into a detailed reading of Nietzsche's untimely revaluation of history (*Historie*) as life's teacher (*historia magistra vitae*) in favour of an understanding of history in the service of life (*historia ancilla vitae*), I think it is important to note that this revaluation includes a rejection of some of the philosophical-historical axioms that at the time had appeared to ground the modern concept of history. Most prominent in this context is his denial of any historical teleology able to grant meaning to history and of any historical necessity capable of injecting a meaning into history that would ultimately exclude human agency (see Koselleck 2018, 189–96).[1]

Agamben furthermore introduces a supplementary definition of contemporariness, which can be seen as an elaboration of the end section of the first part about being able to see one's own epoch: "The contemporary is he who firmly holds his gaze on his own time so as to perceive not its light, but rather its darkness" (Agamben 2009, 44). Through an analogy to our perception of the dark sky at night, where remote galaxies move away from us at a speed that is faster than the speed of the light that emanates from them, he defines the quality of being contemporary as "being able not only to firmly fix your gaze on the darkness of the epoch, but also to perceive in this darkness a light that, while directed toward us, infinitely distances itself from us. In other words, it is like being on time for an appointment that one cannot but miss" (ibid., 46). Thus, the present that the contemporary perceives cannot reach him or her: "The appointment that is in question in contemporariness does not simply take place in chronological time: it is something that, working within chronological time, urges, presses, and transforms it. And this urgency is the untimeliness, the anachronism that permits us to grasp our time in the form of a 'too soon' that is also a 'too late'; of an 'already' that is also a 'not yet'" (ibid., 47). The untimeliness of contemporariness is an urgency that takes place within chronological time while at the same transforming chronological time. In this way Agamben's analysis shares some structural similarities with Derridean deconstruction and the insight that there is no outside (no outside-text; *il n'y a pas de hors-texte*), but it also operates with *one* more or less unified epoch, with one identifiable hegemonic temporality and shared chronological time in which contemporariness takes place and which contemporariness transforms. This concept of time in the singular is a very Western—and male—one: its history includes Nietzsche, Barthes, Pericles, Robespierre, Sade, Mandelstam, Paul, the Messiah, Foucault, and Benjamin, and takes place in Paris, Athens, New York, and so on. It is therefore in a certain sense an undivided or undifferentiated time, which perhaps should be historicised in the light of the present state of globality to which cultures all over the planet have arrived via different historical trajectories.

Interestingly Agamben makes a last qualification of his conception of the contemporary: it is not only the one who perceives a light that cannot reach its destination; the contemporary "is also the one who, dividing and interpolating time, is capable of transforming it and putting it in relation with other

---

1   The Nietzschean critique of modern historicism of course also inspired Michel Foucault in his development of a genealogical approach in "Nietzsche, Genealogy, History" (Foucault 1977). Foucault's rejection of "the metahistorical deployment of ideal significations and indefinite teleologies" (140), however, necessarily still operates within a "pre-global era" and thus within a very Western tradition and cultural sphere. It is therefore—for good historical reasons—unable to take the current condition of contemporaneity into consideration.

times" (ibid., 53). I would claim, however, that today these other times should relate not only to the past—and perhaps the future—on the axis of Western chronological time but also to other cultural times formed along other trajectories.[2] Today chronological recomposition and Hartog's notion of "regimes of historicity" (2015) as changing articulations of the structure of past, present, and future are too reductive to allow us to understand temporal complexity. As I will try to show later, such a complex inclusion or entanglement of different cultural times in the constitution of the present may be said to take place in the work of Kader Attia.

2

As indicated above, Nietzsche's second *Untimely Meditation* should not be read as a critique and rejection of historicism in itself—defined by "the basic thesis that every aspect and expression of human life is unavoidably conditioned by history" (Breazeale 2018, xv)—but rather of the teleology and necessity with which it is often associated. Walter Benjamin's reflections on the concept of history (*Geschichte*), written in 1940 and posthumously published in 1942, provide an elaborated critique of this notion of historicism (Benjamin 1992). As Peter Osborne explains, the use and notion of historicism that Benjamin criticises is the version associated with the Historical School in Germany, developed in the latter part of the nineteenth century in direct opposition to Hegel's philosophy of history (see Osborne 1995, 138–44)—in Hegel, time is self-motivated and unfolds in the form of the workings of the spirit as it moves towards itself through the ages of history (Hegel 1975). The version of historicism that Benjamin addresses is thus a form of historical time-consciousness, which is characterised not only by an objectivism about knowledge of the past "the way it really was (Ranke)" but also by the idea of history as progress (Benjamin 1992, 391). According to Benjamin, the historicist conception of history as progressing through "a homogeneous, empty time" (ibid., 395) involves a naturalisation of chronological, continuous history and an oblivion of the constitutive role of the present in any time-consciousness, as the point from where history is given direction. For Benjamin, history, in Osborne's (1995, 141) formulation, "is an economy of violence dissembling as progress"; needless to say, he regards the idea of progress with contempt. Benjamin is looking for a "different, *qualitative* experience of the 'now' as an *historical* present" (ibid., 143). The instantaneity of the now is thus a historical rather than a merely natural or a priori given form of temporality.

Such a kairotic moment, such untimeliness, may find a part of its conceptual prehistory in Kant. In the *Critique of Pure Reason*, time—alongside space— forms part of Kant's transcendental aesthetics where these two entities are regarded as necessary for cognition: they are required in order for anything to appear before us, thereby being sensed, perceived, and known (1.1.2.4, Kant

---

2 The art historiographical consequences of what I prefer to call the condition of contemporaneity are explored in a recent anthology, *Time in the History of Art: Temporality, Chronology and Anachrony*, edited by art historians Dan Karlholm and Keith Moxey (2018). See also my *Anachrony, Contemporaneity and Historical Imagination* (Lund 2019).

1855, 28–29). Time is a basic condition for the realisation of any phenomenon, but whereas those phenomena may well disappear again, time itself cannot. Kant famously claims that time "is not an empirical conception," but necessarily "exist[s] as a foundation *a priori*," which makes possible axioms of time in general, such as "time has only one dimension" and "different times are not co-existent but successive" (ibid., 28). In Kant's first critique, time is thus an a priori given, independent of our sensory perception.

The concept of contemporaneity of course challenges such a transcendental notion of time and the idea that it is exclusively one-dimensional and that different times cannot co-exist. But Kant's own analysis of the sublime nine years later in the *Critique of Judgement* (Kant 2007) constitutes a challenge to the transcendental notion of time too. Here, the sublime is not only an ungraspable magnitude that exceeds any individual subjective experience or perception but also a moment where simultaneity or coexistence is made intuitable. The intuition of coexistence involves a negation of temporality, a movement beyond the capacities of sensation and conceptual determination to the realm of reason, whereby successive apprehension is replaced by an instantaneous grasping (see Wayne 2014, 121). Thus, "the unstable form of the sublime is," as Michael Wayne remarks in his book *Red Kant*, "inextricably linked with a new and potentially radical conception of temporality and history" (ibid.).

In the *Critique of Pure Reason*, the imagination is linked to time as the form of inner sense. Relative to the understanding, its function is to synthesise the progressive sequence of representations in time. In the sublime, by contrast, the imagination is related to reason and in a reversal of its normal operation institutes what Kant calls a "regression" (*ein Regressus*) that annihilates the condition of time and makes possible the intuition of coexistence (see Makkreel 1984, 303):

> Measurement of a space (as apprehension) is at the same time a description of it, and so an objective movement in the imagination and a progression. On the other hand the comprehension of the manifold in the unity, not of thought, but of intuition, and consequently the comprehension of the successively apprehended parts at one glance [*in einen Augenblick*], is a retrogression that removes the time-condition in the progression of the imagination, and renders *co-existence* intuitable [*und das Zugleichsein anschaulich macht*]. Therefore, since the time-series [*die Zeitfolge*] is a condition of the internal sense and of an intuition, it is a subjective movement of the imagination by which it does violence to inner sense—a violence which must be proportionately more striking the greater the quantum which the imagination comprehends in one intuition. (Kant 2007, 89)

The sublime violates the model of linear temporal progression in the ordering of the manifold that Kant mapped out in the *Critique of Pure Reason* where he emphasised the successive apprehension of percepts in a temporal sequence. The sublime radically shifts to an instantaneous grasping of what is coexisting. Thus "comprehending in one instant what is apprehended successively, is a regression that in turn cancels the condition of time in the imagination's progression" (Kant, *Critique of Judgement* §27, as translated in Wayne 2014, 121).

The sublime involves a radical cancelling of ordinary temporal unfolding and a disruption of our habitual ways of perceiving and experiencing the world; but, rather than annihilating time as such, the regress of the imagination—the comprehension in an instant of what was successively apprehended—suggests a possible negation of the mathematical or linear form of time (see Makkreel 1984, 308).

In this way, Kant's analysis of the sublime might be seen as a tacit model for Benjamin's concept of *Jetztzeit* (translated as "now-time" or the "presence of the now") that describes time at a standstill where the past, in a flash, enters into a constellation with the present, objectively interrupting the mechanical temporal process of historicism (Benjamin 1992; 2002, 262). Just as the sublime interrupts the successive apprehension described in the *Critique of Pure Reason*, dialectics at a standstill interrupt and open the linear continuum of history.

In Benjamin, the dialectical convergence of past and present therefore holds a political potential. His ambition is to explode "the continuum of history" (Benjamin 1992, 395) in order to make it possible to recompose it (see Cox and Lund, forthcoming). His now-time is a constructive form of temporality in which "the slivers of history," as emphasised by political theorist Isabell Lorey in her recent reading of Benjamin's reflections on the concept of history, "are newly composed, in which history persistently emerges. The now-time is the creative midpoint, not a transition of the past into the future" (Lorey 2014). Unlike the presentism described by Hartog, Groys, and others, Benjaminian now-time becomes time filled with emancipatory possibilities (rather than mere probabilities): "History is the subject of a structure whose site is not homogeneous, empty time, but time filled by the presence of the now [*Jetztzeit*]," as Benjamin (1992, 395) remarks in the famous passage that I already quoted in part above. Time is not an empty, homogeneous duration unaffected by the events that fill it. Time itself has a history and politics. It is mediated, constructed, and multiple, not a blank a priori, and there are many different co-existing ways of being in time and belonging to it. The experience of contemporaneity is perhaps sublime in the sense that it is an interruption of unified linearly ordered time, but the contemporary condition does not allow us any distance to that which otherwise would elicit an experience of the sublime—today there is no temporal outside to the sublime spectacle, so to speak.

The difficulty, I argue, of experiencing the Kantian sublime today not only concerns the cancellation of our distance to that which triggers the sublime experience, the loss of a secure position from where to experience something as a sublime spectacle. There is also an important *temporal* aspect in that we no longer enjoy the comfort of a secure position in relation to a one-dimensional time, from where to grasp time or to establish a disjunctive relationship with time, thereby becoming untimely as in Giorgio Agamben's definition of the contemporary. Contemporaneity may, of course, be seen as synchronisation and standardisation of all the world's cultures and time-experiences, in line with a conception of the sublime as "a symptom of the supersensible totality of global capitalism" (Wayne 2014, 118); but, it can also—as an, in principle, shared present, a globally shared experience of co-presence—be seen to hold a potential to interrupt the mechanical progression or rather accumulation and repetition of what is without alternatives.

To be untimely *then*—that is, under the modern regime of historicity—was to not coincide with the present time in the singular; to be untimely *now* is to act on present times in the plural and to counter the time of global capital, which is about standardisation, synchronisation, and accumulation with no other temporal horizon, with no different future, even if imagined. In Peter Osborne's analysis, a large part of what we call "contemporary art" works in the service of such synchronising and standardising global capital. I do not, however, think that we should only deplore that the institutions of contemporary art have created a new kind of cultural space, "dedicated," in the words of Osborne (2013, 27), "to the exploration through art of similarities and differences between geopolitically diverse forms of social experience that have only recently begun to be represented within the parameters of a common world." Osborne (2010, 9) sees the new international biennials as "emblems of capital's capacity to cross borders, and to accommodate and appropriate cultural differences. Art labour," he claims, "is variable cultural capital." The idea of contemporaneity, understood as the "projection of the temporal unity of the present across the planet" (ibid., 7), is no doubt grounded in the interpenetration of social forms and cultural clusters by capital and their consequent interconnection and dependency; but the experience and cultural significance of contemporaneity cannot merely be reduced to the workings of global capital.[3] Some of the most interesting contemporary art explores the possibilities for installing a social imagination beyond capitalism on the conditions of contemporaneity, which largely is the consequence of the development of that very capitalism without being reducible to it. Perhaps it is therefore time to pay attention to and allow for cultural difference in the—at a certain level at least—globally shared present, as the access to this present is still highly unevenly distributed. Anthropologist Marc Augé describes a new condition of radical contemporaneity between peoples and cultures:

> It is only now, in the rather blinding light of a generalized situation of cultural circulation, that we can become aware of what the eruption of the outside world into their societies has meant for certain peoples. Likewise, it is only today that the conditions of a contemporaneous anthropology are emerging, in the sense that the dialogue between observer and observed is inscribed in a universe where both recognize each other, even though they continue to occupy different and unequal positions. Contemporaneity cannot be decreed; the transformation of the world imposes it. (Augé 1999, 50)

The speed of cultural, economic, and migratory circulation has inaugurated *a generalised sharing of time*. "The world's inhabitants have at last become truly contemporaneous," Augé states (ibid., 89). Due to this circulation, there is now an undeniable co-existence of different temporalities.

---

3 Roughly put, Osborne mainly focuses on the damaging dimension of contemporaneity (i.e., on synchronisation and presentism), whereas for instance Terry Smith in his analysis emphasises a co-existence of different temporalities and the possibility of "planetary thinking."

The time in relation to which one should be untimely today is the complex temporality of global capital subjecting all social forms to its standardising logic. Untimeliness today may consist of differentiating the presentist present, opposing colonising synchronisation by marking or articulating a contemporaneity of difference that permits another kind of what art historian Terry Smith calls "world-making" and "coeval composition" (Smith 2015, 2016).

3

Kader Attia is a contemporary artist in the sense that he—unlike modernist artists who produce new work and carry the progressive history of art forward (see Danto 1997, 4–5)—is occupied with establishing relationships, or what he calls restitutions and reparations, with the past and allow it to take part in the present. The pasts that he actualises are, however, pasts that come from places and cultures that do not share the Western point of view on history. The different—and from a modern Western progressivist perspective hitherto "other" and perhaps even developmentally "delayed" or non-coeval (Fabian 1983)—cultural temporalities that are being brought to the fore and become visible and audible in Attia's reconfiguration of "the distribution of the sensible" (Rancière 2004) are not necessarily reduced in their difference. They are not being made to comply with a neocolonial standard set by a Western-dominated notion of art and cultural signification; rather, they enter into relationships while retaining their prehistories and particularities. In Attia's work they often in a certain sense incorporate the otherness of the colonising cultures—which of course also have been the primary motors in the globalisation of capitalism—but leave this incorporation or appropriation visible without covering it up and without wanting to return to an original, "non-contaminated" state of self-identity, to a time and history that is exclusively their own.

Attia's work thus engages in a global dialogue, intervening in and seeking to replace the Western monologue. It addresses cultural questions and global issues concerning the coming together of Occidental and Oriental (or extra-Occidental) cultures with a focus on politics, on living together—including in very concrete ways in works that deal with social housing projects. For instance, in the piece *Oil and Sugar #2* (2007), he worked with the "colonial" materials of oil and sugar. In *Holy Land* (2006) he installed almost a hundred mirrors on a beach on the Canary Islands to help African migrants at sea navigate, but also to complexly signal that this is not any holy land as the mirrors were shaped to look like tombstones—as well as surfboards and the windows of Gothic cathedrals. His work thus aims not only to criticise colonial history but also, and more so, to criticise the coloniality of now—as part of this endeavour he opened the cultural space with the telling name la colonie in Paris in 2016. Central to this is the relationship between injury and repair, concretely as well as psychologically and metaphorically. *Ghardaïa* (2009), for instance, is a fragile model of the "functionalist" eleventh-century Algerian city—which inspired modernist architects like Le Corbusier—made from couscous and thus constituting a kind of repair of the relationship between Western modernity and the ancient Mzab culture and reinstalling time and a historical trace:

> Lack of quotation is lack of acknowledgement. Even today, when Le Corbusier's work is the focus of a retrospective, Mozabite architecture is mentioned succinctly, in the best case. During a huge exhibition of his work in London, you could only see two postcards from Ghardaïa. We should try to imagine this conversation in another context, in Algeria or Congo for instance, so you can see how much Algerian or Congolese people could learn about the extent of their own heritage upon the world. Even though colonization is now over, it is still a fact that entire intellectual territories and areas have not been freed yet, or at least "reappropriated" by the traditional cultures representing the very origins of European "sources of inspiration" (Attia 2014, 180).

Attia's documentary film *Reflecting Memory* (2016), to add another example that deals with establishing relationships with "unacknowledged" pasts in the present, explores the phenomenon of phantom limbs as a way of addressing the phantom limbs of cultural complexes and the hauntings that remain within our consciousness:

> It was by extending to the human psyche the body of my political research on the concept of reparation that I fathomed the importance of the immaterial character of wounds, and the silent cry that they emit between official History and the one lived endlessly in the secret of family and community stories. Mass traumas and injustices or those of simple individuals last far longer than the initial act; they are maintained by the dominant power's stories while the mind imposes, troubles, and hides the necessity of their denunciation. This absolute, quasi-religious conception of science as a factor of modernity dominates the human psyche by the universalism of its conception of progress. This hegemony has led inevitably to the production of opposed reactions. (Attia 2018b)

Repair has thus become a central concept and concern in Attia's poetics and artistic practice (Attia 2014)—a recent piece, *Le grand miroir du monde* (The grand mirror of the world, 2017), simply consists of a large rectangle of broken mirrors covering the whole floor of the gallery space.[4] Attia—who was trained in philosophy—talks of the ambiguity of the concept of repair or reparation and opposes the way in which it is understood in so-called traditional non-Western civilisations to the way it is understood in modern civilisations. The modern repair tries to erase the traces of the injury and bring the object back to its original shape, which according to Attia involves a denial of time as the removing of the injury is actually a removing of time, of the history of the object. The non-Western repair, in contrast, keeps the trace of the injury and acknowledges what has happened to the object. It therefore adds to the history of the object (Attia 2018a).

---

4   The dimensions of the piece vary according to the specific exhibition site.

Historian, philosopher, and political theorist Achille Mbembe writes of the postcolonial present where a multiplicity of co-existing times and traditions (see Chakrabarty 2000, 109) are interconnected and are being brought to bear on the same present as "the *time of entanglement*": "This time of African existence is neither a linear time nor a simple sequence in which each moment effaces, annuls, and replaces those that preceded it, to the point where a single age exists within society. This time is not a series but an *interlocking* of presents, pasts, and futures that retain their depths of other presents, pasts, and futures, each age bearing, altering, and maintaining the previous ones" (Mbembe 2001, 16, his italics).5 Nietzsche's and Agamben's contemporary person were a Western person, or man, who is able to establish a disjunctive relationship with his, or her, *own* time, that is, with a singular, unified Western progressivist time and history. Attia's work of repair complicates this modern untimeliness by introducing other times, other pasts, and by allowing hitherto unheard pre-histories to the present to become audible in a shared, entangled contemporary present. The reparative relationships with different pasts that Attia's artistic practice brings into being somehow interfere with and differentiate an otherwise synchronised present—and thereby imply at least a potential for imagining another, decolonised future where several cultural traditions take part in the constitution of the present.

REFERENCES

Agamben Giorgio. 2009. "What Is the Contemporary?" In *What Is an Apparatus? And Other Essays*, translated by David Kishik and Stefan Pedatella, 39–54. Stanford, CA: Stanford University Press. First published 2008 as *Che cos'è il contemporaneo?* (Rome: Nottetempo).

Attia, Kader. 2014. *Repair*. Edited by Léa Gauthier. Paris: Blackjack éditions.

———. 2018a. "Kader Attia Speaks about the Idea of Repair" (interview with Judith Benhamou-Huet). YouTube video, 2:38, posted by "Judith Benhamou-Huet Reports," 22 May. Accessed 14 March 2019. https://www.youtube.com/watch?v=PBYoL6z4V7Q.

———. 2018b. "The Field of Emotion." Kader Attia homepage. Accessed 14 March 2019. http://kaderattia.de/the-field-of-emotion/.

Augé, Marc. 1999. *An Anthropology for Contemporaneous Worlds*. Translated by Amy Jacobs. Stanford, CA: Stanford University Press. First published 1994 as *Pour une anthropologie des mondes contemporains* (Paris: Aubier).

Benjamin, Walter. 1992. "On the Concept of History." In *Selected Writings, Volume 4, 1938–1940*, translated by Edmund Jephcott and others, edited by Howard Eiland and Michael W. Jennings, 389–400. Cambridge, MA: Belknap Press of Harvard University Press. Essay first published 1942 as "Geschichtsphilosophische Reflexionen," in *Walter Benjamin zum Gedächtnis*, edited by Max Horkheimer and Theodor Wiesengrund Adorno (Los Angeles, CA: Institut für Sozialforschung).

———. 2002. *The Arcades Project*. Translated by Howard Eiland and Kevin McLaughlin. Cambridge, MA: Belknap Press of Harvard University Press. Written 1927–40, first published 1982 as *Das Passagen-Werk*, edited by Rolf Tiedemann (Frankfurt am Main: Suhrkamp).

---

5 On the register of the postcolony as, initially, a reference to a chronological moment that ambiguously signals an end of colonisation and a beginning of the establishment of a new nation-form, see Harootunian (2015, 197–234).

Breazeale, Daniel. 1997. Introduction to Nietzsche 1997, vii–xxxiii.

Chakrabarty, Dipesh. 2000. *Provincializing Europe: Postcolonial Thought and Historical Difference*. Princeton, NJ: Princeton University Press.

Cox, Geoff, and Jacob Lund. Forthcoming. "Time.now."

Danto, Arthur C. 1997. *After the End of Art: Contemporary Art and the Pale of History*. Princeton, NJ: Princeton University Press.

Derrida, Jacques. 1992. "Aphorism Countertime." Translated by Nicholas Royle. In *Acts of Literature*, edited by Derek Attridge, 414–33. New York: Routledge. First published 1986 as "L'aphorisme à contretemps," in *Roméo et Juliette: Le livre* by Gervais Robin after William Shakespeare (Paris: Papiers).

Fabian, Johannes. 1983. *Time and the Other: How Anthropology Makes its Object*. New York: Columbia University Press.

Foucault, Michel. 1977. "Nietzsche, Genealogy, History." In *Language, Counter-Memory, Practice: Selected Essays and Interviews by Michel Foucault*, translated by Donald F. Bouchard and Sherry Simon, edited by Donald F. Bouchard, 139–64. Ithaca, NY: Cornell University Press. First published 1971 as "Nietzsche, la généalogie, l'histoire," in *Hommage a Jean Hyppolite*, 145–72 (Paris: Presses universitaires de France).

Groys, Boris. 2011. "Comrades of Time." In *Going Public*, 84–101. Berlin: Sternberg Press.

Harootunian, Harry. 2015. *Marx after Marx: History and Time in the Expansion of Capitalism*. New York: Columbia University Press.

Hartog, François. 2015. *Regimes of Historicity: Presentism and Experiences of Time*. Translated by Saskia Brown. New York: Columbia University Press. First published 2003 as *Régimes d'historicité: Présentisme et expériences du temps* (Paris: Seuil).

Hegel, Georg Wilhelm Friedrich. 1975. *Aesthetics: Lectures on Fine Art*. Translated by T. M. Knox. 2 vols. Oxford: Clarendon Press. First delivered as lectures 1818–29.

Jameson, Fredric. 1994. *The Seeds of Time*. New York: Columbia University Press.

Kant, Immanuel. 1855. *Critique of Pure Reason*. Translated by J. M. D. Meiklejohn.

London: H. G. Bohn. First published 1781 as *Kritik der reinen Vernunft* (Riga: J. F. Hartknoch).

———. 2007. *Critique of Judgement*. Translated by James Creed Meredith, revised and edited by Nicholas Walker. Oxford: Oxford University Press. First published in 1790 as *Kritik der Urteilskraft* (Berlin: Lagarde und Friederich).

Karlholm, Dan, and Keith Moxey, eds. 2018. *Time in the History of Art: Temporality, Chronology and Anachrony*. New York: Routledge.

Koselleck, Reinhart. 2018. "On the Meaning and Absurdity of History." In *Sediments of Time: On Possible Histories*, translated and edited by Sean Franzel and Stefan-Ludwig Hoffmann, 177–96. First published 1997 as "Vom Sinn und Unsinn der Geschichte" (*Merkur* 51: 319–34).

Lorey, Isabell. 2014. "Presentist Democracy: Exodus and Tiger's Leap." Translated by Aileen Derieg. *Transversal Texts*, June. Accessed 14 March 2019. http://transversal.at/blog/Presentist-Democracy.

Lund, Jacob. 2019. *Anachrony, Contemporaneity and Historical Imagination*. Berlin: Sternberg Press.

Makkreel, Rudolf. 1984. "Imagination and Temporality in Kant's Theory of the Sublime." *Journal of Aesthetics and Art Criticism* 42 (3): 303–16.

Mbembe, Achille. 2001. *On the Postcolony*. Translated by A. M. Berrett, Janet Roitman, Murray Last, and Steven Rendall. Berkeley: University of California Press. First published in 2000 as *De la postcolonie: Essai sur l'imagination politique dans l'Afrique contemporaine* (Paris: Karthala).

Nietzsche, Friedrich. 1997. "On the Uses and Disadvantages of History for Life." In *Untimely Meditations*, edited by Daniel Breazeale, translated by R. J. Hollingdale, 60–123. Cambridge: Cambridge University Press. Essay first published 1874 as "Vom Nutzen und Nachteil der Historie für das Leben," 2nd part of *Unzeitgemässe Betrachtungen* (Leipzig: Fritzsch, 1873–76).

Osborne, Peter. 1995. *The Politics of Time: Modernity and Avant-Garde*. London: Verso.

———. 2010. "Contemporary Art is Post-conceptual Art." Lecture given at Fondazione Antonio Ratti, Villa Sucota, Como, 9 July 2010. Accessed 14 March 2019. http://www.fondazioneratti.org/mostre/103/contemporary_art_is_post-conceptual_art. Page numbers refer to the PDF transcript.

———. 2013. *Anywhere or Not at All: Philosophy of Contemporary Art*. London: Verso.

———. 2015. "Existential Urgency: Contemporaneity, Biennials and Social Form." *Nordic Journal of Aesthetics* 24 (49–50): 175–88.

Rancière, Jacques. 2004. *The Politics of Aesthetics: The Distribution of the Sensible*. Edited and translated by Gabriel Rockhill. London: Continuum. First published 2000 as *Le partage du sensible: Esthétique et politique* (Paris: La Fabrique).

Smith, Terry. 2015. "Defining Contemporaneity: Imagining Planetarity." *Nordic Journal of Aesthetics* 24 (49–50): 156–74.

———. 2016. *The Contemporary Composition*. The Contemporary Condition 2. Berlin: Sternberg Press.

Wayne, Michael. 2014. *Red Kant: Aesthetics, Marxism and the Third* Critique. London: Bloomsbury.

Experimental Systems

Contemporaneity, Untimeliness, and Artistic Research

Michael Schwab
Journal for Artistic Research (JAR)

Arguably, "contemporary art" is today's standard model for artistic practice. As in physics, where its "standard model" combines various—but not all—phenomena into a coherent theory, a standard model acts as a norm against which new findings are to be evaluated. Given the historical stability of such standard models, the most likely outcome will be that they absorb what initially looked like departures. However, given their restriction, on the one hand, and their reflectiveness, on the other, such "standard models" can also act as a springboard for historical change. Paradigm shifts become inevitable when standard models lose traction.

However, despite the term's ubiquity, claiming that "contemporary art" is art's current standard model is perhaps problematic since clear definitions of how it is to be practised are missing. For instance, in places where contemporary art is taught—such as the art schools at which I have worked—nobody ever teaches definitions of contemporary art that a student could apply. At the same time, there has been a recent wave[1] of research into contemporaneity and writing about contemporary art that has started to affect the situation, lending concepts to practitioners who want to evaluate how what they do fits those concepts, and vice versa. Despite the various philosophical positions taken in this development, it seems clear to me that on the ground "contemporary art" is seen as a shared historical phenomenon rather than some form of ongoing "ending" of (art's) history, which may have been modernity's utopian or postmodernism's dystopian narrative from which we have been recovering.[2]

However, despite acting as such a strong point of reference, at least to me, "contemporary art" does not look like a coherent whole. In moving away from those narratives, contemporary art seems to have managed to bind together two seemingly opposing forces, the aesthetic and the epistemic, without

---

1   Recent books on the topic include Smith, Enwezor, and Condee (2008); Smith (2009); Aranda, Wood, and Vidokle (2010); Osborne (2013a); Cox and Lund (2016).

2   Postmodernism's historical relevance to the development of notions of contemporaneity is unclear. While the literature seems to suggest postmodernism's role is reducing—say, from Antonio Negri's text "Contemporaneity between Modernity and Postmodernity" (2008) to Peter Osborne's *Anywhere or Not At All* (2013a. 17)—it is also the case that postmodernism must be put into perspective when assessing contemporaneity.

installing a meaningful relationship between them that could act as a fail-safe at its borders. On the aesthetic side, contemporary art seems to flirt with the spectacle (Guy Debord), which even when aiming at critical practice risks being quickly absorbed into the marketplace; on the other, epistemic side—sometimes in relation to aesthetics defined as *inaesthetics* (Alain Badiou) or *anaesthetics* (Wolfgang Welsch)—we may have political art or institutional critique, in which art risks being overdetermined and made to fit into particular political programmes. (Although with a different aim in mind, Walter Benjamin already defined these two extremes in *The Work of Art in the Age of Mechanical Reproduction* when in the epilogue he says: "This is the situation of politics which Fascism is rendering aesthetic. Communism responds by politicizing art" [Benjamin 1999, 235].) The problem, though, is not the existence of such extremes; rather, it is that in the centre both paradigms seem to sit side by side without a discernable relationship of a kind that could be open to a critique comparable to the one that might be deployed in the aesthetic or the epistemic alone. The aesthetic and the epistemic almost act as independent variables within contemporary art.

Assuming that there are limits to contemporary art and that notions of "contemporaneity" express historical conditions (as suggested in Geoff Cox's and Jacob Lund's Danish research project The Contemporary Condition[3] and also in the writings of Peter Osborne [2013a] and Terry Smith [2009]), space is created for "artistic research" practices *not* to simply and automatically be part of contemporary art but rather to potentially be a border phenomenon during times of historical change. As such, artistic research may be a symptom indicating cracks in the standard model and shifting relationships to contemporaneity in artistic practice if not on even larger scales. This chapter explores this possibility.

To be sure, the field of artistic research that I am referring to is itself highly diverse to the degree that in a recent thread on the PhD-design JISC mailing list, Ken Friedman (2017) sought to find "articles, reports, and documents of any kind on the topics of 1) practice based research, 2) practice led research, 3) practice as research, 4) artistic research" in order to sort out "confusing" uses of terms and to determine how they may be differentiated. Given this confusion, it is crucial that a particular approach, for instance the UK approach to practice-led research, is not generalised so it can capture parallel developments. Personally, I have been part of a group of people that prefers option 4 ("artistic research"), with the caveat that this is not meant to ontologise what counts as artistic research, but, by also adapting Friedman's third option, seeks *articulations* of practice as research. Combining two of the four options will surely add to the confusion that Friedman experiences.

With respect to such notions of artistic research, its practices may be seen as being outside contemporary art, part of contemporary art, or in a position at a distance from such inside–outside dialectics suggesting that "artistic research" can be *completely* understood neither from an exclusively academic perspective

---

3 See http://contemporaneity.au.dk.

nor from an exclusively artistic one. In "A Brief Survey of the Current Debates on the Concepts and the Practices of Research in the Arts," Henk Borgdorff (2013, 148) seems to also follow this logic when he distinguishes academic, *sui generis*, and critical perspectives; nevertheless, it is problematic—as expressed in his careful wording—to conflate this set of perspectives with national research agendas, which he, however, does. While Borgdorff's "critical perspective" seems to be driven more by a critique of the ongoing capitalisation of knowledge and less by questions of contemporaneity, it is noteworthy that even here, the *sui generis* perspective is breached by a third, critical variant at a distance to what I conceived as the standard model of contemporary art.

Approaches to artistic research tend to be top-down: that is, they tend to start from concepts or institutional realities rather than from concrete articulations of research to hand. In contrast to this, I would characterise my own work as a bottom-up approach that is engaged as deeply as possible in concrete research projects in my various functions as an artistic researcher in the Transpositions[4] research project and the ERC-funded MusicExperiment21[5] research project, as well as the Editor-in-Chief of the *Journal for Artistic Research* (JAR).[6] Across these projects, my colleagues and I have been investigating articulations of artistic practice as research, that is, how research can be made evident in artistic practice and in the secondary formats of artistic production in particular (artist's books, journal articles, lecture performances, etc.). Using the concept of *expositionality* or *exposing practice as research* (Schwab 2011, 2012b; Schwab and Borgdorff 2014), JAR subjects both the form and the content of research articulations to a rigorous peer-review process (Schwab 2018a). However, to understand the epistemological implications of expositionality, I have also been investigating how Hans-Jörg Rheinberger's theory of experimental systems (1997) may be methodologically deployed, how it may help characterise what is happening in artistic research, and how, conversely, such a theory would have to be critiqued from the point of view of artistic research practice (Schwab 2014b). In what follows, I will develop aspects of my work in these different contexts in order to argue for the specific role artistic research can play in the current discourse on contemporary art.

Rather than starting from contemporary art and developing an epistemological basis within it—the paths here seem to invariably cross around 1800 either through Benjamin's focus on Novalis and Friedrich Schlegel (Benjamin 2004) or Jean-Luc Nancy and Philippe Lacoue-Labarthe's focus on Johann Gottlieb Fichte (Lacoue-Labarthe and Nancy 1988), or even a variant that favours Hölderlin (Blanchot [1982] 1989, 269–76)[7]—here, I propose to use Rheinberger's approach to historical epistemology as developed in the context of the sciences, to first seek comparable patterns of contemporaneity in contemporary art and, then, to speculate about alternative perspectives. It is striking that most discourses that seek to emphasise or even supply an epistemology

---

4 See https://www.researchcatalogue.net/view/94538/94539.
5 See https://musicexperiment21.eu/.
6 See http://www.jar-online.net/.
7 Leslie Hill (1997) calls Blanchot an "extreme contemporary."

for contemporary art are more likely to approach it from an idealist rather than empiricist perspective, for which in particular the experimental sciences may stand.

Regardless of the approach, though, science and art in our *idea* of "c.1800" seem both to stem from the shifting *episteme* at the time—modernity—without suggesting, however, that their different subsequent historical trajectories would be historically overcome in a "re-examination" of the Renaissance (Wilson 2002) or a "third culture" (Snow [1959] 1998), a proximity also idealised in Helga Nowotny's foreword to *The Routledge Companion to Research in the Arts* (2011). Rather, the suggestion is that as modernity has historically unfolded and the disciplines have diversified to a degree where integration seems virtually impossible, they may still harbour a relationship to a once-shared cultural space, which today needs to be constructed either as historically in the past or outside history in a temporal space that could be referred to as "the contemporary." Historically, such a space could be suggested in the proximity of artistic and scientific practices in, for instance, Novalis, who was both a writer and a geologist, as well as, more than one hundred years later, in Kafka, where geology—through photography—and writing seem to have productively engaged each other.[8]

Those different disciplines, or cultures, are not so much shared than mutually informative of a space where strata—or words, or disciplines—are formed. It seems to me that in the same manner, in "Answering the Question: What is Postmodernism?" Jean-François Lyotard ([1983] 2001, 79) refuses to give the now outdated notion of postmodernism a historical definition, when he says that "Postmodernism thus understood is not modernism at its end but in the nascent state, and this state is constant." In other words, modernity and contemporaneity are structurally and not historically distinct giving validity to an approach that transposes a structure from one discipline—or its history—into another. More specifically, in this text, I am testing how a structure conceptualised in the history of science to describe temporal phenomena in early-twentieth-century laboratories may help shed light on something in art that is seemingly unrelated.

Experimental systems

When engaging with Rheinberger's philosophy, the concept of *epistemic things* seems arguably to be the most productive to artistic researchers (Borgdorff 2012; Schwab 2013, 2014a). An epistemic thing appears as an as (yet) unknown

---

8   Franz Kafka was engaged in accident prevention in quarrying through his work at the Arbeiter-Un-fallversicherungs-Anstalt für das Königreich Böhmen in Prague. "Kafka's extensive use of photography as a source of information on accident prevention is remarkable. He ingeniously exploits the fact that in the case of quarrying, photography is not restricted to producing the surface (the horizontal dimensions of a terrain) but can reproduce the depth as well (the vertical layers of the soil). Here is a model of a Kafkaesque literary text: like the image of the quarry, the text yields its full richness only to a gaze directed both to the surface and the depth—the multitude of verbal citations and echoes evoked and concealed by this surface. Indeed Kafka himself used quarrying to denote the empirical pole of his empirical-transcendental model of aesthetic production" (Corngold, Greenberg, and Wagner 2009, 299–300; see also, Caygill 2017).

material trace in an experimental system, which over time as it is increasingly understood is rendered into what Rheinberger calls a *technical object*, that is, a blackboxed, functional unit ready to be deployed either in future experimental systems or the marketplace.

An epistemic thing implies the future. While it is insufficiently known to be understood, it is known enough that it promises future understanding. To Rheinberger, a thing could not be called *epistemic* without such an anticipatory horizon. In effect, science or understanding in general may be seen as *consuming* epistemic anticipation, so that as it is more and more understood, the weaker a thing's epistemic potential might be said to be. Attention usually moves on as epistemic potential is lost; but Rheinberger is quite clear that epistemic potential can return should the closure (the blackbox) around the epistemic thing that makes it a technical object not retain its specific functional place in the ensemble of the experimental system—sporadic points of excess that float on an imperfectly connected, precarious network of functional units. However, below epistemic things is yet another procedural layer.

Experimental systems are material systems of differential play designed to register *unprecedented events*. Being unprecedented, those events must be of a type that exceeds what is currently known; thus, they tend to first appear as disturbance, irritation, contamination, or noise—that is, as by-products of what knowledge can already cover. Out of those traces that mark unprecedented events, epistemic things emerge as initial, tentative supplements to what is seen as the cause of those events. In line with Jacques Derrida's (1997) thinking, paradoxically, "origin" is always also after the fact. In other words, an unprecedented event becomes the origin for future knowledge not at the moment when it happens but later when a point in time becomes an origin; a structure of delay or deferral is part of the objects themselves and not a secondary effect of, for instance, a lack of knowledge on our part or communicative difficulties. Epistemic things can exist only as delay, which is the very reason why knowledge must structurally be positioned in the future: research as knowledge-to-come rests on an origin-already-passed.

The journey from trace (comparatively unknown) to technical object (comparatively known) is described by Rheinberger (1994) as *historial*, that is, history-making rather than *historical*, that is, made-in-history. The notion of historial here is also loaned from Derrida in order to express two different, simultaneous currents of history. The first looks forward into a future, open horizon built on past facts and secured by the chronological passing of time. The second looks backward into a rich bed of possible origins that need to be actualised should the future be possible. A historical perspective values only the first current, where events happen in history and affect only the future; a historial perspective, in contrast, accounts for both currents. An event looked at historially may be seen like a temporal mirror with time running both forward to a future and backward to its past.

These descriptions may sound very abstract, but they quickly become concrete when looking at a historian's work or even that of an artist researcher retracing his or her steps in a research project. Will I be aware of the difference between a past before today, and a past that "belongs" to today as if history, that is, historical difference, had not occurred? Rheinberger also quotes the words of Georges Canguilhem, who says that "the past of a science of today is not to be confounded with that science in its history" (as quoted in Rheinberger 2009, 182). Or, in Rheinberger's own words, "the recent is made into the result of something that did not so happen. And the past is made into a trace of something that had not (yet) occurred" (Rheinberger 1997, 178). In "Translating Derrida," Rheinberger also notes how Derrida saw in the late writings of Husserl (his *Origin of Geometry*, which Derrida translated into French) a move beyond phenomenology due to the effects of history that will always offset the meaning of a point in time depending on whether we encounter it up- or downstream. Maurice Merleau-Ponty made a similar point in his late, unfinished book *The Visible and the Invisible* when he says that "operations of reconstitution or of re-establishment which come second cannot by principle be the mirror image of its internal constitution and its establishment, as the route from the Etoile to the Notre-Dame is the inverse of the route from the Notre-Dame to the Etoile: the reflection recuperates everything except itself as an effort of recuperation" (Merleau-Ponty 1968, 33). And later: "The whole reflective analysis is not false, but still naïve, . . . as long as, in order to constitute the world, it is necessary to have a notion of the world as preconstituted" (ibid., 34).

This challenge to phenomenology puts into doubt a whole strand of artistic research methodologies that rely heavily on experience, affect, or embodiment, as well as reflection of the kind suggested, for instance, in Donald Schön's often-quoted book *The Reflective Practitioner* (1983). While it is clear that these phenomena exist and are valued, they may not be sufficiently problematised to carry more advanced epistemic claims. In fact, the need to account for deferral and historiality discussed above precludes historical approaches that take their object as constituted in history. Rather, it seems that the only suitable forms of historical epistemology are those that problematise the knowledge that can be had of the past. Historical epistemology is also not to be confused with classical epistemology, which seeks trans- or ahistorical theories of knowledge. Derrida puts it like this: "If we take for granted the philosophical nonsense of a purely empirical history and the impotence of an ahistorical rationalism, then we realize the seriousness of what is at stake" (Derrida 1989, 51). In this sense, historical epistemology represents a more advanced approach of going "back to the 'things themselves,'" as Husserl ([1970] 2001, 1:168) famously put it, one that takes into account the temporal operations by which things come into being in the first place.

From a critical position we can thus not afford to pretend that history (and with it its origins) is simply given. Worse—and this is where my argument switches to Nietzsche—a simplistic understanding of history, best called "historicism," is not historical in any meaningful sense at all since it misses precisely the fundamental quality of history: its plastic character. Nietzsche is quite direct with such historicists or "historical men" as he calls them: "looking to the past impels them towards the future and fires their courage to go on living and their hope that what they want will still happen, that happiness lies behind the hill they are advancing towards. . . . they have no idea that, despite their preoccupation with history, they in fact think and act unhistorically" (*UB* II.1, as translated in Nietzsche 1997, 65).

In the context of the argument about artistic research that I am attempting here, at least two aspects deserve attention. First, with regard to research, failures to engage with deeper, historial notions of history risk impoverishing the research to a degree at which it becomes impossible. Hence, Rheinberger (2016) argues for necessary encounters between the sciences and humanities to find an approach to knowledge objects mindful of their own inherent dynamism that neither an empiricist nor rationalist image of research can touch. Because of this, Rheinberger insists on the impossibility of technoscience, that is, the industrialisation of knowledge production. While new objects may emerge from "innovation incubators" and so on, historically speaking nothing new may have happened. As Rheinberger (1997, 32) says with reference to Helga Nowotny, "If the momentum of science gets absorbed into technology, we end up with 'extended present,'" which is of course reminiscent of Martin Heidegger's notion of "perpetual ending" ([1938–48] 1999, 113; Verendung[9]), that is, the ending of history in technology's "enframing" (Heidegger [1953] 2000).

A historical standstill in the name of progress in which technology seems to be codified may be the consequence of fundamental misunderstandings of how history comes about precisely through the success of the experimental apparatus, which in producing technology distracts us from fundamental atechnological necessities. Nietzsche already says as much when in his "An Attempt at Self-Criticism" from 1886 he says: "for the problem of science cannot be recognized within the territory of science" (Nietzsche 1999, 5). (I leave aside the point that for Nietzsche art is necessary for this recognition, which is not important to my argument.) Hence, when positioning artistic research, the issue might be that, for some, the notion of "research" is already too instrumental, too emptied of historical potentials in its institutional framework; or, conversely, when speaking of "artistic research," expectations may be raised about possible (seamless) integrations of art into the knowledge economy as if artistic positions could be had in the limited theatre of technology.

And, leaving questions of research aside, with regard to art one may wonder whether historical narratives still have traction and, if so, how. Thinking back to avant-garde times, one could imagine how a painting such as Picasso's *Les Demoiselles d'Avignon* (1907) offered new formal solutions to painting—a new technical object of sorts relevant and usable for other painters. However, from the moment the historical gesture of the avant-garde was problematised (Bürger 1984), and despite arguments regarding the possibility for change in what has been termed the "neo-avantgarde" (Buchloh 1984), historical claims must at least be seen as problematic. Does the repetition of avant-garde gestures still promise the future history that they once had? And if yes, from where can the

---

9   The German word *Verendung* also denotes the (slow) solitary death of an animal.

historical relevance of art be recovered? Crudely, I would use the term *modernist* to describe what in retrospect—that is, as a continuing residue—looks like a future-directed but historicist notion of art, according to which, *very* generally speaking, formal solutions (of the kind that could be described as *technical objects*) appear as valid outcomes. Ironically, modernist art would tie *so* much better into policy-maker's ideas about artistic research—another Bauhaus, anybody?—were it not for the fact that, artistically, modernist approaches have very little current relevance.

In terms of art history (and in the field of my own practice) that paradigm seems at the latest to have been done away with around 1970, when conceptual art and Art and Technology came close in exhibitions such as *Software* (Jewish Museum, New York, 16 September–8 November 1970, curated by Jack Burnham) and *Information* (Museum of Modern Art, New York, 2 July–20 September 1970, curated by Kynaston McShine). These exhibitions suggested that art could be programmable, not only in the sense that concepts and rules could replace the actual making of the work as suggested in conceptual art, but also, more profoundly, where the aesthetic experience became technology's target. Such "generative aesthetics" was theorised by, for instance, Abraham Moles (1966) and Max Bense (1971) and put into action by the pioneers of early computer art. Nevertheless, it looks as if the modernist residue that gave technology such a prominent platform was not suitable to describe the art that was already emerging, and which—in retrospect—the exhibition *Open Systems: Rethinking Art c.1970* (Tate Modern, London, 1 June–18 September 2005, curated by Donna DeSalvo) tried to frame and which should be described as post-conceptual.

Contemporaneity in experimental systems

Bracketing out historicist positions seems to be the easy part, although in terms of funding for artistic research and the general tendency toward "outputs" and "impact" we may have a long fight on our hands. However, as indicated at the start of this chapter, while concerns about sufficiently complex notions of research and art suggest a possible affinity between artistic research and contemporary art, I would like to use the remainder of this chapter to complicate things. However, let's first look at the space they share.

As suggested by the above critique of a modernist approach, emphasis has to be moved from objects with a more or less stable historical identity—like "masterworks" that represent the achievements of the research—to more precarious, ambivalent, or provisional things. In line with this thinking, Borgdorff understands artworks as epistemic things rather than technical objects, as could also have been claimed. As Borgdorff (2012, 193) says, "within artistic practices, artworks are the hybrid objects, situations, or events—the epistemic things—that constitute the driving force in artistic research." He attests a lack of completeness that indicates (via Adorno) both their status as art and their potential to continue to unfold into knowledge. However, there is also a modernist residue in Borgdorff's work concept, which, through registers of non-identity still rescues on a "higher" level the identity of the work of art.

Paulo de Assis's assemblage theory goes a step further here (Assis 2018). To him, works are virtual entities, which can only be reconstructed from iterative, selective, and always different actualisations. Hence, because of the necessary inconsistencies between these material assemblages, a work can only be understood as a multiplicity rather than an identity, that is, there is no single and simple original point of reference. In my own practice I offered the notion of "proto-object"[10] to replace the notion of "work," suggesting that since some assemblages made in a research setting may be registered as a work while others will not, aesthetic judgements concerning "art" may need to be suspended in order to appropriately engage with emergent and as-yet unidentified things. Esa Kirkkopelto (2018) goes as far as to suggest that in artistic research the very notion of "art" may need to be jeopardised. Regardless of how one may finally decide on the ontology of contemporary works of art, when linking it to Rheinberger's philosophy, these diverse positions agree in one point: value lies with what is unknown, underdetermined, and open, as associated with epistemic things, and not with what is known, identified, and closed, which is the functional position of technical objects.

So what about an epistemic thing's temporal structure? To answer the question, it is important to remember that an epistemic thing is not a material object but an event emergent from the differential play of the experimental system and its resultant traces or *graphemes*, as Rheinberger prefers to call them. In effect, the event isn't first of all an abrupt rupture in the fabric of knowledge, although it may be retrospectively narrated as such (Rheinberger 2013, 203). Rather, traces have to resonate (Rheinberger 1997, 65) and come together within the different spaces of representation employed in the system as well as in its temporal structure. The event has to be multiple, that is, recurrent, since this is how difference is registered in time. Still, without such a coming together, there is no event and no epistemic thing. At the same time, and according to the Derridean framework that Rheinberger uses, this confluence is only accessible as delay, that is, regarding a future point at which we will know that something has happened. Hence, the coming together isn't actually happening, or if it is, it is diverted into a projected future. This means that this coming together is not synchronicity but a more or less focusable temporal distribution. This also means that "noise" is an epistemic phenomenon rather than an epistemic adversary, which corrupts channels of communication (Serres 1982; Malaspina 2018).

As a consequence, "time" does not refer to a universal chronology within which things are situated, but rather time is a quality of the things themselves. (In the last consequence, chronology itself is historicist and it is no surprise that "the clock" is linked to modernity both in terms of spatial order [the clock as a prerequisite for establishing longitude and, hence, navigation and global trade] and social order [the clock in the workplace and industrialisation] [Rossum 1996].) With reference to Ilya Prigogine and Isabelle Stengers, Rheinberger (1997, 179) advocates "localized and situated time" where temporality is a quality of an entity that at first enables relations, that is, resonances.

---

10   https://www.researchcatalogue.net/view/186304/186305. See also Schwab (2012a).

In very broad terms, such a theory sees time not as a measure (a quantity) but as a quality. Without this move, the coming together of the traces of the experimental system would not really happen, since they would have come together already in the time in which they were measured. In other words, epistemic things can only be understood in their temporal structure if time is qualified rather than quantified. Usually, since time is represented in *chronos*, we will think of such time structures as singular events with associated time points, but this is just a way of representing them; when attention moves to aspects lost in chronology, that is, representation—or at least lost in the limited, universalising representational orders we usually refer to—phenomena that seemed secured need reassessment. If we accept, as Foucault or, differently, Rancière do, that our world has moved beyond "representational regimes," it is on this level that representation needs to be challenged and new epistemic regimes described.

When it comes to the time structure of epistemic things, Rheinberger's theory does not mention contemporaneity. If at all, he mentions the concept only in very general terms, such as "an epistemology of contemporary experimentation" (Rheinberger 1997, 1); but it should be clear from my analysis just now that in my eyes this also means "contemporaneity *in* experimentation." When stepping across into the field of art, we may, however, feel handicapped by Rheinberger's fairly frequent references to George Kubler's *The Shape of Time* (1962), which proposes historical series of *forms* rather than something much less representationally stable. With it comes a certain emphasis on the artwork, or more generally, artefact, which as stated earlier has at least modernist connotations.

One may read Rheinberger's interpretation as a contemporary critique on Kubler where "form" is seen much more as a "grapheme" rather than an "aesthetic form" in line with, for instance, Robert Smithson's interest in Kubler. As Stefanie Stallschuss suggests, Kubler's "temporal definition of form opens his theory to contemporary art production" (Stallschus 2013, 24), which to some degree requires us to look away from his examples to the way in which he approaches time. However, when citing Kubler, Rheinberger does not refer to the importance of Kubler's work to many artists of the 1960s and the way this encounter prepared "c.1970" (Lee 2001), creating the link to contemporary art that I am suggesting here.

Ultimately, Rheinberger as well as Kubler—both as historians, either of science or of art—approach the objects of their investigations from a moment *after the fact*, that is, starting from and adhering to a historical perspective potentially limiting insights into processes of making. As Kubler says, "we cannot clearly descry the contours of the great currents of our own time: we are too much inside the streams of contemporary happening to chart their flow and volume. We are confronted with inner and outer historical surfaces. Of these only the outer surfaces of the completed past are accessible to historical knowledge" (Kubler 1962, 30). At the same time, approaching historical objects also as a historical epistemologist (with the knowledge and experience of a trained biologist), the "inner surfaces" that Kubler refers to are perhaps not as remote to Rheinberger, preparing, as it were, a step *through* those surfaces into "graphematic spaces" (Rheinberger 1997, 1998) that need not necessarily be historically represented (Schwab 2013).

THE CONTEMPORARY IN ART

Not through art historical references, but through Rheinberger's focus on temporality, can a link to the recently emerging debates about contemporaneity in art be made. I will take Peter Osborne's book *Anywhere or Not At All: Philosophy of Contemporary Art* (2013a) as my guiding text. Before looking at contemporary art's particular temporality, though, I should stress that for Osborne, through a genealogical link to early German Romanticism of the kind that Walter Benjamin (2004) identified, contemporary art is seen foremost as an epistemic rather than aesthetic enterprise (Osborne 2013a, 44). While we may not necessarily define this enterprise as "research" we can say that with the Romantic project surely a demand against art has risen that sees art not so much only on the side of perception or imagination and not even located in a (Kantian) harmony between imagination and understanding, but in the understanding proper as a *special* way to think the world in the making of art (by romanticising it, as Novalis says). This approach bore the risk of drifting from somewhat innocent but politically potent art- and world-making to religion and mysticism of a kind against which Nietzsche would later revolt.

Second, Osborne sees contemporary art as a historical phenomenon against possible readings, which claim contemporaneity as an effect of the ending of history. As suggested above, from a critical point of view that aims to understand how the artistic may negotiate the aesthetic and the epistemic if both appear as independent variables, it is difficult to find contemporaneity's historical dimension. It seems particularly difficult from a strictly philosophical position that may not be able to easily unpack in propositional language historial notions of history of the kind Derrida suggests. Hence, Osborne's text is admittedly experimental. He uses, as he says, an "experimental method of montage as the means of production of historical intelligibility" (Osborne 2013a, 55), which I find very interesting: the historicity of contemporary art, in suspending history, cannot be engaged with using hermeneutic, that is, *passive* modes of understanding. Interestingly, Rheinberger also sees his major book as a writing experiment (Rheinberger 1997, 2).

Osborne accepts, as an effect of globalisation, a differentiated world, also on the level of temporality. As he says: "The root idea of the contemporary as a living, existing, or occurring together 'in' time, then, requires further specification as a *differential* historical temporality of the present: a coming together of different but equally 'present' times, a temporal unity in disjunction, or a disjunctive unity of present times" (Osborne 2013a, 22). Thus, in principle, we are dealing with a fairly similar differential spatio-temporal structure of contemporaneity across Osborne's and Rheinberger's writings. However, there are a number of differences between the two, which help me describe a possible pressure point of artistic research in contemporary art.

In a different way to Rheinberger, who highlights the materiality of traces, epistemic things, and technical objects, as well as the coming together of times in them, Osborne relates to the *fictional* character of the contemporary. He argues, given the emphasis on delay and the resulting speculative or projective attitude, that there is no will for *actual* historical action. In other words, Osborne does not understand contemporaneity historically as suggested in relation to Rheinberger's theory, but rather, he sees a "disavowal" at play (Osborne 2013a, 23). Hence, the coming together is historically negative and not historially productive. I will at this point not discuss other approaches to contemporary art and only mention with Boris Groys another theorist who sees in contemporary art a similarly negative expression, describing it in terms of "nostalgia" (Groys 2016, 21). These are indications that notions of contemporary art are constructed around passive rather than active responses to the problem of history. (In Nietzsche, as is well known, a distinction between active and passive nihilism is crucial for a move beyond nihilism.)

A critique of the notion of "fiction" in this context does not mean that the importance of the literary needs to be neglected. Rheinberger, too, stresses the need for narratives ("stories") and so does the wider field of science and technology studies, where, for instance, Steven Shapin (1984) emphasises the importance of what he calls "literary technology." However, Rheinberger does not question to the same degree notions of reality, which via unexpected incursions feature in experimental systems. For example, while he challenges the notion of "data" as a (passive) input into a scientific system, the term *facta*, with which Rheinberger (2004, 6) replaces it—from the Latin *factum* as "something done or made"—does not have the status of something fictional despite having been made; if anything, the opposite is true. In a similar vein, a "matter of fact," a notion that Shapin highlights in Robert Boyle's work, is something produced by an experimental apparatus, which we paradoxically must take as real. In other words, historiality's lack of historicity does not give it less agency, only a different one.

Second, and to some degree related to the problem of "fiction" is the ontological status of *contemporaneity* and *the contemporary*. Experimental systems border each other in what Rheinberger calls a "patchwork" but they are otherwise fairly isolated, specific, and fragmented, which to Rheinberger following Bachelard enables the epistemic complexity of modern science. In what I said above, I applied the notion of *contemporaneity* only to processes inside an experimental system, that is, the very limited and concrete space of a system and *not* the patchwork of experimental systems—micro- rather than macro-structures. In fact, when I asked Rheinberger in my interview with him whether the patchwork could itself be understood as an experimental system, he was very hesitant. "I prefer to characterise this higher level as an experimental culture. Its structure feeds back into its elements, but there is no mimicry between the levels" (Rheinberger 2013, 204). While an experimental system to Rheinberger is not (and, in fact, must not) be void of contradictions, it has to be sufficiently coherent to work. Epistemic cultures that combine experimental systems in a patchwork, in contrast, can be less coherent and their objects can be less concrete, resulting in a less resonant temporal structure. Scale matters here—contemporaneity may locally be achieved but remains globally elusive.

Hence, slippages can be detected from smaller to larger constellations if attention is not paid to the qualitative changes that accompany such upscaling. Thus, "fiction" need not be associated with contemporaneity as such but only when it happens on the global scale of the kind Osborne is interested in, that is, when material, temporal structures are extended into more conceptual spheres, such as, for example, when the notion of "art" is at stake. In fact, in Osborne's text such upscaling to the totalising perspective of the global can only ever happen in the mode of "as if" and, hence, as fiction. As he says, "there is no actual shared subject-position from the standpoint of which its relational totality could be lived *as* a whole, in whatever futural, temporally fragmented or dispersed a form. Nonetheless, the idea of the contemporary functions *as if* there is" (Osborne 2013b, 80). Assuming that contemporaneity is a temporal effect within a materially concrete situation, and as such is historically real, it is perhaps not surprising that when moving to the global scale one has to treat contemporaneity *as if* it were a locale, when, in fact, it is not, due to the lack of a possible subject-position as indicated. More simply put, we cannot inhabit "the globe" despite the famous image beamed back to us from Apollo 8.

So, what is behind the drive to a global contemporary art? Interestingly, if we discount the contemporary as having this kind of reach while maintaining its historical reality, contemporary art must, as a matter of fact, be a modernist residue. The disavowal or the nostalgia mentioned above as part of it is then an effect not of contemporaneity but of a *very* late stage of modernity just before what is happening on the ground has managed to shift, for instance, notions of art. The "global" is first of all a *modern* fiction as the imaginary perimeter of capitalist expansion. As suggested with reference to *experimental cultures*, such a global perspective is not required to explain the conglomeration of disjuncted temporalities. Furthermore, the associated problem of colonisation needs to be highlighted and the fact that "the globe" remains in the possession of the coloniser. Should (some) contemporary art be taken seriously in aspiring to postcolonial practices, assuming a global stage would miss representing those practices in their specificity (either by assuming an implicit global stage or by withdrawing notions of contemporaneity and ultimately art from it).

Finally, can *contemporaneity* really be treated as a concept or is it more like an event structure that is only accessible from within its locale and by no means something that repeats itself across events connected up externally? If, as argued above, we are dealing with more or less focused temporal distributions, contemporaneity always has a specific texture—things don't come together in a single point, but enter a spatially as well as temporally distributed play in the concrete. While this play will have some spatio-temporal perimeter, claiming that it covers the globe misses its dynamic aspects of moving in time and space across its material basis. When challenging the existence of a global contemporary art, it is not that a global experimental system/contemporaneity categorically could not exist. However, first, we have to ask whether we actually have any experience of it, or whether it is not an abstract projection from concrete experience; second, if we had it, would we not lose a degree of complexity that a looser ensemble of multiple systems offers? What is the actual experience of contemporary art? Do we still find this on a global scale? This kind of slippage may actually reflect a more general problem of philosophy rather than an issue with contemporary artistic practice: it could be that philosophy finds it hard to focus on the concrete and that, as suggested by Laruelle (2010), even under conditions of difference it tends to opt for transcendental and ultimately representational solutions. What might a local philosophy look like? Or, what might philosophy as locality look like? Is there agency between history and its end?

A philosophy of contemporary art certainly overlaps with a philosophy of experimental systems, but there is also reason to question how much these philosophies actually share. When the focus is on artistic research one may perhaps point out that aspects of fictionality and the speculative nature of the concept of contemporaneity move the focus away from the epistemic grounding that experimental systems provide. In turn, however, a philosophy of experimental systems seems to be hampered by notions of knowledge that require technical objects, without which it would amount to nothing. In the following last part, I will try to position artistic research in a particular relationship to contemporaneity through a further engagement with Nietzsche's second *Untimely Meditation*.

UNTIMELINESS AND ARTISTIC RESEARCH

In taking Roland Barthes's statement "the contemporary is the untimely" as a starting point, Giorgio Agamben emphasises the relevance of Nietzsche in this context (Barthes quoted in Agamben 2009, 40). I have dealt with one aspect already, namely chronology: "It is important to realize that the appointment that is in question in contemporariness does not simply take place in chronological time: it is something that, working within chronological time, urges, presses, and transforms it" (Agamben 2009, 47). Second, Agamben also re-emphasises the disjointedness of time as the prerequisite for the coming together of times in the contemporary. The metaphor Agamben uses here is cosmological: points in time are as removed from one another as stars in the sky, which due to their distance can only be seen as darkness. So Nietzsche, in his self-declared untimeliness, at the same time breaks with his own time as he is able to bring times together—in his case, probably first of all, ancient texts as part of his work as a philologist, but beyond this, perhaps also in a more ethical dimension, as a suggested mode in which to encounter what is now.

But does "the contemporary is the untimely" do justice to Nietzsche's second *Untimely Meditation*? In order to answer this question, I want to first bracket and put aside the historicist position (which Nietzsche calls the *antiquarian species of history* [see Nietzsche 1997, 67]). Furthermore, for the two other positions (the *monumental* and the *critical species of history*), we have to be clear that the notion of the contemporary is not of Nietzsche's time and does not feature in Nietzsche's text in any meaningful way. Instead, I propose to use those two positions in Nietzsche's conception to critique notions of the contemporary that I previously introduced with Rheinberger and Osborne, using them to "split" a broader notion of contemporaneity into the supra-historical and the untimely, or the monumental and the critical notions of history.

According to Nietzsche, all modes of history are grounded in the ahistorical (*unhistorisch*), a ground only against which history becomes possible. That is, history is a representational figure suspended over, but nevertheless connected to, an ahistorical ground. I would compare this ground to Rheinberger's graphematic space, the space in which traces occur and resonate and from which epistemic things emerge, which ultimately turn into technical objects. As argued above, if an event's temporality is what emerges in this space, the space itself cannot have a fixed time (*chronos*) within which such an event would already have its place and where the different times as traces (of the experimental system) would come together. On this level, the emergent events in their nascent states (epistemic things) are connected, since if there is no history as yet, there is also no historical difference. Agamben (2009, 50) expresses this as the contemporaneity of "historical becoming." Nietzsche refers to it as "monumental history" since to him at the time of writing (i.e., the late nineteenth century), it was still monumental works of art that were historically relevant. He claims "that the great moments in the struggle of the human individual constitute a chain, [and] that this chain unites mankind across the millennia like a range of human mountain peaks" (Nietzsche 1997, 68). For this reason, in the first section of the text, Nietzsche refers to what he calls monumental history also as "supra-historical" (ibid., 66). Furthermore, he assesses this position as "wise," that is, that it *understands* contemporaneity as history's substrate. I propose, in order not to get stuck with Nietzsche's nineteenth-century idea of monuments, to side with Robert Smithson's updated version. As Smithson says: "Instead of causing us to remember the past like the old monuments, the new monuments seem to cause us to forget the future" (Smithson [1966] 1996, 11). I think this plays precisely into Osborne's contention regarding that lack of a historical perspective in contemporary art, when he classifies the temporal unity as fictional and not materially real as we have heard. The untimely understood in this way, that is, supra-historically, may indeed be seen as the contemporary.

Nietzsche, however, proposes next to the monumental and antiquarian mode of history, a third, critical mode, which adds a crucial shift to the contemporary. The contemporary in being able to bring together different times in the time of the contemporary—the mountain peaks—may be philosophically right, but it pays a price in weakening one's plastic powers (as also stated by Osborne). In effect, if the unity of times, that is, the contemporary, is believed to exist, it cannot be challenged by anything new—which would become just another mountain peak were it not for the fact that to become a mountain peak the category of the supra-historical/contemporaneity would need to be departed from. In other words, "discovering" contemporaneity as the basis for history precisely disables its making. As Nietzsche says: "A historical phenomenon, known clearly and completely and resolved into a phenomenon of knowledge, is, for him, who has perceived it, dead" (Nietzsche 1997, 67). It is because of unity, completion and, ultimately—in Nietzsche's words—death that what Osborne defines as contemporary art needs to be challenged. Nietzsche's untimely, despite the confusion that the Barthes quotations create in Agamben's text, *can only be the contemporary as reality* in the sense in which I discussed it above with Rheinberger—and which includes literary elements—and *not as fiction*. Barthes/Agamben may not have wanted to associate the contemporary with the supra-historical, but Osborne's analysis makes this unavoidable.

Hence, rather than suggesting that "the contemporary is the untimely," the drift that Nietzsche gives the untimely splits the contemporary in two, a supra-historical, transcendental contemporary as philosophical speculation and an untimely contemporary experienced in concrete spatio-temporal acts of creation. Both can fold into each other insofar as the one does not exclude the other, but if looked at principally it is only the latter that promises to connect the aesthetic with the epistemic dimensions of artistic practice. To be sure, "the aesthetic" then is to be understood in the sense neither of *aisthesis* nor of philosophy of art, but "as part of the sense of world created through art" (Schwab 2018b, 194); while "the epistemic" does not offer a system of knowledge, but a project interested in expanding what can be understood—and how it can be understood.

Artistic research situated at this very point offers an untimely extension and critique of the contemporary. It sits within but on the fringes of contemporary art, at times accepted and at times rejected by the dominant narratives that act as its gatekeepers. The crucial assessment to be made when being confronted with a particular case is not whether it is or isn't contemporary art, but whether a materially situated time structure of contemporaneity is presented and what this actually means to both our future and past. In this way, artistic research does not extend history in some form of aspired replacement of contemporary art (innovation); instead, artistic research makes different histories and futures possible (invention). How they may historically be acted upon is a different matter.

References

Agamben, Giorgio. 2009. "What Is the Contemporary?" In *What Is an Apparatus? and Other Essays*, translated by David Kishik and Stefan Pedatella, 39–54. Stanford, CA: Stanford University Press. Essay first published 2008 as *Che cos'è il contemporaneo?* (Rome: Nottetempo).

Aranda, Julieta, Brian Kuan Wood, and Anton Vidokle, eds. 2010. *E-Flux Journal: What Is Contemporary Art?* Berlin: Sternberg Press.

Assis, Paulo de. 2018. *Logic of Experimentation: Rethinking Music Performance through Artistic Research*. Orpheus Institute Series.

Leuven: Leuven University Press.

Benjamin, Walter. (1968) 1999. "The Work of Art in the Age of Mechanical Reproduction." In *Illuminations: Essays and Reflections*, edited by Hannah Arendt, translated by Harry Zohn, 211–44. London: Pimlico. Essay first published 1936 as "L'œuvre d'art à l'époque de sa reproduction mécanisée" (*Zeitschrift für Sozialforschung* 5 [1]: 40–68). This translation first published 1968 (New York: Harcourt Brace Jovanovich).

———. 2004. "The Concept of Criticism in German Romanticism." In *Selected*

Writings, Volume 1, 1913–1926, edited by Marcus Bullock and Michael W. Jennings, 116–200. Cambridge, MA: Belknap Press of Harvard University Press. First published 1920 as *Der Begriff der Kunstkritik in der deutschen Romantik* (Berlin: A. Scholem; Bern: Francke).

Bense, Max. 1971. "The Project of Generative Aesthetics." In *Cybernetics, Art and Ideas*, edited by Jasia Reichardt, 57–60. London: Studio Vista.

Blanchot, Maurice. (1982) 1989. *The Space of Literature*. Translated by Ann Smock. Lincoln: University of Nebraska Press. First published 1955 as *L'espace littéraire* (Paris: Gallimard). This translation first published 1982 (Lincoln: University of Nebraska Press).

Borgdorff, Henk. 2012. *The Conflict of the Faculties: Perspectives on Artistic Research and Academia*. Leiden: Leiden University Press.

———. 2013. "A Brief Survey of Current Debates on the Concepts and Practices of Research in the Arts." In *SHARE: Handbook for Artistic Research Education*, ed. by Mick Wilson and Schelte van Ruiten, 146–52. Amsterdam: ELIA. Accessed 4 February 2019. http://www.elia-artschools.org/userfiles/Image/customimages/products/120/share-handbook-for-artistic-research-education-high-definition.pdf.

Buchloh, Benjamin H. D. 1984. "Theorizing the Avant-Garde." *Art in America* (November) 19–21.

Bürger, Peter. 1984. *Theory of the Avant-Garde*. Translated by Michael Shaw. Minneapolis: University of Minnesota Press. First published 1974 as *Theorie der Avantgarde* (Frankfurt am Main: Suhrkamp).

Caygill, Howard. 2017. *Kafka: In Light of the Accident*. London: Bloomsbury Academic.

Corngold, Stanley, Jack Greenberg, and Benno Wagner. 2009. "Commentary 14." In *Franz Kafka: The Office Writings*, edited by Stanley Corngold, Jack Greenberg, and Benno Wagner, 299–300. Princeton, NJ: Princeton University Press.

Cox, Geoff, and Jacob Lund. 2016. *The Contemporary Condition: Introductory Thoughts on Contemporaneity and Contemporary Art*. Berlin: Sternberg Press.

Derrida, Jacques. 1989. *Edmund Husserl's Origin of Geometry: An Introduction*. Translated by John P. Leavey, Jr. New ed. Lincoln: University of Nebraska Press. First published 1962 as *Introduction à "L'origine de la géométrie" de Husserl* (Paris: Presses universitaires de France).

———. 1997. *Of Grammatology*. Translated by Gayatri Chakravorty Spivak. Corrected ed. Baltimore: Johns Hopkins University Press. First published 1967 as *De la grammatologie* (Paris: Minuit).

Friedman, Ken. 2017. "Research Request." Email to the PhD-Design JISCMail list, 11 April 2017. Accessed 4 February 2019. https://www.jiscmail.ac.uk/cgi-bin/webadmin?A2=ind1704&L=phd-design&F=&S=&P=23948.

Groys, Boris. 2016. *In the Flow*. London: Verso.

Heidegger, Martin. (1938–48) 1999. *Gesamtausgabe: III. Abteilung Unveröffentliche Abhandlungen. Bd. 67. Metaphysik und Nihilismus*. Edited by Hans-Joachim Friedrich. Frankfurt am Main: Vittorio Klostermann. Volume contains the unpublished texts "Die Überwindung der Metaphysik" (1938/39) and "Das Wesen des Nihilismus" (1946–48).

———. [1954] 2000. "Die Frage Nach Der Technik." In *Gesamtausgabe: 1. Abteilung Veröffentliche Schriften 1910–1976; Bd. 7. Vorträge und Aufsätze*, edited by Friedrich-Wilhelm v. Herrmann, 5–36. Frankfurt am Main: Vittorio Klostermann. Essay first published 1954 in *Vorträge und Aufsätze* (Pfullingen: Günther Neske). Translated by William Lovitt as "The Question Concerning Technology" in *Martin Heidegger: Basic Writings*, edited by David Farrell Krell (London: Routledge, 2011), 213–38.

Hill, Leslie. 1997. *Blanchot: Extreme Contemporary*. London: Routledge.

Husserl, Edmund. (1970) 2001. *Logical Investigations*. Translated by John N. Findlay. 2 vols. Abingdon, UK: Routledge. First published 1900–1901 as *Logische Untersuchungen* (Halle: M. Niemeyer). This translation first published 1970 (London: Routledge & Kegan Paul).

Kirkkopelto, Esa. 2018. "Abandoning Art in the Name of Art: Transpositional Logic in Artistic Research." In *Transpositions: Aesthetico-Epistemic Operators in Artistic Research*, edited by Michael Schwab, 33–40. Orpheus Institute Series. Leuven: Leuven University Press.

Kubler, George. 1962. *The Shape of Time: Remarks on the History of Things*. New Haven, CT: Yale University Press.

Lacoue-Labarthe, Philippe, and Jean-Luc Nancy. 1988. *The Literary Absolute: The Theory of Literature in German Romanticism*. Translated by Philip Barnard and Cheryl Lester. Albany: State University of New York Press. First published 1978 as *L'absolu littéraire: Théorie de la littérature du romantisme allemand* (Paris: Seuil).

Laruelle, François. 2010. *Philosophies of Difference: A Critical Introduction to Non-philosophy*. Translated by Rocco Gangle. London: Continuum. First published 1986 as *Les philosophies de la différence* (Paris: Presses universitaires de France).

Lee, Pamela M. 2001. "'Ultramoderne': Or, How George Kubler Stole the Time in Sixties Art." *Grey Room* 2 (winter): 46–77.

Lyotard, Jean-François. (1983) 2001. "Answering the Question: What is Postmodernism?" Translated by Régis Durand. Appendix to *The Postmodern Condition: A Report on Knowledge*, translated by Geoff Bennington and Brian Massumi, 71–82. Manchester: Manchester University Press. Chapter first published 1982 as "Réponse à la question: Qu'est-ce que le postmoderne?" (*Critique* 419). Translation first published 1983 in *Innovation/Renovation: New Perspectives on the Humanities*, edited by Ihab Hassan and Sally Hassan (Madison: University of Wisconsin Press).

Malaspina, Cecile. 2018. *An Epistemology of Noise*. London: Bloomsbury Academic.

Merleau-Ponty, Maurice. 1968. *The Visible and the Invisible*. Edited by Claude Lefort. Translated by Alphonso Lingis. Evanston, IL: Northwestern University Press. First published 1964 as *Le visible et l'invisible* (Paris: Gallimard).

Moles, Abraham A. 1966. *Information Theory and Esthetic Perception*. Translated by Joel E. Cohen. Urbana: University of Illinois Press. First published 1958 as *Théorie de l'information et perception esthétique* (Paris: Flammarion).

Negri, Antonio. 2008. "Contemporaneity between Modernity and Postmodernity." In Smith, Enwezor, and Condee 2008, 23–29.

Nietzsche, Friedrich. 1997. "On the Uses and Disadvantages of History for Life." In *Untimely Meditations*, edited by Daniel Breazeale, translated by R. J. Hollingdale, 60–123. Cambridge: Cambridge University Press. Essay first published 1874 as "Vom Nutzen und Nachteil der Historie für das Leben," 2nd part of *Unzeitgemässe Betrachtungen* (Leipzig: Fritzsch, 1873–76).

———. 1999. *The Birth of Tragedy*. In *The Birth of Tragedy and Other Writings*, edited by Raymond Geuss and Ronald Speirs, translated by Ronald Speirs, 1–116. Cambridge: Cambridge University Press. First published 1872 as *Die Geburt der Tragödie* (Leipzig: Fritzsch). "An Attempt at Self Criticism" added to 2nd ed., first published 1886 (Leipzig: Fritzsch).

Nowotny, Helga. 2011. Foreword to *The Routledge Companion to Research in the Arts*, edited by Michael Biggs and Henrik Karlsson, xvii–xxvi. London: Routledge.

Osborne, Peter. 2013a. *Anywhere or Not At All: Philosophy of Contemporary Art*. London: Verso.

———. 2013b. "Global Modernity and the Contemporary: Two Categories of the Philosophy of Historical Time." In *Breaking Up Time: Negotiating the Borders between Present, Past and Future*, edited by Berber Bevernage and Chris Lorenz, 69–84. Schriftenreihe Der FRIAS School of History 7. Gottingen: Vandenhoeck & Ruprecht.

Rheinberger, Hans-Jörg. 1994. "Experimental Systems: Historiality, Narration, and Deconstruction." *Science in Context* 7 (1): 65–81.

———. 1997. *Toward a History of Epistemic Things: Synthesizing Proteins in the Test Tube*. Stanford, CA: Stanford University Press.

———. 1998. "Experimental Systems, Graphematic Spaces." In *Inscribing Science: Scientific Texts and the Materiality of Communication*, edited by Timothy Lenoir, 285–303. Stanford, CA: Stanford University Press.

———. 2004. "Experimental Systems: The Virtual Laboratory." The Virtual Laboratory: Essays and Resources on the Experimentalization of Life; Max Planck Institute for the History of Science, Berlin. Accessed 7 February 2019. http://vlp.mpiwg-berlin.mpg.de/essays/data/enc19.

———. 2009. "Translating Derrida." *CR: The New Centennial Review* 8 (3): 175–87.

———. 2013. "Forming and Being Informed: Hans-Jörg Rheinberger in Conversation with Michael Schwab." In *Experimental Systems: Future Knowledge in Artistic Research*, edited by Michael Schwab, 198–219. Orpheus Institute Series. Leuven: Leuven University Press.

———. 2016. "Culture and Nature in the Prism of Knowledge." *History of Humanities* 1 (1): 155–81.

Rossum, Gerhard Dohrn-van. 1996. *History of the Hour: Clocks and Modern Temporal Orders*. Translated by Thomas Dunlop. Chicago: University of Chicago Press. First published 1992 as *Die Geschichte der Stunde: Uhren und moderne Zeitordnungen* (Munich: Carl Hanser).

Schön, Donald A. 1983. *The Reflective Practitioner: How Professionals Think In Action*. New York: Basic Books.

Schwab, Michael. 2011. "Editorial JAR 0." *JAR* 0. Accessed 4 February 2019. http://www.jar-online.net/issues/0.

———. 2012a. "Between a Rock and a Hard Place." In *Intellectual Birdhouse: Artistic Practice as Research*, edited by Florian Dombois, Ute Meta Bauer, Claudia Mareis, and Michael Schwab, 229–47. London: Koenig Books.

———. 2012b. "Exposition Writing." In *Yearbook for Artistic Research and Development*, 16–26. Stockholm: Swedish Research Council.

———. 2013. Introduction to *Experimental Systems: Future Knowledge in Artistic Research*, edited by Michael Schwab, 5–14. Orpheus Institute Series. Leuven: Leuven University Press.

———. 2014a. "Artistic Research and Experimental Systems: The Rheinberger Questionnaire and Study-Day—A Report." In *Artistic Experimentation in Music: An Anthology*, edited by Darla Crispin and Bob Gilmore, 111–23. Orpheus Institute Series. Leuven: Leuven University Press.

———. 2014b. "The Exposition of Practice as Research as Experimental System." In *Artistic Experimentation in Music: An Anthology*, edited by Darla Crispin and Bob Gilmore, 31–40. Orpheus Institute Series. Leuven: Leuven University Press.

———. 2018a. "Peer-Reviewing in the 'Journal for Artistic Research.'" In *Evaluating Art and Design Research: Reflections, Evaluation Practices and Research Presentations*, edited by Walter Ysebaert and Binke van Kerckhoven, 52–59. Brussels: VUB Press.

———. 2018b. "Transpositionality and Artistic Research." In *Transpositions: Aesthetico-Epistemic Operators in Artistic Research*, edited by Michael Schwab, 191–213. Orpheus Institute Series. Leuven: Leuven University Press.

Schwab, Michael, and Henk Borgdorff. 2014. Introduction to *The Exposition of Artistic Research: Publishing Art in Academia*, edited by Michael Schwab and Henk Borgdorff, 8–20. Leiden: Leiden University Press.

Serres, Michel. 1982. *Parasite*. Translated by Lawrence R. Schehr. Baltimore: Johns Hopkins University Press. First published 1979 as *Le parasite* (Paris: Grasset).

Shapin, Steven. 1984. "Pump and Circumstance: Robert Boyle's Literary Technology." *Social Study of Science* 14 (4): 481–520.

Smith, Terry. 2009. *What Is Contemporary Art?* Chicago: University of Chicago Press.

Smith, Terry, Okwui Enwezor, and Nancy Condee, eds. 2008. *Antinomies of Art and Culture: Modernity, Postmodernity, Contemporaneity*. Durham, NC: Duke University Press.

Smithson, Robert. (1966) 1996. "Entropy and the New Monuments." In *Robert Smithson: The Collected Writings*, edited by Jack Flam, 10–23. Berkeley: University of California Press. Essay first published 1966 (*Artforum*, June).

Snow, C. P. (1959) 1998. *The Two Cultures*. Cambridge: Cambridge University Press. First published 1959 (Cambridge: Cambridge University Press).

Stallschus, Stefanie. 2013. "A Theory of Experimentation in Art? Reading Kubler's History of Art after Rheinberger's Experimental Systems." In *Experimental Systems: Future Knowledge in Artistic Research*, edited by Michael Schwab, 15–25. Orpheus Institute Series. Leuven: Leuven University Press.

Wilson, Stephen. 2002. *Information Arts: Intersections of Art, Science, and Technology*. Cambridge, MA: MIT Press.

177

Paulo de Assis is a research fellow at the Orpheus Institute. He was the Principal Investigator of the European Research Council project MusicExperiment21 (musicexperiment21.eu), which investigated experimental performance practices, innovative modes of presentation, and transdisciplinary encounters between art, research, and philosophy. He is an experimental performer, pianist, and musicologist, with wider interests in composition, aesthetics, and philosophy. In addition to his artistic practice, he is the author of *Logic of Experimentation* (2018), *Luigi Nono's Wende* (2006), and *Domani l'aurora* (2004), and the editor of *Aberrant Nuptials: Deleuze and Artistic Research 2* (forthcoming, 2019), *Virtual Works—Actual Things* (2018), *The Dark Precursor: Deleuze and Artistic Research 1* (2017), *Experimental Affinities in Music* (2015), *Sound and Score: Essays on Sound, Score and Notation* (2013), and *Dynamics of Constraints: Essays on Notation, Editing and Performance* (2009).

Babette Babich teaches philosophy at Fordham University in New York City. On occasion, she also teaches at the Humboldt University in Berlin and is Honorary Professor of philosophy at the University of Winchester in England. She has published widely on philosophy of science and life-size ancient Greek bronzes, as well as art and museum theory. Recent monographs include *The Hallelujah Effect: Music, Performance Practice, and Technology* (2016) and *Un politique brisé* (2016). She has edited fourteen collective volumes, including *Hermeneutic Philosophies of Social Science* (2017), in addition to editing *The Observable* (2016), a posthumous volume by Patrick Aidan Heelan, S.J. (1926–2015) on Heisenberg's philosophy of quantum mechanics, along with Bohr and Einstein. Founder, in 1996, and editor of the journal *New Nietzsche Studies*, she has just finished two issues celebrating Nietzsche's *Birth of Tragedy* and a new edited book collection, *Reading David Hume's "Of the Standard of Taste"* (2019).

Zsuzsa Baross is Professor Emerita, Cultural Studies Department, Trent University, Canada. She is the author of *Posthumously: For Jacques Derrida* (2011) and *Encounters: Gerard Titus-Carmel, Jean-Luc Nancy, Claire Denis* (2015); her work on temporality, memory, and history and on the future in and of cinema and the thought of Jean-Luc Godard has appeared in numerous anthologies and journals; she conducted seminars ("Le Cinéma selon Jean-Luc Godard," "Il y a du rapport sexuel") at the Collège International de Philosophie, Paris. She has been collaborating with researchers on artistic research at the Orpheus Institute, Ghent, since 2016. Her two volumes *On Contemporaneity, after Agamben* are forthcoming in 2019 and 2020, published by Sussex Academic Press.

Pol Capdevila is a senior lecturer at the Humanities Department at Universitat Pompeu Fabra (Barcelona) where he teaches contemporary art. He also teaches image theory (BA) at the Communication Department at the same university. He is also currently teaching on the Research in Arts and Design MA (Eina) and Communication Aesthetics in Literary Journalism,

Communication, and Humanities MA (UAB). He obtained a BA in philosophy and a PhD in aesthetics and art theory from Universitat Autònoma de Barcelona. He held a position as a predoctoral research fellow at Potsdam University, Berlin (with a "la Caixa" award in 2003 and a DAAD fellowship in 2004) and postdoctoral fellowships at Potsdam University and the University of Cambridge University with the Beatriu de Pinós programme. His research interests revolve around aesthetic experience, hermeneutics, and theory of reception, and manifestations of temporality in contemporary art and culture, about which he has published various academic papers and book chapters.

Geoff Cox is Associate Professor/Reader in Fine Art at Plymouth University (UK) and Associate Professor/Lektor in Digital Design at Aarhus University (Denmark), where he is currently engaged (with Jacob Lund) on a research project, The Contemporary Condition, funded by the Danish Council for Independent Research. As part of this, he published *The Contemporary Condition: Introductory Thoughts on Contemporaneity and Contemporary Art* (2016, with Jacob Lund) as the first in a series of small co-edited books published by Sternberg Press. He co-runs a yearly workshop/publication in collaboration with the transmediale festival in Berlin and is co-editor of the associated open-access online journal APRJA (with Christian Ulrik Andersen). He is editor for the open-access DATA browser book series (Open Humanities Press; with Joasia Krysa), is currently working on a multi-authored book project about live coding, a book on aesthetic programming (with Winnie Soon), and a research project on machine seeing.

Composer and director **Heiner Goebbels** is among the most important exponents of the contemporary music and theatre scene. His compositions for ensemble and orchestra published by Ricordi Berlin are performed worldwide, as are several of his music theatre works and staged concerts, which have been produced by Théâtre Vidy Lausanne, Ensemble Modern, and the Ruhrtriennale—International Festival of the Arts, among others. He has created a great variety of sound and video installations, which have been displayed by Artangel London, MAC Lyon, Museum Mathildenhöhe Darmstadt, and Albertinum Dresden, among others. The music theatre production *Stifters Dinge* is still in the repertoire of Théâtre Vidy. *Schwarz auf Weiss*, *Eislermaterial*, and *Landschaft mit entfernten Verwandten* are in the repertoire of the Ensemble Modern. The London Sinfonietta and the Orchestra of the Age of Enlightenment and many other European ensembles perform *Songs of Wars I Have Seen* and the Ensemble Klang performs an ensemble version of *Walden*. His latest productions, *John Cage: Europeras 1&2*, *Harry Partch: Delusion of the Fury*, and *Louis Andriessen: De Materie* are distributed by the Ruhrtriennale, of which Goebbels was the artistic director between 2012 and 2014. Currently, he works as a professor at the Institute for Applied Theatre Studies, Justus Liebig University, Giessen, Germany, and is President of the Theatre Academy Hessen. heinergoebbels.com.

Jacob Lund is Associate Professor of Aesthetics and Culture and Director of the research programme Contemporary Aesthetics and Technology at the School of Communication and Culture, Aarhus University, Denmark. He is also Editor-in-Chief of *The Nordic Journal of Aesthetics*. Lund has published widely on aesthetics, art history, critical theory, and comparative literature. Currently he is engaged on a research project, The Contemporary Condition (with Geoff Cox), which focuses on the concept of contemporaneity and changes in our experiences of time as these might be seen to be registered in contemporary art (www.contemporaneity.au.dk). His publications as part of this project include *The Contemporary Condition: Introductory Thoughts on Contemporaneity and Contemporary Art* (2016, with Geoff Cox) and *Anachrony, Contemporaneity and Historical Imagination* (2019).

Ryan Nolan is a musician and PhD student at the University of Plymouth (UK). His current research project operates at the intersection between art theory, music studies, and philosophy of history, which intends to critically redefine the concept of contemporary music in the wake of increased philosophical interest in "the contemporary" as a form of historical time. He is an affiliated researcher within The Contemporary Condition research project at Aarhus University (Denmark).

Peter Osborne is a professor in and the Director of the Centre for Research in Modern European Philosophy (CRMEP), Kingston University London. His books include *The Politics of Time: Modernity and Avant-Garde* (1995; 2011), *Philosophy in Cultural Theory* (2000), *Conceptual Art* (2002), *Marx* (2005), and *Anywhere or Not at All: Philosophy of Contemporary Art* (2013), and *The Postconceptual Condition* (2018).

Andrew Prior is a digital/sound artist and musician. His research practice explores the transformative potential of media and technology. In particular, his work is concerned with the use of noise and artefacts involved in digital mediation, as a raw material for sound works. Another key aspect of his current thinking is around the creative affordances of networked digital files. His work ranges between online works and installations to performative pieces. He is currently a member of the Kurator/Art and Social Technologies research group at the University of Plymouth, UK.

Michael Schwab is a London-based artist and artistic researcher who investigates postconceptual uses of technology in a variety of media including photography, drawing, printmaking, and installation art. He holds an MA in philosophy (Hamburg University) and a PhD in photography (Royal College of Art, London) that focused on post-conceptual post-photography and artistic research methodology. He is the founding Editor-in-Chief of the *Journal for Artistic Research* (JAR), co-editor of *Intellectual Birdhouse: Artistic Practice as Research* (2012), co-editor of *The Exposition of Artistic Research: Publishing Art in Academia* (2013), and the editor of *Experimental Systems: Future Knowledge in Artistic Research* (2013) and *Transpositions: Aesthetico-Epistemic Operators in Artistic Research* (2018).

Index

Editors
Paulo de Assis
Michael Schwab

Authors
Paulo de Assis
Babette Babich
Zsuzsa Baross
Pol Capdevila
Geoff Cox
Heiner Goebbels
Jacob Lund
Ryan Nolan
Peter Osborne
Andrew Prior
Michael Schwab

Production manager
Heike Vermeire

Managing editor
Edward Crooks

Series editor
William Brooks

Lay-out
Studio Luc Derycke

Cover design
Lucia D'Errico

Cover image
© Carlo Scarpa, detail of
the restoration of
Museo di Castelvecchio
Courtesy of Museo di Castelvecchio,
Verona
Photo by Lucia D'Errico

Typesetting
Friedemann bvba

Printing
Wilco, Amersfoort
(The Netherlands)

© 2019 by Leuven University Press /
Universitaire Pers Leuven /
Presses Universitaires de Louvain.
Minderbroedersstraat 4
B-3000 Leuven (Belgium)

ISBN 978 94 6270 183 0
eISBN 978 94 6166 286 6
https://doi.org/10.11116/9789461662866

D/2019/1869/23
NUR: 664

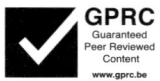

*This book is published in the Orpheus Institute
Series.*